Georg
The

ibrary Byelaws and Regulations apply to th'
't should ' 'turned or renewed on or '
' may be

14

ANALYSING TEXTS
General Editor: Nicholas Marsh

Published

Chaucer: The Canterbury Tales   *Gail Ashton*

Aphra Behn: The Comedies   *Kate Aughterson*

Webster: The Tragedies   *Kate Aughterson*

John Keats   *John Blades*

Shakespeare: The Comedies   *R. P. Draper*

Charlotte Brontë: The Novels   *Mike Edwards*

E. M. Forster: The Novels   *Mike Edwards*

George Eliot: The Novels   *Mike Edwards*

Shakespeare: The Tragedies   *Nicholas Marsh*

Shakespeare: Three Problem Plays   *Nicholas Marsh*

Jane Austen: The Novels   *Nicholas Marsh*

Emily Brontë: *Wuthering Heights*   *Nicholas Marsh*

Virginia Woolf: The Novels   *Nicholas Marsh*

D. H. Lawrence: The Novels   *Nicholas Marsh*

William Blake: The Poems   *Nicholas Marsh*

John Donne: The Poems   *Joe Nutt*

Thomas Hardy: The Novels   *Norman Page*

Marlowe: The Plays   *Stevie Simkin*

Analysing Texts
Series Standing Order ISBN 0–333–73260–X
(*outside North America only*)

You can receive future titles in this series as they are published by placing a standing order.
Please contact your bookseller or, in case of difficulty, write to us at the address below
with your name and address, the title of the series and the ISBN quoted above.

Customer Services Department, Macmillan Distribution Ltd
Houndmills, Basingstoke, Hampshire RG21 6XS, England

George Eliot: The Novels

MIKE EDWARDS

First published 2003 by
PALGRAVE MACMILLAN
Houndmills, Basingstoke, Hampshire RG21 6XS and
175 Fifth Avenue, New York, N.Y. 10010
Companies and representatives throughout the world

PALGRAVE MACMILLAN is the global academic imprint of the Palgrave Macmillan division of St. Martin's Press, LLC and of Palgrave Macmillan Ltd. Macmillan® is a registered trademark in the United States, United Kingdom and other countries. Palgrave is a registered trademark in the European Union and other countries.

ISBN 1–4039–0056–6 hardback
ISBN 1–4039–0057–4 paperback

This book is printed on paper suitable for recycling and made from fully managed and sustained forest sources.

A catalogue record for this book is available from the British Library.

Library of Congress Cataloging-in-Publication Data

Edwards, Mike, 1942–
    George Eliot: the novels / Mike Edwards.
        p.   cm. – (Analysing texts)
    Includes bibliographical references and index.
    ISBN 1–4039–0056–6 – ISBN 1–4039–0057–4 (pbk.)
    1. Eliot, George, 1819–1880 – Criticism and interpretation.
    2. Women and literature – England – History – 19th century.
    3. Didactic fiction, English – History and criticism.   I. Title.
    II. Analysing texts (Palgrave Macmillan (Firm))

PR4   273
823

10
12   1

Printe

Contents

General Editor's Preface   vii

How to Use This Book   viii

Part 1: Analysing George Eliot's Novels

1   Beginnings   **3**
    The Mill on the Floss, pp. 53–4   4
    Silas Marner, pp. 5–6   10
    Middlemarch, pp. 7–8, 3   16
    Conclusions   25
    Methods of Analysis   29
    Further Work   31

2   Characters   **32**
    The Mill on the Floss, pp. 119–20   33
    Silas Marner, pp. 20–1   40
    Middlemarch, pp. 13–14, 83–4   46
    Conclusions   54
    Methods of Analysis   57
    Further Work   58

3   Relationships   **60**
    The Mill on the Floss, pp. 437–8   60
    Silas Marner, pp. 114–16   67
    Middlemarch, pp. 267–9, 425   73
    Conclusions   83
    Methods of Analysis   86
    Further Work   87

4   Society   **89**
    The Mill on the Floss, pp. 619–21, 611   90
    Silas Marner, pp. 23–4   96

Middlemarch, pp. 741–2, 735–6   101
Conclusions   110
Methods of Analysis   114
Further Work   115

5 **Morality**   **117**
The Mill on the Floss, pp. 603–4   118
Silas Marner, pp. 169–70   124
Middlemarch, pp. 614–15, 264, 211   131
Conclusions   138
Methods of Analysis   141
Further Work   143

6 **Conclusions**   **145**
The Mill on the Floss, pp. 656–7   146
Silas Marner, pp. 181–3   150
Middlemarch, pp. 837–8   155
Conclusions   161
Methods of Analysis   166
Further Work   166

Part 2: The Context and the Critics

7 **George Eliot's Life and Work**   **171**

8 **The Context of George Eliot's Work**   **181**

9 **Some Critical Approaches**   **192**
Barbara Hardy   192
Michael Wheeler   197
Kate Flint   200

Further Reading   207

Index   210

General Editor's Preface

This series is dedicated to one clear belief: that we can all enjoy, understand and analyse literature for ourselves, provided we know how to do it. How can we build on close understanding of a short passage, and develop our insight into the whole work? What features do we expect to find in a text? Why do we study style in so much detail? In demystifying the study of literature, these are only some of the questions the *Analysing Texts* series addresses and answers.

The books in this series will not do all the work for you, but will provide you with the tools, and show you how to use them. Here, you will find samples of close, detailed analysis, with an explanation of the analytical techniques utilised. At the end of each chapter there are useful suggestions for further work you can do to practise, develop and hone the skills demonstrated and build confidence in your own analytical ability.

An author's individuality shows in the way they write: every work they produce bears the hallmark of that writer's personal 'style'. In the main part of each book we concentrate therefore on analysing the particular flavour and concerns of one author's work, and explain the features of their writing in connection with major themes. In Part 2 there are chapters about the author's life and work, assessing their contribution to developments in literature; and a sample of critics' views are summarised and discussed in comparison with each other. Some suggestions for further reading provide a bridge towards further critical research.

Analysing Texts is designed to stimulate and encourage your critical and analytic faculty, to develop your personal insight into the author's work and individual style, and to provide you with the skills and techniques to enjoy at first hand the excitement of discovering the richness of the text.

NICHOLAS MARSH

How to Use This Book

This book is designed to be used in close conjunction with the novels it discusses. Each chapter is based on detailed analysis of passages from four novels. The aim is to show how understanding of the writer's ideas and skill emerges from close study of selected passages. The approach and techniques used are clearly demonstrated so as to help you to embark confidently on independent study of other parts of the novels. You can use similar approaches to work on other writers too.

You will gain most benefit from this book if you have done some preliminary work of your own. Of course, you should have read the novels under discussion, and preferably more than once. If you are studying Eliot for examination purposes you should certainly make yourself thoroughly familiar with them. It will be useful, too, to reread each passage discussed and check on its context. You will need to have the relevant passage ready to hand as you read, so that you can refer back and forth easily between the analysis and the text.

There is much you can do beyond that. Study each passage in detail, first as a self-contained piece, then in the context of the novel. Think about its structure, its language, the balance of description, narrative and dialogue, and the links between these. You will probably find it useful to make a few informal notes. In this way you can develop a feel for the atmosphere, mood and tone of the passage, and about the treatment of character and theme. You will also develop insight into the author's ideas and the techniques he uses.

No doubt you have a method of study of your own that you have regularly used. By all means apply it to the passages discussed here. But remember that no programme of study is to be followed slavishly. Use all the means available to suggest approaches that may have slipped your attention, but keep an open mind and be ready to follow where your own imagination leads. Many things come to mind when you study novels. Don't be too ready to dismiss stray thoughts as trivial or foolish. Pursue them and work out their implications. Even if they turn out in the end to be misguided, you will have gained a great deal in the process of developing them. The more you explore your ideas, the richer they will grow and the more thoroughly they will be your own.

Having done some preparatory study you will be in a better position to read the analysis in this book with understanding, and critically. In each chapter emphasis is placed on one specific feature of Eliot's work, but seen always in relation to others and not in isolation. Each extract is considered first as an independent piece of writing, then as part of the novel to which it belongs. The aim, in the end, is to see how the extract relates to its chapter and to its novel, and so deepen your ideas about the whole book.

There is a great deal of room for diversity of approach and interpretation in the process of analysis. You are unlikely to find your responses mirrored precisely in the discussions, though it would be strange if there were no resemblance at all. Certainly you will now be in a position to disagree or agree for good independent reasons with what is said in the analyses that follow, and you will be able to build on them and develop further ideas of your own. Remember finally that disagreement is an essential part of the process: criticism exists to be contested.

Editions

Penguin editions are used for page references to the novels discussed in this book. There are several different Penguin editions of Eliot's novels, and it will be easiest for you to use the specific editions listed below. Here are the original dates of publication of the novels discussed, followed by the editions from which page numbers are taken:

The Mill on the Floss: first published 1860; Penguin Classics 1979, revised 1985
Silas Marner: first published 1861; Penguin Classics 1996
Middlemarch: first published 1872; Penguin Classics 1994

Note that some, but not all, earlier Penguin editions of these novels have the same pagination, so it is important to check that your edition matches those quoted. However, the major passages used for detailed analysis are identified by chapter and part of chapter as well as page number so that you can find them easily no matter which Penguin or other edition you use.

There are page references to the following other works by George Eliot:

Adam Bede: J. M. Dent, Everyman Edition, 1960
Daniel Deronda: J. M. Dent, Everyman Edition, 1964 (2 vols)

Where it is clear which book, or, in the chapter on critical approaches, which essay, is under discussion, reference is usually by page number alone. Otherwise books are fully identified at the time of reference, and reappear in the recommendations for further reading.

PART 1

ANALYSING GEORGE ELIOT'S NOVELS

1

Beginnings

Three of the best-known of George Eliot's seven novels have been selected for this study: *The Mill on the Floss, Silas Marner* and *Middlemarch*. The first two of these novels illustrate contrasting aspects of her early work, and the third is the pinnacle of her later writing. *The Mill on the Floss*, Eliot's second full novel, was published in 1860, the year after *Adam Bede*. It is distinctive in two fundamental respects. With some close parallels in the earlier pages between the protagonist and the author, it is her most autobiographical novel. Its emotive title singles it out not only from Eliot's other works, but also from the undemonstrative inclination of Victorian writers in general to name novels after a protagonist; it was, indeed, suggested by Eliot's publisher, John Blackwood. After *The Mill on the Floss*, next in order of publication was *Silas Marner* (1861); though it, too, took its origin from Eliot's childhood, it is a more consciously objective book than its predecessor, with rather more of the feeling of a parable. *Middlemarch* dates from much later, 1872, after Eliot had produced two further books. It is unique among her novels in taking the name of a town for its title and this reflects its broader scope. The complexity of *Middlemarch* shows a fully mature control of the elements of structure and theme. It evolved, however, from two stories originally conceived as separate.

These novels will be discussed in order of publication. In each chapter a topic or theme common to the novels will be studied by means of detailed analysis of extracts. At the end of Part 1 a chapter on the conclusions will review the outcome of the analysis and explore the final effect of the novels. The business of this first chapter is to analyse the opening paragraphs and consider how they relate to the nature of the novels they introduce and how they reflect the concerns of Eliot's work in general.

(i)   *The Mill on the Floss*

George Eliot considered several alternative titles for the novel, including 'Sister Maggie', 'The Tullivers', 'St Ogg's on the Floss', 'The House of Tulliver', 'The Tulliver Family' and 'Life on the Floss'. A stronger emphasis on location and setting is implied in the final title than in the others, and is confirmed in the first chapter, 'Outside Dorlcote Mill'. It opens with descriptions of the Floss and its associated town of St Ogg's, and moves on to describe Dorlcote Mill and the ordinary life – vegetable, human and animal – of the region. It is not quite devoid of characters: there are the anonymous waggoners, who have a representative function; and there are the little girl and the dog, who, though yet unnamed, are to play an important part in the novel. Only in the last sentence of the chapter is there reference to the central family of the novel, the Tullivers. These are the opening two paragraphs:

> A wide plain, where the broadening Floss hurries on between its green banks to the sea, and the loving tide, rushing to meet it, checks its passage with an impetuous embrace. On this mighty tide the black ships – laden with the fresh-scented fir-planks, with rounded sacks of oil-bearing seed, or with the dark glitter of coal – are borne along to the town of St Ogg's, which shows its aged, fluted red roofs and the broad gables of its wharves between the low wooded hill and the river brink, tingeing the water with a soft purple hue under the transient glance of this February sun. Far away on each hand stretch the rich pastures and the patches of dark earth, made ready for the seed of broad-leaved green crops, or touched already with the tint of the tender-bladed autumn-sown corn. There is a remnant still of the last year's golden clusters of bee-hive ricks rising at intervals beyond the hedgerows; and everywhere the hedgerows are studded with trees: the distant ships seem to be lifting their masts and stretching their red-

brown sails close among the branches of the spreading ash. Just by the
red-roofed town the tributary Ripple flows with a lively current into
the Floss. How lovely the little river is with its dark, changing wavelets!
It seems to me like a living companion while I wander along the bank
and listen to its low placid voice, as to the voice of one who is deaf and
loving. I remember those large dipping willows . . . I remember the
stone bridge . . .

And this is Dorlcote Mill. I must stand a minute or two here on the
bridge and look at it, though the clouds are threatening, and it is far
on in the afternoon. Even in this leafless time of departing February it
is pleasant to look at – perhaps the chill damp season adds a charm to
the trimly-kept, comfortable dwelling-house, as old as the elms and
chestnuts that shelter it from the northern blast. The stream is brim
full now, and lies high in this little withy plantation, and half drowns
the grassy fringe of the croft in front of the house. As I look at the full
stream, the vivid grass, the delicate bright-green powder softening the
outline of the great trunks and branches that gleam from under the
bare purple boughs, I am in love with moistness, and envy the white
ducks that are dipping their heads far into the water here among the
withes – unmindful of the awkward appearance they make in the drier
world above.

(pp. 53–4)

The first purpose of these introductory paragraphs is to set the scene
for the narrative which is to follow. They are primarily descriptive,
introducing the Floss and the town of St Ogg's in paragraph one and
Dorlcote Mill in paragraph two as significant elements in a rich environment mingling human activity and natural phenomena. These
two features, the river and the mill, one natural, the other man-made,
will dominate the whole of the novel and determine its conclusion.

Discussion of a passage like this will naturally tend to focus on the
mood that emerges from the description – on the keynote established
here, which will influence the mood of the rest of the novel. There
is another element, too, that demands attention: the nature of the
observing eye, the narrator, who intrudes and participates both
explicitly and implicitly in the description.

First impressions of this passage are likely to be strongly influenced
by its unhurried pace – a feature it shares with many another
nineteenth-century novel. There is space to consider the mental

picture at length, from the obvious bridge to the less obvious fir-planks. The senses are engaged by rich colours, green, soft purple, red-brown, golden and red alongside more subtle shades, by the movement of the river and the scent of fir. There is considerable particularity of detail. Notice, for example, that Eliot is not satisfied with general descriptions, but uses compounds to try to convey the particularity of what she describes in her references to 'fresh-scented fir-planks', 'tender-bladed autumn-sown corn'. Trees are referred to by species: ash, willow (also here called 'withy', 'withe'), elm and chestnut. It is easy to believe that this scene is drawn from life. (As it was, of course: Eliot travelled far to find an actual geographical model for the Floss and its mill.)

But there is more behind the leisureliness than convention only. Spaciousness in both mood and rhythm dominates the first paragraph from the first phrase to the end in a sequence of cumulative adjectives ('wide . . . broadening . . . mighty . . . broad . . . spreading . . . large'). At the same time there is a sense of richness in the 'dark glitter of coal' and of fertility in 'rounded sacks' of seed, seemingly somewhat at odds with the season: the mood of this damp February seems poised between the plenitude of a Keatsian autumn and the incipience of spring: both seasons are caught in the reference to the tint and tenderness of the newly sprouting corn sown in the autumn. The promise of new growth stands side by side with the recollection of 'last year's golden cluster'. There is a powerful awareness here of the changing seasons and their meaning for the lives of people bound into them. Equally there is a powerful sense of the richness, variety and complexity of the life of the countryside.

Eliot takes time to engage us in the natural world, to make us feel its evolution. Nature itself is brought to life. Personification is the cold name for the device used but how vividly poetic is the effect! The Floss 'hurries' against a tide 'rushing' to meet it and seems to the narrator 'a living companion', its sound a 'placid voice'; the February sun casts a 'transient glance' at the earth; the Ripple flows with a 'lively' current; even the distant ships, 'lifting their masts and stretching their red-brown sails' seem to share in the animation of nature. The imagery deepens into sexual or emotional significance with the 'loving' tide that meets the Floss in 'an impetuous embrace' and has the voice of a 'loving' companion. Eliot, like the characters she is to write of, is used to close contact with the natural world and has an intimate knowledge of its ways and changing moods. The environment is like that to which she formed a powerful emotional attachment in her own childhood, and it is one to which Maggie will be seen to be indissolubly tied.

The theme of change develops in the second paragraph. Here the emphasis rests more evenly between promise and menace. There is still colour in the 'delicate bright-green' powdering the tree-trunks that 'gleam' from under purple boughs, but the boughs are bare. The clouds threaten rain or storm in this 'chill damp season', this 'leafless time'. At the same time, the stream is brim full, the grass vivid, and trees shelter the dwelling-house from the cold north wind. Thus inspired with the fruitfulness that grows out of the chill and damp of winter, the narrator may speak of being 'in love with moistness'. The mood changes too. Though there remain hints of the leisureliness of the opening paragraph (the full stream, the great trunks, the age of house and trees), there is a stronger focus on the near and small. Dorlcote Mill is homely: pleasant, trim, comfortable, its withy plantation little. The season adds 'charm' rather than power or greatness to the house. The atmosphere of the paragraph lightens with the concluding picture of the rather comical white ducks. With this second paragraph we have moved from the sublime to the homely – with just a hint of the ridiculous.

As a whole, this passage clearly has a complex mood, embracing grandeur, threat, richness, restlessness, a mild touch of comedy; there is sensuality as well as sensuousness. The narrator is conscious of the changing seasons and the broader movement of time; intensely conscious of the personality of the natural phenomena she describes, and in an intimacy bordering on sexual with them. Always she is conscious of impermanence, movement and variety: of the transient sunshine, of the rushing and checking of waters and their 'changing wavelets'; at one moment she is aware of the promise of the young shoots of corn, at another of the 'remnants' of last year's ricks; everything is in flux, February 'departing', and in this damp season, suggestive of the seasonal cycle as a whole, the brimming stream looks forward to a time when its level will have sunk in a dry warm summer.

The description is detailed, vivid and thus persuasive; more than that, it is striking because it is so intensely felt by an eye that understands the countryside.

The features that emerge from these paragraphs are to do chiefly with the natural world. A locality and its life are described with a sense of nostalgia at a time of year redolent of the transience of nature; the mood is complex, divided between consciousness of the decaying remnants of a dead season and delight in the promise of spring. There are also thematic points here. There is something ominous about the rushing river and in the sense of change itself, which always promises death as well as renewal. And the language of love that runs through the passage points to a major theme of the novel. Love and death are encapsulated here as keynotes for what is to follow. It is clear from the nature of the passage that, though the eye of the narrator recalls in St Ogg's aspects of her own past, her memories are fully disciplined by her artistic intentions and thematic interests.

The perspective of the narrator is far from easy to identify. The past recalled in this novel is Eliot's own, and it is unprofitable to attempt to distinguish between narrator and author: for all practical purposes the narrator is Eliot. However, the nature of her recall is not at all straightforward. Her influence is felt long before the blatant 'it seems to me' and repeated 'I remember' at the end of the first paragraph. Her voice is present earlier in the ecstatic exclamation drawn from her by the spectacle of the plain of the Floss, 'How lovely the little river is . . . !' It is felt from the beginning in the present tense of the paragraph, and in the opening phrases: without a finite verb, they suggest a limitless present containing the world of change and movement about to be described. Although the scene purports to be remembered and the presence of the narrator grows more insistent in the second paragraph ('I must stand', 'As I look', 'I am in love'), a different impression emerges later in the chapter when the narrator is described dozing in a chair, recalling the whole scene. This opening, then, is not an actuality being described, but an episode in the infinite present of the imagination. That 'I remember' repeated at the end of the first paragraph is ambiguous: the narrator is remembering visiting a place she remembers: thus the remembering embraces and contains the scene as well as being contained within it.

In these opening paragraphs Eliot achieves an interesting double effect. On the one hand she establishes the environment in which the action of the novel is to evolve – and indeed a little later in the introductory chapter Maggie and Yap appear though unnamed, followed by the Tullivers. At the same time she dramatises her authorship as a form of daydream, imagining herself as a traveller recognising ground trodden long ago.

It is worth giving weight to the element of self-consciousness here. *The Mill on the Floss* is, as I mentioned earlier, the most autobiographical of Eliot's novels. But this scene is not autobiography in any straightforward sense, for she is not, in fact, describing her own past. We know that Eliot and Lewes found the location on the Tweed, far from the scene of the novel. We are dealing here, then, not with raw experience, but with an imaginative construct. If it seems real, vivid and powerful, it is not because it transmits raw experience, but because of the art of the writer. The Floss and Dorlcote Mill appear here not because they recall originals in Eliot's childhood, but because they are central to the events of the novel. Artistry is evident in the choice of subject as well as its treatment. Already there are pointers to the nature of the book and its central themes. The characters, when they are introduced, appear as part of a social and natural environment: they grow from it and will reflect its qualities. The river itself, of course, makes its presence felt in every part of the novel, in its events and in its imagery, and thus will provide a fitting environment for its climactic events; its unpredictability expresses more powerfully than any other phenomenon the pervading theme of change. The resonances of love at the beginning of the extract hint at the subject of much that is to come, and the headlong rushing of the river and its checking by counter-currents foreshadow the stumbling progress of Maggie, by turns eager, headstrong and thwarted in the energy of her charge towards the crises of her life; there is, too, in this meeting and clashing of natural forces something which touches on the conflict between Maggie and Tom, and on the social pressures that bear upon them. At the same time, the emphasis on change that permeates the passage suggests a large perspective, embracing the individual stories of Tom and Maggie as well as the general cycle of birth and death, growth and decay, and the emotions associated with them. The narrator, remembering and imagining, already contains in her balanced consciousness the best and the worst in human experience.

(ii) *Silas Marner*

Though it too takes its origin from Eliot's childhood – the story was suggested by her recollection of seeing a weaver in her early years – the opening of *Silas Marner* strikes a very different note. Instead of beginning with an infinite present and recreating a personal past, it takes us back to an earlier era very different from Eliot's present. Instead of describing a natural scene it outlines the life of a community. Now the tone, rather than nostalgic or pastoral, has something of the quality of fable:

> In the days when the spinning-wheels hummed busily in the farm-houses – and even great ladies, clothed in silk and thread-lace, had their toy spinning-wheels of polished oak – there might be seen in districts far away among the lanes, or deep in the bosom of the hills, certain pallid undersized men, who, by the side of the brawny country-folk, looked like the remnants of a disinherited race. The shepherd's dog barked fiercely when one of these alien-looking men appeared on the upland, dark against the early winter sunset; for what dog likes a figure bent under a heavy bag? – and these pale men rarely stirred abroad without that mysterious burden. The shepherd himself, though he had good reason to believe that the bag held nothing but flaxen thread, or else the long rolls of strong linen spun from that thread, was not quite sure that this trade of weaving, indispensable though it was, could be carried on entirely without the help of the Evil One. In that far-off time superstition clung easily round every person or thing that was at all unwonted, or even intermittent and occasional merely, like the visits of the peddler or the knife-grinder. No one knew where wandering men had their homes or their origin; and how was a man to be explained unless you at least knew somebody who knew his father and mother? To the peasants of old times, the world outside their own direct experience was a region of vagueness and mystery: to their untravelled thought a state of wandering was a conception as dim as the winter life of the swallows that came back with the spring; and even a settler, if

he came from distant parts, hardly ever ceased to be viewed with a remnant of distrust, which would have prevented any surprise if a long course of inoffensive conduct on his part had ended in the commission of a crime; especially if he had any reputation for knowledge, or showed any skill in handicraft. All cleverness, whether in the rapid use of that difficult instrument the tongue, or in some other art unfamiliar to villagers, was in itself suspicious: honest folk, born and bred in a visible manner, were mostly not overwise or clever – at least, not beyond such a matter as knowing the signs of the weather; and the process by which rapidity and dexterity of any kind were acquired was so wholly hidden, that they partook of the nature of conjuring. In this way it came to pass that those scattered linen-weavers – emigrants from the town into the country – were to the last regarded as aliens by their rustic neighbours, and usually contracted the eccentric habits which belong to a state of loneliness.

(pp. 5–6)

This paragraph is by way of prelude, taking us back into a past only vaguely defined to set a social scene before Silas is introduced in the second paragraph in a more specific era – 'the early years of this century'. The social environment is a strange one, seemingly primitive, dominated by the everyday and the practical, imbued with the sense of magic in a world only partially understood. There is no evidence of the kind of social refinement or sophistication that education and breadth of experience might bring. Most people in this community know about the weather and little else, and thus they view with mistrust anyone who has special abilities. The feeling of fable arises partly from the simplicity of the world Eliot presents, and partly from the fearful sense of an unseen world of powers and dominations that feeds on the naivety of the populace.

The nature of the past Eliot presents is characterised by sharp contrasts. The paragraph begins with an opposition between the spinning-wheels in the farmhouses and the toy machines of 'great ladies clothed in silk and thread-lace'. This opposition foreshadows a contrast between poorer and richer classes that will run through the story and culminate in Godfrey Cass's ill-considered offer to relieve Silas of the company of Eppie. The remainder of the paragraph contrasts the ways of travellers with the homely, familiar lives of 'the brawny

country-folk', whose weathered minds distrust the 'pallid undersized
. . . pale' men who haunt their country: the pallor is insisted on, suggesting an unnatural, indoor life of secret and hidden things; 'undersized' contrasts directly with 'brawny' and suggests something stunted
and therefore unnatural, a sport. The local folk know who they are,
and they know who everybody else's relatives are, unlike the weavers,
who are 'wandering men' and therefore barely identifiable. Not
understanding the wanderers, they regard them as 'alien' (the word
appears twice), 'eccentric'. To the community cosily nestled in the
comfortable 'bosom of the hills', the aliens from the towns seem as
far distant in their nature as in their origin and are thus viewed with
intense suspicion. The effect is accentuated by their trade. Weaving
is considered a more mysterious trade than that of other visitors such
as the knife-grinder or peddler and thus forms one pole of a further
opposition, between cleverness, either of tongue or hand, and the
stolid ordinariness of the rustic community.

It is the sense of the strangeness and estrangement of the weavers
that emerges most strongly from the passage, for Eliot insists on it in
so many ways. Apart from their separateness in physique and habits,
they have a mystical power that frightens their hosts. They appear
'dark against the early winter sunset', carrying a 'mysterious burden'
– as it were of sin, and reminiscent of Faithful's burden in *The
Pilgrim's Progress*. They are felt to be in league with 'the Evil One',
their work is 'an art unfamiliar to villagers' and 'part[akes] of the
nature of conjuring'. Distrust, suspicion, vagueness and mystery cling
to them. In such a context, their wandering achieves something of a
biblical echo of the wanderings of Cain or the expulsion of Adam
from Paradise, and so it would occasion no surprise if a weaver of
unimpeachable life were suddenly discovered in 'the commission of
a crime'. Thus it is that weavers are condemned, in this inflexible
community, to wither in the 'state of loneliness' with which the paragraph emphatically concludes.

The society presented here is clearly an unsophisticated one. The
hostile reaction of people towards the weavers is aptly represented by
the barking of the shepherd's dog, for they, too, are moved by unreasoning instinct. In comparing people's knowledge of the lives of
weavers with their knowledge of the migrations of swallows, Eliot

confirms the impression of a way of life not far removed from the merely instinctual. In this context, religion is not a matter of discussion or exploration: it, too, is instinctual, mixed up with magic and conjuring, and more a matter of primal fear than of reason, faith or morality. In the story that is to follow, religion comes rather to be still more a matter of convention: Silas Marner's church-going, or lack of it, are a matter of grave communal concern and an index of the degree of his acceptance by his community. The suspicion attaching to travel in this rural world has more than a mere geographical meaning. People do not like psychological travel either, preferring to stick to what they know, which is the weather; they do not like clever talk or odd giftedness; they prefer 'honest folk, born and bred in a visible manner'. Eliot finds a telling phrase to encapsulate the ways of this world: 'untravelled thought' embraces a broad range of ideas including distrust of visitors, intellectual unreceptiveness, lack of education, narrow experience and resistance to change.

All the features adumbrated in the opening paragraph point to significant elements in the story that follows. The isolation of Silas, the difficulties of his relationship with people in the community at different levels, the odd half-light of the religious world are essential themes. He is no more sophisticated than the community he has become part of (consider, for example, his failure to see the connection between church and chapel in his conversation with Mrs Winthrop in Chapter 10, p. 83) but, with his protruding eyes, bent posture and strange fits, he is the alien carried to the extreme. The reference made in this paragraph to the knowledge of people's relatives has direct relevance to the questions over the origins of Eppie on which much of the story hangs. Though there is one crucial element in the story, gold and its meaning, that finds no place here, its mysterious disappearance and discovery are part of the texture of mystery that is established in the opening paragraph and colours the whole novel.

This architectural strength reveals the organising power of the author. Though Eliot's personal involvement in what is described is far less evident at the beginning of *Silas Marner* than in the opening description of *The Mill on the Floss*, what is given is nevertheless a very personal view. This is in no sense a complete picture of the society of Raveloe, nor of its region, nor of a period. Eliot attempts to generalise her story by making reference to 'that far-off time', alluding in general to 'certain pallid undersized men', great ladies, villagers, honest folk and so on, and thus tries to give the impression of presenting a complete society. In fact, what we are given is a few very specific features of a community, all related to the single issue of its intolerance of intruders. Eliot's skill here is to persuade us that we are receiving an objective picture of a society when in fact we are being given a squint-eyed interpretation of a few aspects of a small community. There is a severe selectivity at work in the service of the architecture of the whole.

Superficially simpler than in *The Mill on the Floss*, the posture of the narrator here is more complex than may appear at first sight. As in the earlier novel, there is a species of double vision. Is she of the social world she sketches, or above it? Often she appears to adopt the position of the villagers when she speaks of 'brawny country-folk' as if approvingly in contrast with the unhealthy-looking weavers, and of 'honest folk' in contrast with incomprehensible strangers. Her rhetorical questions, 'what dog likes a figure bent under a heavy bag?' and 'how was a man to be explained unless you at least knew somebody who knew his father and mother?', appear to adopt the tone of the indigenous populace. The statement that 'No one knew where wandering men had their homes' seems to support a vision of the world quite as circumscribed as that of the people of Raveloe, for whom Raveloe and the world are practically identical. On the other hand, the opening of the next sentence, 'To the peasants of old times', establishes distance, revealing the intelligence residing behind the narrative and separated from it. This double vision finds expression in the pervasive irony of the passage. The irony is obvious in the reference to 'that difficult instrument the tongue', and the likening of speech to an 'art unfamiliar to villagers'. It appears also in the ingrained distrust of foreigners which would be unsurprised if a crime were to cap a life of inoffensive conduct. It lies always beneath the insistent stress on the diabolical oddity of weavers – their mysterious burden, their unnatural pallor, their magical skill – and thus pervades the whole.

There is a parallel complexity in the style of the passage. It passes from the narrative mode of the first sentence to a more discursive style comparable with that of the historian when Eliot begins a sentence with 'To the peasants of old times'. Towards the conclusion it develops, with 'In this way it came to pass', towards a quasi-biblical manner. The vocabulary is often simple and concrete in representing the views of rural people, but varies towards the abstract, as Eliot generalises about the nature of the society she is describing, or into ironic circumlocution; contrast the simplicity of the barking of the shepherd's dog with the periphrasis of 'a region of vagueness and mystery', for example. In the whole, however – and specifically in the phrase 'superstition clung easily round every person' – abstract and concrete sit happily side by side, each enhancing the other. Thus flaxen thread and rolls of strong linen form a 'mysterious burden'; migrations of swallows represent the 'conception . . . dim' of a life of wandering. There is figurative language but it rarely leaps to the eye. Notice, for example, the personification of the spinning-wheels that 'hummed busily' on the farms, which contrasts with the reference to the great ladies who merely 'had' their 'toy' wheels – neither humming nor busy. The contrast between town and country appears in the opposing of the attractive 'bosom of the hills' against the town which, without epithets, would be neutral were it not for the emigration thence of weavers. There is a comparable contrast in sounds and images – the homely humming of spinning-wheels against the alarmed barking of the farm dog, linen and thread against the stark figure 'dark against the early winter sunset', the friendliness of conversation rendered awkward and strange by the reference to the tongue as a 'difficult instrument'. Eliot presents an eerie landscape in which primitive characters meet in a half-light of subterranean fears born of suspicion and mistrust, brought together by the needs of trade and not by preference or expectation of comfort, and communicating only haltingly.

Despite the extravagant, almost violent, mood of the opening, there is a sense of balance in the voice of the narrator, and despite the restricted scope of the presentation of the community there is a element of realism in its treatment. The final effect of these disturbing contrasts of mood and style is to present the society in which the story is set with a mixture of criticism and sympathy. Eliot understands the shepherd's fears that weavers have some compact with the devil but does not share it; rather, she recognises for what they are the imagined terrors that beset those without access to education or information. There is sympathy, too, for the difficulties that can be imposed on eccentric individuals by the limitations of a rigid society. Sympathy, indeed, is the feeling towards which the emphatic final word of the passage, 'loneliness', reaches. The passage mingles realism and understanding with the strange and wild, but it is on sympathy and understanding that the mood settles before Silas is ushered in. Despite the breadth implied in the opening paragraph, then, he initially appears on this bleak stage rather as an individual than a representative of the effects of a general social evil.

In the sequel, of course, it is insight and understanding that take precedence over the mythical qualities of the story. In the novel as a whole, realism takes precedence over fable.

(iii)   *Middlemarch*

Middlemarch at once presents a problem: may it more properly be said to 'begin' with the Prelude, or with Chapter 1? The Prelude appears to have nothing to do with the action. Chapter 1, however, begins in a direct manner distinctly at variance with Eliot's approach in the earlier two novels:

> Miss Brooke had that kind of beauty which seems to be thrown into relief by poor dress. Her hand and wrist were so finely formed that she could wear sleeves not less bare of style than those in which the Blessed Virgin appeared to Italian painters; and her profile as well as her stature and bearing seemed to gain the more dignity from her plain garments, which by the side of provincial fashion gave her the impressiveness of a fine quotation from the Bible, – or from one of our elder poets, – in a paragraph of to-day's newspaper. She was usually spoken of as being remarkably clever, but with the addition that her sister Celia had more common-sense. Nevertheless, Celia wore scarcely more trimmings; and it was only to close observers that her dress differed from her sister's, and had a shade of coquetry in its arrangements; for Miss Brooke's plain dressing was due to mixed conditions, in most of which her sister

shared. The pride of being ladies had something to do with it: the Brooke connections, though not exactly aristocratic, were unquestionably 'good': if you inquired backward for a generation or two, you would not find any yard-measuring or parcel-tying forefathers – anything lower than an admiral or a clergyman; and there was even an ancestor discernible as a Puritan gentleman who served under Cromwell, but afterwards conformed, and managed to come out of all political troubles as the proprietor of a respectable family estate. Young women of such birth, living in a quiet country-house, and attending a village church hardly larger than a parlour, naturally regarded frippery as the ambition of a huckster's daughter. Then there was well-bred economy, which in those days made show in dress the first item to be deducted from, when any margin was required for expenses more distinctive of rank. Such reasons would have been enough to account for plain dress, quite apart from religious feeling; but in Miss Brooke's case, religion alone would have determined it; and Celia mildly acquiesced in all her sister's sentiments, only infusing them with that common-sense which is able to accept momentous doctrines without any eccentric agitation. Dorothea knew many passages of Pascal's *Pensées* and of Jeremy Taylor by heart; and to her the destinies of mankind, seen by the light of Christianity, made the solicitudes of feminine fashion appear an occupation for Bedlam. She could not reconcile the anxieties of a spiritual life involving eternal consequences, with a keen interest in gimp and artificial protrusions of drapery. Her mind was theoretic, and yearned by its nature after some lofty conception of the world which might frankly include the parish of Tipton and her own rule of conduct there; she was enamoured of intensity and greatness, and rash in embracing whatever seemed to her to have those aspects; likely to seek martyrdom, to make retractations, and then to incur martyrdom after all in a quarter where she had not sought it. Certainly such elements in the character of a marriageable girl tended to interfere with her lot, and hinder it from being decided according to custom, by good looks, vanity, and merely canine affection. With all this, she, the elder of the sisters, was not yet twenty, and they had both been educated, since they were about twelve years old and had lost their parents, on plans at once narrow and promiscuous, first in an English family and afterwards in a Swiss family at Lausanne, their bachelor uncle and guardian trying in this way to remedy the disadvantages of their orphaned condition.

(pp. 7–8)

The contrast with the earlier novels is easy to see. Here there is no
preliminary description of a scene or a society. Instead, Eliot at once
places Dorothea in a web of social, historical and psychological con-
texts. The sheer quantity of information communicated, the range
and variety of ideas touched on and the complexity of the relationships suggested in this opening paragraph are astonishing and
demand careful analysis. Structurally the passage falls naturally into
four sections: the opening dealing primarily with Miss Brooke's and
Celia's dress; second, a passage dealing with the 'mixed conditions'
from which the sisters' ideas have grown; a third section, the longest,
dealing with Dorothea's mind and aspirations; and a final note on the
sisters' education.

Within this simple structural analysis the paragraph generates a
rich variety of meaning. In the first section, the basic contrast between
Dorothea's appearance and dress gives rise to a series of contrasts,
some of them extraordinary. The most obvious of these is the contrasting of Dorothea with her younger sister, Celia, who is reputed
to be less clever, but to possess more common sense. The distinction
is of a commonplace kind, but becomes an interesting one because
of the doubts Eliot generates about its precise significance. Consider,
particularly, how the distinction appears in the light of the 'shade of
coquetry' in Celia's dress: does this imply that there is more common
sense in coquetry than in Dorothea's refinement? and if so, is it so in
the eyes of the narrator, or in the eyes of the community? Already,
the phrase 'she was spoken of' presents the sisters in the perspective
of a community that makes judgements on its members. There is
doubt, too, how far the narrator shares the ideas of the community:
the reference to 'provincial fashion' implies a broader perspective
on the part of the narrator – a perspective which embraces Italian
painters in this section, and Pascal, Jeremy Taylor, Bedlam and Lausanne elsewhere. These questions, doubts and uncertainties develop
incrementally in the passage as a whole so that what seemed to begin
as a conventional character portrait rapidly becomes anything but
straightforward. In this context, it is hard to be sure what is meant
by Dorothea's being 'remarkably clever', for there is no way to assess
the parameters by which she appears so. Clear it is, however, both
that Dorothea is in some way exceptional and that the narrator is to

some degree reserving judgement on her. There are hints of this doubt in the repetition of 'seemed': her beauty 'seemed to be thrown into relief' by her plain dress; 'her stature and bearing seemed to gain the more dignity' from her simple attire. There is a much broader hint in the outrageous comparison between Dorothea and the Blessed Virgin of the Italian renaissance. The hyperbole illustrates Dorothea's exceptional quality but stresses that, like a biblical quotation in a daily newspaper, she is exceptional in relation to a thoroughly unremarkable provincial society. A linked doubt arises over the religious elements in this first section. Dorothea's quasi-religious zeal is yet to be developed; here, the Blessed Virgin is diminished to the worldly vision of painters, and biblical quotation is diminished by being undifferentiated from quotation from 'one of our elder poets'. More broadly, the reference invites inquiry about the status of religious faith in this society of which Dorothea is a member. In this opening section, then, simple and direct though it may appear on a cursory reading, Eliot's primary achievement is to raise questions and awaken doubts.

These uncertainties are set aside for a time while the background of the Brooke sisters is addressed – but only to be replaced by a different group of uncertainties. This, the second section of the paragraph, focuses on two sources of the Brooke sisters' preference for modest dress: the 'pride of being ladies' and 'well-bred economy'. The good family background of the Brookes – by no means aristocratic, but far from undistinguished – is covered with mild irony. There is a sardonic acceptance of simple means of measuring a family when Eliot denies, without overt question, the existence of anything savouring of trade, or 'lower than an admiral or a clergyman' in the family history; and there is a hint of the possibly questionable origins of fortune in the reference to the Puritan gentleman who had 'managed to come out of all political troubles as the proprietor of a respectable family estate'. 'Respectable' is a problematic word whenever it appears because of all the assumptions it encompasses. In this instance its use implies an economic comfort large rather than entirely untarnished, and raises a range of questions about the nature of respectability in Middlemarch and about the Brookes' idea of their own position in that world. Eliot refers to the prominence of the Brookes in a restricted environment – 'attending a village church hardly larger than a parlour' – as a source of the sisters' sense of superiority, and voices their own estimate of themselves in contrasting their views of fashion with those of 'a huckster's daughter'. The Brookes, then, have a high estimate of their own standing, but Eliot reminds us that they inhabit an undemanding realm: Middlemarch is only a small pool for such fish. In this section, as in the first, Eliot is busily avoiding simple definitions. Here she undermines the certainties of middle England: all that is associated with 'the pride of being ladies' opens the possibility of a range of valuations involving wholesome and unwholesome pride, vanity and conceit, and throws disturbing doubt on the shifting meaning of 'ladies' in this or other social groupings.

In the third section Eliot looks more closely at Dorothea herself. Again, she begins with dress, for the external appearance reflects an internal truth. Now, however, the truth is personal rather than social or familial. Dorothea has 'religious feeling'. By this phrase it is evident that Eliot means a serious and deep preoccupation with the practice of Christianity to better the human lot. Though Dorothea is described as having a 'theoretic' mind it is clear from what follows in the novel that she has practical aims in view as a means of expressing her spiritual aspirations. Here Eliot focuses on Dorothea's spiritual world with fine ambiguity. For Dorothea, pretty clothes are no more than 'artificial protrusions' when seen *sub specie aeternitatis*: in likening fashion to a matter fit for Bedlam, Eliot is thinking of a house of madmen, not simply of confusion. Dorothea's clearmindedness in her higher ambitions makes a sharp contrast. She is seen as better in being consumed not with the vagaries of fashion but with 'the destinies of mankind' and 'the anxieties of a spiritual life involving eternal consequences'. Clearly, then, she is indeed exceptional, and even admirable. Perhaps the earlier reference to the Blessed Virgin was not entirely ironic. Nevertheless, there are heavy hints of irony in this section. If her mind is theoretic, does that not imply impracticality? Such is the implication of the vivid language employed by Eliot in speaking of Dorothea's reaching towards a 'lofty conception' of 'intensity and greatness', even towards a tortuous route to martyrdom. This language is in itself too grand to be entirely transparent. The doubt is sharpened by the passionate tone of Dorothea's aspirations: she is 'enamoured of' an intense life, 'rash in embracing' it. And what is to be the theatre of this idealistic urge? Why, 'the parish of Tipton' which is set 'frankly' side by side with the nobility of Dorothea's visions. Of course, the parish must be the scene of the formulation in action of Dorothea's 'own rule of conduct', and there we see a genuine, sincere motive in play; yet Tipton is most unlikely to be the scene of a nineteenth-century martyrdom. In this incongruity of great and small, Eliot registers a serious question about the realism of Dorothea's ambitions. As the course of the novel shows, however, Eliot is also concerned with the general nature of martyrdom and greatness.

The incongruity reaches its climax in the fourth section of the paragraph. Despite the preceding ironies, it is a little shock to be brought to earth by Eliot's flat reference to Dorothea as 'a marriageable girl', and by the prosaic outlines of the upbringing of her and her sister that conclude the paragraph. The contrast of great and small modulates now into a contrast of passion with practicality. The noble inclinations of Dorothea's spirit are now considered with heavier irony as factors that merely 'interfere with her lot' and 'hinder it' from being determined by any ordinary range of factors, among which Eliot lists 'custom, good looks, vanity', and finally, and extraordinarily, 'merely canine affection'. It is hard not to hear in this violent phrase a tone of personal disgust on the part of the author; yet we may wonder if, despite her idealistic dreams, Dorothea follows Casaubon with much more than a spaniel's nose. The paragraph concludes, significantly, on a note of bleak realism, with Mr Brooke's trying to 'remedy the disadvantages of their orphaned condition'. Suddenly, Dorothea is seen from a different perspective: here we have a personality spurred into exaltation by a practical lack; having neither father nor mother, she appears psychologically, to borrow a phrase from *Silas Marner*, a member of a disinherited race, and thus it is that she tries to reframe her heritage in a spiritual realm. In presenting this aspiration from the point of view of society as merely an obstacle to Dorothea's proper goal as the wife of a suitable husband, Eliot suggests a complex of questions touched on in the novel as a whole: the meaning of marriage, the status of women and the validity of individual ambition.

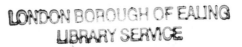

Stylistically the paragraph matches its complex subject. Much of its phrasing seems to stem from the Bible or the elder poets referred to near the beginning, but these more lofty phrases stand ironically alongside the language of today's newspaper. See how often a fine beginning descends into bathos: in, for example, the sentence which deals with Dorothea's studying Pascal and Jeremy Taylor, and speaks of 'the destinies of mankind, seen by the light of Christianity' before contrasting them with 'the solicitudes of feminine fashion [as] an occupation for Bedlam'; or the next sentence where 'eternal consequences' contrast with 'artificial protrusions of drapery'. Irony is everywhere in this passage. Consider the use of negations: the Brooke family is 'not exactly aristocratic'; among its forebears 'you would not find any' tradesmen; Dorothea 'could not reconcile' fashion with eternity. All these negations invite us to make judgements about the standards and attitudes underlying them, for every negative implies a positive standard from which there is divergence or dissent. Consider, finally, the implications of the sentence in which Dorothea is contrasted with Celia, who 'mildly acquiesce[s]' in Dorothea's feelings, but 'without any eccentric agitation': is it Celia or Dorothea who is less flattered? Should we think of Celia as superior because she is more in tune with the world and her own nature, or of Dorothea as more noble because she transcends these trivial standards? The judgement is a fine one.

The picture we have of Dorothea in this opening paragraph is remarkably complex, and remarkably balanced. Clearly she is to be the protagonist of the novel, and clearly is admirable for her noble mind and virtuous soul. At the same time Eliot presents her as something of the innocent, more than a little naive in the ways of the world: aware of her social position she undoubtedly is, but she has yet to learn of the importance of custom, convention and the demands of human vanity. Pascal and Jeremy Taylor cannot prepare her for the limitations of Edward Casaubon, nor for the varieties of perfidy housed in the rest of the society of Middlemarch. Almost before we have begun, it seems, Dorothea runs the risk of dismissal as an over-emotional girl. Her religious tendencies are perhaps not rational, but the product merely of an over-sensitive nature. Eliot's language ('eccentric', 'anxieties', 'theoretic', 'yearned', 'lofty', 'enam-

oured', 'rash', 'martyrdom') implies excess, lack of judgement, immaturity. Some of these words, however, may express more about the
unambitious laziness of observers than about Dorothea. After all, a
degree of eccentricity is probably essential to any kind of greatness:
to be without it would be unexceptional. We are invited, then, not
uncritically to admire a heroine, but to understand and sympathise
with an imperfect protagonist.

That Dorothea is a character of serious status is at once evident
from the way her portrait is prepared in the Prelude, which opens
thus, preparing the odd reference to the Blessed Virgin noted above:

> Who that cares much to know the history of man, and how the mys-
> terious mixture behaves under the varying experiments of Time, has
> not dwelt, at least briefly, on the life of Saint Theresa, has not smiled
> with some gentleness at the thought of the little girl walking forth one
> morning hand-in-hand with her still smaller brother, to go and seek
> martyrdom in the country of the Moors? Out they toddled from rugged
> Avila, wide-eyed and helpless-looking as two fawns, but with human
> hearts, already beating to a national idea; until domestic reality met
> them in the shape of uncles, and turned them back from their great
> resolve. That child-pilgrimage was a fit beginning. Theresa's passion-
> ate, ideal nature demanded an epic life: what were many-volumed
> romances of chivalry and the social conquests of a brilliant girl to her?
> Her flame quickly burned up that light fuel; and, fed from within,
> soared after some illimitable satisfaction, some object which would
> never justify weariness, which would reconcile self-despair with the
> rapturous consciousness of life beyond self. She found her epos in the
> reform of a religious order.
>
> (p. 3)

There is a close parallel with the portrait of Dorothea in the linking
of the 'little girl', Teresa, with an 'epic life'. Teresa's childishness is
stressed: she and her brother 'toddled . . . wide-eyed and helpless-
looking as two fawns' to seek their fate. Here, as in the description
of Dorothea, the word 'martyrdom' appears; so does the concept of
life as epos, which in the portrait takes the form of Dorothea's 'lofty
conception' of her place in the world. Here, as in the action of the
novel, there is conflict between a 'great resolve' and 'domestic reality'

that is adumbrated in the portrait of Dorothea. As in the novel and
its opening portrait, 'life beyond self' is essential for the spiritual
health of noble individuals; Dorothea and Lydgate are both powerful exemplars of this view.

As the Prelude proceeds, its relevance to Dorothea becomes more
pointed. Eliot speaks of the many Teresas who have failed to find fulfilment, whether because of lack of opportunity or because of mistaken action or because of dissipation in countless obstacles, and of
the many others who have remained unrecognised and unsung. The
difficulties propounded are peculiar to, or at least are intensified in,
women. Women, says Eliot, often find their ardour caught between
'a vague ideal and the common yearning of womanhood', and many
potential Teresas finish as 'foundress[es] of nothing'. (Do not be
misled by the note in the Penguin Classics edition or Eliot's spelling:
the reference is to Teresa of Avila who founded convents but not an
order, and not to Theresa of Lisieux who was not born when the novel
was published: the convent in Avila was Carmelite when Teresa
entered it, though she later reformed the rule.) This feminist aspect
of Dorothea's story is picked up in the epigraph to Chapter 1:

> Since I can do no good because a woman,
> Reach constantly at something that is near it.
>
>   (p. 7)

For Eliot, writing as she was under a male pseudonym, the problem
of making a mark in the world as a woman is particularly pointed.
To that extent if not otherwise, the story of Dorothea has autobiographical elements.

The Prelude is thus not a gratuitous ornament. Eliot uses it to set
the intensely individual portrait of Dorothea with which the novel
proper begins in a context which invites us to think of her representative status. No matter how idiosyncratic she may be, she stands for
everyone who needs to experience life as epos; and more particularly,
she stands for women who find themselves cut off from their epic
aspirations by trivial convention or by brutal circumstance. Eliot is
no soap-box orator, however, and maintains always a healthy balance.
In likening Teresa's inheritors to 'a cygnet' in a 'brown pond' in the

Prelude, Eliot acknowledges that Dorothea's story is one among many, and that there is a wider world outside the pond – we may interpret the image on many levels – than Dorothea is aware of.

The homely image of the pond brings the Prelude that began in such fine style finally down to earth. The effect of bathos is one we have seen repeated in Dorothea's portrait. The image also establishes a register in which the portrait can be placed. In seeing the Brookes as the swans of the brown pond of Middlemarch, Eliot accepts both their significance and their unimportance. Dorothea is not so much a big fish in the modest environment of her local pond as merely a cygnet aspiring to become something more than just another swan. Thus Eliot diminishes her status as a heroine; and thus also her epos, at the beginning of the novel, has more than a touch of mock-epic about it.

Conclusions

Middlemarch begins with a narrower field of vision than the earlier novels, for it concentrates on one character, whereas *The Mill on the Floss* begins with a region and *Silas Marner* with a society. Yet it is already apparent that *Middlemarch* is to be a bigger, more complex work than the other two novels. The portrait of Dorothea touches on so many social, familial, moral, intellectual and psychological impli-cations that a large structure is clearly envisaged. In addition, the Prelude on St Teresa shows that Dorothea is to be seen as represent-ing her class and her sex, and not merely as an individual; her story has ramifications outside her own history and outside the fictional world. There is a curious parallel between the cygnet and swans of *Middlemarch* and the white ducks in the second paragraph of *The Mill on the Floss*. Both moments are comic: but the range of relevant resonance in the later novel is much wider. George Eliot here pre-sents herself uncompromisingly as a very serious writer with concerns about the real world. Her tone of ironic humour does nothing to diminish the impression, and rather strengthens it.

Each of the earlier novels opens in a distinctive manner. The opening of *The Mill on the Floss* is marked out by Eliot's sensitivity to the natural environment, to the seasons and their effect on rural life. From the technical point of view, it shows Eliot's ability to play on the symbolic potential in description of the natural world. The novel begins by recalling a personal past and contains an element of nostalgia; however, there is also a sense of involvement in the community life and work associated with the river Floss and the surrounding countryside that carries the novel beyond the merely personal. In *Silas Marner* the recall of the past is less personal. Here Eliot focuses on a period of social change – specifically the displacement of the weavers from the towns to the countryside – that brings about social conflicts. The mood of this opening is darker, sketching a rural society uneducated, unreceptive, suspicious of the unknown and dyed with prejudice. The narrative tone is complex: Eliot adopts the voice of the rural folk she is writing about, but always with an ironic distance, presenting them as objects for consideration and not identifying with them or their views.

What common features emerge from these beginnings? These are the basic ideas that strike me most forcibly:

- The past. The power of the past is obvious in the openings of the earlier novels, but not yet in *Middlemarch*. In that novel, too, however, it will become important. For example, Dorothea is a product of a background, and will be heavily influenced by a man obsessed with the past.
- Community. Eliot deals in all three novels with carefully documented societies with individualised standards, habits and influence. All her protagonists are seen in relation to a community, endeavouring to find a place in it or reacting against it. There are major differences in nature among the communities: family is crucial in *The Mill on the Floss*, religion in *Silas Marner*, while *Middlemarch* stands out as possessing the most complex social world.
- Alienation. Dorlcote Mill is brought before us in a nostalgic tone to represent a past that cannot be reclaimed. The world of Silas Marner is characterised by friendlessness and isolation. *Middlemarch* begins like a typical Victorian story of orphanage; but we

cannot be sure of its ending with the rediscovery of a lost patron-
age. This consistent strand in Eliot's writing may be linked to
her own history.

- Moral vision. George Eliot's moral perspective does not emerge
  at all clearly from the opening of *The Mill on the Floss*, but is
  implied in *Silas Marner* in references to the Evil One, and in
  Middlemarch in allusions to St Teresa, the Bible and the Blessed
  Virgin as background to Dorothea's aspirations to live by the
  light of Christianity. Moral questions stand at the heart of all
  the novels, whether in the story of a comparatively uncultivated
  man, such as Silas Marner, or in that of a young lady of high
  intelligence and strong moral sense such as Dorothea Brooke.
  Maggie Tulliver contains a little of both characters: anxious to
  learn, and captivated by Thomas à Kempis, yet essentially a rural
  lass. In this consistent focus of Eliot's work we see a serious
  concern with social ethics and personal morality.
- Narrative complexity. Though superficially simple and similar –
  they are all cast as conventional third-person narrative – the
  openings of these novels all show a disturbing volatility in tone.
  The Mill on the Floss begins with a strange clashing of past and
  present, and obscure allusion to the location of the scene in the
  narrator's past. In *Silas Marner* the narrator appears to adopt the
  tone and prejudices of the community she presents, while at
  the same time standing critically outside it. The beginning of
  Middlemarch finds a deeply ironic tone in which the parish
  of Tipton can figure largely in the eschatological ruminations of
  Dorothea, and she and the Blessed Virgin have wrists in
  common: this points to the broad range of concerns in the rest
  of the narrative.
- Allusiveness. In the passages from *Middlemarch* discussed above
  there are overt references to the Bible, St Teresa, Pascal and
  Jeremy Taylor. Every chapter has its own epigraph: in Chapter
  1, it is from *The Maid's Tragedy*; in many cases, however, the
  epigraph is Eliot's own. *Silas Marner* takes its epigraph from
  Wordworth's *Michael*, and the opening has echoes of the Bible
  and Bunyan. These allusions are the obvious expression of the

broad erudition of the writer. She read widely and moved in circles in which discussion and argument were a normal part of everyday life. Her novels are often naturalistic or homely, but they are above all novels of ideas – chiefly moral and social ideas – such as those towards which Eliot gestures at the beginning of *Middlemarch*.

- Variety of style. Eliot can write very simply and directly. We can find many examples of straightforward statements like 'I remember the stone bridge . . . And this is Dorlcote Mill' at the beginning of *The Mill on the Floss*. At other times we find lengthy suspensions, compounded with parentheses and comparisons, that make serious demands on the attention of the reader. Look, for example, at the final sentence of the first paragraph of Chapter 1 of *Middlemarch*. The Prelude to *Middlemarch* offers a violent contrast of styles. Compare the suspension and parallelism of the lengthy opening rhetorical question ('Who that cares much to know . . .') with the down-to-earth simplicity of the phrase that follows, 'Out they toddled'. The diction of the Prelude shows a similar variety, embracing both 'toddled', 'epos' and 'illimitable satisfaction'. In part this variety is related to differences in subject matter. A more homely style is appropriate to the story of Silas Marner than to that of Maggie Tulliver, and a more sophisticated mode matches the mind of Dorothea Brooke. If we take into consideration the models she had before her, such as Fielding and Austen, and the common source of the nineteenth century, the Authorised Version of the Bible, we see in Eliot a marked preference for mingling the sophisticated or theoretical with the concrete and vivid. She was highly educated, but she never lost contact with the concrete language of the region in which she grew up, and she represents it vividly in conversations among the characters in all these novels.

- Structural implications. The basis of the plot of *Silas Marner* is already present in the epigraph and opening paragraph. The first paragraph of *Middlemarch* shows Eliot touching many different notes in the course of what begins as a straightforward character portrait, and so foreshadows the wide range of complex patterns that grew from its original two stories. *The Mill on the Floss* begins with the river that closes the action, and thus offers itself as an example of unity of conception.

- Irony. Different kinds of irony appear in each of the openings. It is most evident in the opening of *Middlemarch* where it sometimes takes the conventional form. There and in the other passages discussed it also appears in its more general form in the creation of doubts about the implications of what is being said, and in the juxtaposition of conflicting levels of meaning.

These are some of the features that we explore in future chapters.

Methods of Analysis

There are many ways of approaching literary analysis. It is best to build on methods that you have found successful from experience, so these notes should be viewed only as suggestions.

- Begin with simple things. Decide what kind of narrative you are looking at: whether first- or third-person, whether in the present tense or the past. What kind of thing is discussed: characters or ideas, action or setting? Is the interest dominated by one character or spread among a few?
- Then it is often useful to see whether the passage under study seems to fall into sections, as the paragraph from *Middlemarch* above does. Then you can more easily look at the development of ideas from one section to another. Often the passage will be split physically into convenient separate paragraphs.
- Think about the setting. Is it town or country, social or environmental, realistic or imaginary? How much detail is there? Is the setting used to generate a mood or to create a sense of actuality? Are there any symbolic features in it? Notice how widely different in their use of setting are the passages discussed in this chapter.
- Consider the author's use of language. This includes syntax and diction: the length, organisation and complexity of sentences and the choice of words. Eliot often makes demands on her

readers in both syntax and diction but is equally capable of writing with extreme simplicity.

- Look for striking, emotive, resonant or unusual words, particularly those loaded words that make you reassess the nature of what is being said. In the extracts considered above, words like 'placid', 'threatening', 'disinherited', 'loneliness', 'respectable' and 'orphaned' fall into this general category.

- Many other stylistic considerations may suggest themselves. Two features emerge strongly from the passages discussed above. Irony is an inseparable part of the weave of her writing and finds varying tones depending on her view of the subject. Negation forms a consistent part of her style. In the opening paragraph of *Middlemarch* there is an entertaining example of both features in the statement that Celia is 'able to accept momentous doctrines without any eccentric agitation'.

- The mood of a passage depends on several of the qualities mentioned above and is not always easy to describe. The three novels we have discussed begin with different moods. Notice, however, that humour is always present, even in the bleak world of *Silas Marner*.

- Narrative voice is probably one of the last things to consider, for it depends on all the others. In Eliot you will find the author constantly intruding, either in person as an 'I' rather than merely an 'eye' or by implication in general comments. It is already clear that this is a writer who sees it as her task to comment on the action as well as to describe it.

- Finally, try to sum up how the beginning of the novel prepares for the rest of the narrative: what kind of keynote it establishes for the mood of the whole, whether in any way it envisages the conclusion or important future events, whether it introduces the major characters, and how much of the subject of the novel it contains in embryonic form.

These are ideas to think about, select from and add to. When you come to write about a passage from a novel, you will not necessarily wish to include them all mechanically. You will almost certainly wish to include other ideas of your own.

Further Work

The Mill on the Floss

Look the last three paragraphs of Chapter 1 ('The rush of the water ... I have been dreaming of', pp. 54–5) and see how the ideas considered in the discussion above are developed. In particular, consider the increased prominence of the role of the narrator and the implications of the way the characters are introduced at the end.

Silas Marner

Study paragraph two of the novel ('In the early years of this century ... could raise the phantasm of appetite', pp. 6–7). There are many interesting features in this paragraph, which includes among other things a description of Silas and a local anecdote from the narrator's own experience. How is the narrator's stance modified here? What can we discover about Silas? And how does his portrait develop ideas seen earlier about the relationship between weavers and the local community?

Middlemarch

Consider how the concerns of the early part of Chapter 1 are developed in the five paragraphs following the one discussed above ('It was hardly a year since they had come to live at Tipton Grange . . . and always looked forward to renouncing it', pp. 8–10). You will find that the passage deals largely with Dorothea, but notice also how aspects of the political, religious and social background are touched on, and be aware of the ironic point of view that colours the whole narrative. Look at the second half of the Prelude, too, if you wish.

2

Characters

George Eliot's characters in the novels discussed here fall within the range of normality of the kind of people among whom she grew up. She does not deal with extremes of good or evil, wealth or poverty, and avoids the extreme ends of the social spectrum, preferring to describe the modest aspirations, moderate habits and average acumen of the rural communities of the midlands; the very title of *Middlemarch* points unambiguously to her intention. Significantly broader than Jane Austen's, Eliot's field of vision is nevertheless restricted. The rich, glittering variety of London life with which Eliot was familiar makes no appearance in these novels. Only in *Middlemarch* do the protagonists travel farther than locally.

Within her chosen field, however, Eliot develops a vast range of fully realised characters vividly portrayed and minutely differentiated. Even minor characters are given sufficient space to develop a realistic presence and voice. Eliot portrays manners with vividness and humour. The idiomatic dialogue that develops among her rural characters strikes the ear with the directness of transcription. On a more serious level, major characters are marked out by a steady focus on the complex of realistic moral, social and personal concerns peculiar to each.

This chapter explores the means used by Eliot to portray character. It deals with the emergence of character from portrait, dialogue and symbolism; it considers the use of commentary by other characters and the use of direct comment by the author or narrator. Attention is paid also to the structural aspects of characterisation: the use of parallels and contrasts between characters, particularly when they are related by family or friendship.

(i) *The Mill on the Floss*

In *The Mill on the Floss* Eliot shows a marked inclination to treat characters in pairs. The most obvious pairing is that of Maggie and Tom, whose relationship, troubled as much by their similarities as their differences, dominates the novel. There are several other important pairings of different kinds, such as the parallels between Maggie and Lucy, Tom and Stephen, and Philip and Stephen, and the conflict between Tom and Philip, itself a reflection of the conflict between their fathers. The Tulliver uncles and aunts stand out individually by contrast, as do the fathers or father surrogates like Mr Tulliver, Mr Deane, Mr Wakem and Doctor Kenn. The following passage from the middle part of Chapter 7 in Book One recounts the cutting of Maggie's hair and shows how the common and distinctive qualities of the characters are expressed in action and dialogue:

'Maggie,' said Mrs Tulliver, beckoning Maggie to her and whispering in her ear as soon as this point of Lucy's staying was settled, 'go and get your hair brushed – do, for shame. I told you not to come in without going to Martha first, you know I did.'

'Tom, come out with me,' whispered Maggie, pulling his sleeve as she passed him, and Tom followed willingly enough.

'Come upstairs with me, Tom,' she whispered when they were outside the door. 'There's something I want to do before dinner.'

'There's no time to play at anything before dinner,' said Tom, whose imagination was impatient of any intermediate prospect.

'O yes, there's time for this – do come, Tom.'

Tom followed Maggie upstairs into her mother's room, and saw her go at once to a drawer from which she took out a large pair of scissors.

'What are they for, Maggie?' said Tom, feeling his curiosity awakened.

Maggie answered by seizing her front locks and cutting them straight across the middle of her forehead.

'O, my buttons, Maggie – you'll catch it!' exclaimed Tom. 'You'd better not cut any more off.'

Snip! went the great scissors again while Tom was speaking, and he couldn't help feeling it was rather good fun: Maggie would look so queer.

'Here Tom, cut it behind for me,' said Maggie, excited by her own daring and anxious to finish the deed.

'You'll catch it, you know,' said Tom, nodding his head in an admonitory manner, and hesitating a little as he took the scissors.

'Never mind – make haste!' said Maggie, giving a little stamp with her foot. Her cheeks were quite flushed.

The black locks were so thick – nothing could be more tempting to a lad who had already tasted the forbidden pleasure of cutting the pony's mane. I speak to those who know the satisfaction of making a pair of shears meet through a duly resisting mass of hair. One delicious grinding snip, and then another and another, and the hinder locks fell heavily on the floor, and Maggie stood cropped in a jagged uneven manner, but with a sense of clearness and freedom, as if she had emerged from a wood into the open plain.

'O Maggie,' said Tom, jumping round her and slapping his knees as he laughed, 'O, my buttons, what a queer thing you look! Look at yourself in the glass – you look like the idiot we throw our nutshells to at school.'

(pp. 119–20)

In the action of this scene, Maggie's mood and character are vividly represented in her violent act of self-mutilation, from the manner in which she performs it and from Tom's reactions. A mood of secrecy and urgency is developed at the outset by Maggie's whispered entreaties and the force of her will, overcoming his reluctance with her assurance, 'Oh yes, there's time for this'. Then the magnitude of the act is reinforced by the heroic instrument Maggie selects to shear herself: it is 'a large pair of scissors', later 'the great scissors'. Maggie is decisive in her behaviour, 'seizing' the locks on her brow and cutting 'straight across'. This is no time for ceremony. The deed must be done on the spur. The onomatopoeic 'Snip!' of the scissors drives home the irrevocable moment. Maggie, carried away by the excitement of her transgression and 'anxious to finish the deed', gets Tom to help her, stamping her foot to hurry him on. At last the shearing is completed, with an echoing of the snipping of the scissors, and Maggie emerges 'with a sense of clearness and freedom'. Though in the immediate sequel to the passage Maggie 'felt an unexpected pang' (p. 120), there is at this point nothing in her heart but triumphant satisfaction.

Maggie's act appears the more significant by contrast with the behaviour of Tom. He thinks of the occasion as 'rather good fun': for Maggie, 'quite flushed', this is much more than fun. He capers about, slapping his knees and laughing, and twice exclaiming 'Oh, my buttons', both because Maggie looks so 'queer' (the word is used twice), and because she will 'catch it' (twice also). Maggie in contrast is at this point unmoved by the threat of retribution to come – 'Never mind – make haste!' – absorbed as she is in the accomplishment of what for her is an emotional necessity. Although Tom implicates himself as an accessory in her crime, he does so with hesitation; indeed, in his manner as he stands 'nodding his head in an admonitory manner' there is a premonition of his later behaviour as the rigid autocrat who banishes his sister. There is a level at which Maggie's act is an excessive act of primitive vengeance. Though primitive, however, it is not simple: there are many layers of meaning in the scene.

What is the significance of this act, so powerfully dramatised, for Maggie? It is partly explained in the paragraph following the extract, where reference is made to Maggie's seeking 'deliverance from her teasing hair and teasing remarks about it' (p. 121). The opening of the extract suggests a richer mine of motives, however. Secrecy is a dominant note in the passage, but at the beginning it is of a different kind from the secrecy of Tom and Maggie in their mischief. Mrs Tulliver beckons and whispers to Maggie to get her hair brushed 'for shame'. She will not speak aloud before the uncles and aunts because to do so would fall short of the standards of polish and propriety she deems appropriate to the Tulliver station in life. Further, in reminding Maggie that 'I told you' to see Martha before coming in she seeks to exonerate herself from blame in this family disgrace. It is in truth only a minor disgrace – Maggie appears in company looking characteristically dishevelled instead of neat as the little lady her mother would wish her to be – but it is large in Mrs Tulliver's mind, and it is therefore large also in Maggie's. From this point of view, Maggie's deed is a rejection of the expectations of mother, uncles and aunts together. Failing to be the little lady, she determines on an exaggerated antithesis, and makes herself 'a queer thing', as she stands 'cropped in a jagged uneven manner'.

Another spur to Maggie's deed is, as the reference to her at the beginning of the passage hints, Lucy. Despite Maggie's deep fondness for her, Lucy is a living reproach to her cousin. The words that dominate her portrait (p. 117) are 'neat' and 'little'. She has a 'little rosebud mouth' which she dutifully puts up to be kissed. She has a 'little straight nose, not at all snubby', and 'little clear eyebrows'; at her 'little round neck' are coral beads. Shorter than Maggie by a head, she seems to Maggie like the queen of fantasy land. In short, she is everything Maggie is not. In Chapter 2, Mrs Tulliver directly contrasts Maggie with Lucy who has 'a row o' curls round her head, an' not a hair out o' place' (pp. 60–1). Beside this 'white kitten' Maggie appears an 'overgrown puppy' (p. 117).

There is more to it than a neat appearance. Lucy is the little lady that Maggie so signally fails to be. She meets the demands of respectability and thus matches the expectations of her parents. In her whispered instruction to Maggie, Mrs Tulliver implies that Maggie ought to be more like Lucy, even that she would prefer a daughter like Lucy for her own. Maggie, though she loves Lucy, knows that she cannot be like her. When she cuts off her hair, then, Maggie is making a statement to her mother and to the world: she is not, and will not be, a Lucy; she does not accept the expectations of her mother; she does not accede to the demands of propriety or respectability. The point is stressed by the direct rebellion against her mother: told to brush her hair, she does quite otherwise. Instead of acceding, she insists on being herself. Trivial in itself, an entertainment for the uncles and a passing distress for the aunts, the cutting of her hair is psychologically and morally irrevocable. The meaning of her act is utterly different for her and for the company at the mill. Her hair will grow back, but she cannot again be the same person.

There is a powerful sense of transgression in the secrecy, the daring and excitement, and the reference to 'the forbidden pleasure of cutting the pony's mane', which recalls the description in Chapter 2 of Maggie's habit of incessantly tossing her hair with 'the air of a small Shetland pony' (p. 61). Superficially, the transgression is that of mischievous children bent on plotting ways of circumventing adult authority. There are other resonances here, however, of maturation and eroticism. The need for privacy, the feverish insistence of Maggie as she entices Tom upstairs, the awakening of Tom's curiosity, the impatience and force of will of Maggie in completing the mutilation, the intimacy of collusion between the two, the change wrought in Maggie, followed by the sudden return to cold reality and the subsequent retreat from what later appears unwisdom – all suggest a powerful emotional experience. Eliot's use of the metaphor of 'emerg[ing] from a wood into the open plain' implies much: the wood in this context is restrictive but safe; the plain is more exciting, with broad prospects, but dangerous because it is exposed. In keeping with the resonances of the episode, the simile suggests in general the emergence from a sheltered childhood into the wider perspectives and responsibilities of adulthood. More specifically, it suggests an emotional or sexual awakening. There is the resonance of a further kind of transgression in the hinting at an incestuous vein, never fully given substance in the novel, in Maggie's feelings and in Tom's delight in 'forbidden pleasure'.

At the end of the episode, Maggie has become a different person, 'a queer thing' in Tom's eyes and, when he encourages her to 'Look at yourself in the glass', in her own. Tom's reference at the end of the extract to 'the idiot we throw our nutshells to' provokes a sudden transformation in Maggie's feelings. Where a moment before she has a 'sense of clearness and freedom', now she feels naked, shorn for the scorn and derision of the world. She looks at herself in the glass and suddenly, excitement withered away, perceives herself objectively. She appears now in a guise familiar to her, for she is regularly perceived as strange and comical. The image of Maggie as an idiot is a mutation of her mother's sense of the oddity of an intelligent, sensitive child whom she only partially understands. Mrs Tulliver expresses her feelings about her daughter most vividly in Chapter 2, when she describes Maggie abstracted, sitting in the sunshine singing and plaiting her hair, and thinks of her as 'half a idiot i' some things . . . like a Bedlam creatur' . . . like a mulatter . . . so comical' (p. 60) – a kind of child never known in her family. Instead of being transported by her own daring, she is cruelly restored to the state that she sought to escape.

Maggie realises that what she has done will lay her open to criticism and mockery. She is used to being in the wrong. Her skin is too
brown, she is too big, she is too untidy and, in the discussion immediately preceding the extract, she has too much hair. Only her father
takes her part as 'a straight black-eyed wench as anybody need wish
to see', and is proud that she 'can read almost as well as the parson'
(both p. 60); but even he thinks her hair should be shorter. In the
aftermath of the episode, she is criticised again, laughed at and threat-
ened with punishment, however playfully. She is considered 'a
naughty child as'll break her mother's heart' (p. 125) by Mrs Tulliver
with tears in her eyes, and 'more like a gypsy nor ever' (p. 125) according to Mrs Pullet. Aunt Glegg thinks that 'Little gells as cut their own
hair should be whipped and fed on bread and water – not come and
sit down with their aunts and uncles' (p. 125) and her husband ironically suggests that gaol would be a solution, since there the job of
cutting her hair would be completed efficiently. The menfolk, indeed,
are more amused than appalled, but it is only her father who, with a
hint of perverse pride in her rashness, comforts and supports her.

Cutting her hair is evidently a complex response to the criticism
she receives, and her rebellion is thus of a subtle kind. On one level
it is an attempt to meet the repeated demand that she should be tidy
and get on with her patchwork like a conventional young lady; her
father more than once says that her hair should be cut off. However,
no one expects her to take this radical step herself, and in doing so
she is wreaking vengeance for the burden of expectation placed upon
her. On another level it is a denial of herself: she cuts off her hair
because she wants to discipline its disorderliness. Yet again, she is
denying her sexuality to the extent that hair is conventionally associated with sexuality and sexual difference. From another point of
view, she is asserting her right to define herself, and it is this view
that matches the mood of the extract most nearly. Maggie's intense
excitement shows that she understands that she is transgressing; her
change of mood after the event shows that she expects retribution.
Thus her cutting of her hair expresses conflicting impulses towards
both rebellion and conformity.

Those conflicting impulses underlie the pattern of rebellion and
submission that dominates the novel. As often as Maggie strays, she

returns to the bounds of the convention she offends. The sequence is apparent in the extract, where Mrs Tulliver's cliché at the beginning, 'for shame', which helps to inspire Maggie's actions, becomes transmuted at the end into real shame into which she has been betrayed by 'passionate impulse' (p. 121). Though her act derives from resentment against Mrs Tulliver's slavery to convention as well as against the idolisation of the Lucy figure, she nevertheless loves Lucy dearly and remains always loyal to her mother. She will not willingly offend them, or her brother. Her hair is again an indicator of moral posture later in the novel, when, back home after her father's failure, and after her stay at Kings Lorton and the development of her fondness for Philip Wakem, Maggie feels 'obliged to give way to her mother about her hair and submit to have the abundant black locks plaited into a coronet on the summit of her head after the pitiable fashion of those antiquated times' (p. 388). The personal tone of the remark – and the judgement in 'pitiable' – recalls the personal comment in the extract, in which Eliot directly addresses her reader in 'I speak to those who know the satisfaction of making a pair of shears meet through a duly resisting mass of hair'.

The meaning of Maggie's act is supported by the language and imagery of the extract. The sense in this episode of her being borne along by the force of her will, 'excited by her own daring', refers the event to the primary symbol of the book, the flood of emotion or passion that carries Maggie repeatedly into uncharted waters whence, suddenly taking fright, she retreats – as she does immediately after the extract, when her 'cheeks began to pale, and her lips to tremble' (p. 121). Mrs Pullet's description of the new Maggie as a gypsy points directly to her next escapade when she runs away to the gypsy camp. There are broader implications, too. The pattern of daring and decision followed by retreat and shame is repeated in Maggie's experiences later in the novel with Philip and Stephen. Equally, the results of those experiences repeat the principle of denial of self realised in the extract. Finally, the covert hints of incest help to explain Tom's jealousy of Maggie's relationships with Philip and Stephen, and her inability to commit herself to those relationships.

In this episode, Eliot's powers are fully engaged. The scene is vividly evoked, and its language supports the emotional intensity of the action. It helps to define the relationship between Maggie and Tom: they are linked by their shared delight in daring, but it is clear that the deed means more to her than to him; she is already a deeper character, and Tom shows himself, here as later, the more conventional of the pair. The episode also develops the feelings of Maggie about her background, the relationship between Maggie and her mother, and the parallel between Maggie and Lucy. Eliot uses the imagery of rural life to explore the feelings of Maggie and Tom, referring to the cutting of a pony's mane, and to the wood and plain that form part of the natural environment of the novel. Despite its varied resonances, the episode is thoroughly realistic, and thoroughly convincing. After the depths of the incident are explored, it remains, at bottom, a vivid evocation of a piece of mischief concocted by two children on the brink of adolescence. Eliot shows here the capacity to communicate effectively on multiple levels, combining simple realism with deeper psychological truths and implications.

(ii) *Silas Marner*

It is a persuasive and simple view that the protagonist of the novel must *ipso facto* be the eponymous Silas. He first appears in the second paragraph of the novel and is present in the final scene. Yet Henry James, among others, was aware that Godfrey Cass, not present at the beginning and conspicuously absent from the end, is a more complex character. Godfrey will be considered in later chapters. Here it is more appropriate to give consideration to Silas. The following extract, two paragraphs from near the end of Chapter 2, summarise the preceding account of Silas's life since settling in Raveloe, and then introduce a new turn in his fortunes:

> So, year after year, Silas Marner had lived in this solitude, his guineas rising in the iron pot, and his life narrowing and hardening itself more and more into a mere pulsation of desire and satisfaction that had no relation to any other being. His life had reduced itself to the functions of weaving and hoarding, without any contemplation of an end towards which the functions tended. The same sort of process has

perhaps been undergone by wiser men, when they have been cut off from faith and love – only, instead of a loom and a heap of guineas, they have had some erudite research, some ingenious project, or some well-knit theory. Strangely Marner's face and figure shrank and bent themselves into a constant mechanical relation to the objects of his life, so that he produced the same sort of impression as a handle or a crooked tube, which has no meaning standing apart. The prominent eyes that used to look trusting and dreamy, now looked as if they had been made to see only one kind of thing that was very small, like tiny grain, for which they hunted everywhere: and he was so withered and yellow, that, though he was not yet forty, the children always called him 'Old Master Marner'.

Yet even in this stage of withering a little incident happened, which showed that the sap of affection was not all gone. It was one of his daily tasks to fetch his water from a well a couple of fields off, and for this purpose, ever since he came to Raveloe, he had had a brown earthenware pot, which he held as his most precious utensil among the very few conveniences he had granted himself. It had been his companion for twelve years, always standing on the same spot, always lending its handle to him in the early morning, so that its form had an expression for him of willing helpfulness, and the impress of its handle on his palm gave a satisfaction mingled with that of having the fresh clear water. One day as he was returning from the well, he stumbled against the step of the stile, and his brown pot, falling with force against the stones that overarched the ditch below him, was broken in three pieces. Silas picked up the pieces and carried them home with grief in his heart. The brown pot could never be of use to him any more, but he stuck the bits together and propped the ruin in its old place for a memorial.

(pp. 20–1)

The structural pattern of these paragraphs is clear from their opening words. 'So, year after year' concludes Eliot's account of the direction Silas Marner's life has followed in the fifteen years leading to the fictional present of the novel. The second paragraph, beginning 'Yet even in this stage', introduces a new element, admitting that what appeared to be Marner's life is not the summation of his story, and suggesting a deeper complexity in his life and character than appears on the surface. The paragraph ends with the incident of the broken pot, which assumes broad symbolic significance.

In the first paragraph Eliot focuses chiefly on the narrowing of Marner's ideas and life. Absorbed in building his hoard of gold, he becomes enslaved by his own obsession. Eliot writes vividly of the 'narrowing and hardening' of his life, finding ironically sensual language, in the phrasing of 'the pulsation of desire and satisfaction', to render the rhythm of a will that has nothing to do with human desire or affection. Towards the end of the paragraph, she describes him as 'withered and yellow' as if she is thinking of a tarnished echo of the gold he gathers. Instead of the vague idealism they once expressed ('trusting and dreamy'), his eyes have adapted to the search for coin, which, as it seems, they 'hunted everywhere', and in the reference to 'the tiny grain' his eyes search for there is an implicit evaluation of the object of his lust as trivial. There is no hint of admiration for this soul-deadening labour: Eliot's language ('narrowing and hardening . . . cut off . . . reduced . . . shrank . . . bent . . . withered') is of atrophy and loss. In the pursuit of his gold, Marner becomes little more than a machine. His life merely embodies 'the functions of weaving and hoarding', as his physical presence seems to mirror his work in a 'constant mechanical relation to the objects of his life'; the comparison of his frame with 'a handle or crooked tube' intensifies the impression of the dehumanisation of his existence. Further, there is a diabolical balance between what he is and what he does: and as the gold increases in quantity, it takes over more of the core of his being. There is no overt expression of sympathy for his situation. Yet it is implicit in the intensity of the portrait, in the status of the earthenware brown pot as Silas's only friend, and in the consciousness of waste in Eliot's sharp depiction of the descent from past trust in people to present recluse isolation.

The first paragraph extends beyond Silas himself, however, in ways that deepen the sense of sympathy. Though he is treated as exceptional, he is compared with 'wiser men' who, engaged in the pursuit of some more elevated goal, are like him in being 'cut off from faith and love'; and the reference to 'erudite research' here irresistibly suggests Edward Casaubon. At the same time, because he is exceptional, Marner lives a life of solitude, divorced from the society here hinted at only in the children who, schooled in the reserved culture described in the opening paragraph of the novel, call him 'Old Master Marner' because, withered as he is, he looks much older than his years; thus he is portrayed both from his own subjective point of view and from the objective point of view of the children. Eliot's language, too, suggests perspectives much beyond Marner's own vision. His obsessiveness is pityingly portrayed in the eyes that hunt constantly in moral blindness. The phrasing of the 'pulsation of desire and satisfaction' ironically adapts the language of love to the imperative demands of his barren business that has as yet 'no relation to any other being'. Eliot, then, constantly suggests perspectives beyond Marner's, while strengthening the force of a portrait of a man performing the rituals of his restricted life without a sense of purpose: 'without contemplation of an end towards which the functions tended'. The first paragraph as a whole generates a background of love, trust, faith and productive work which can give meaning to life, and from which Marner is cut off; his life is essentially empty and, despite his growing heap of gold and despite Eliot's sympathy, pointless.

It is the declared aim of the second paragraph of the extract to demonstrate that, despite the advanced stage the 'withering' of Silas has reached, 'the sap of affection was not all gone' – that there is still in him the need for something beyond the mechanical accumulation of gold, even some vestigial desire for emotional nutrition. The object chosen to represent the flickering of warmth in Silas, an old brown earthenware pot, is an unlikely one, yet Eliot succeeds in investing it with the worth of something much greater. It is described as 'his most precious utensil', and thus contrasts with his gold, which is precious in a materialistic sense. More remarkably, it is personified in Silas's mind as 'his companion' for twelve years; it 'lend[s]' its handle to him. Its shape 'had an expression for him of willing helpfulness', as if it had a human countenance. It is worth noticing the difference in meaning here from saying, for example, that its form expressed helpfulness: the noun 'expression' implies a face, and 'willing' a heart. It is worth recalling, too, the contrasting manner in which Silas is bent to the shape of his loom: in this instance the human is reduced to a mechanism. The brown pot that assumes such significance for Silas expresses both the emotional poverty of his life and the stubborn residual urge towards relationship that survives in the recesses of his being. Thus he experiences a strange 'satisfaction' associated with the drinking of 'fresh clear water' in handling the utensil. There is more than the mere pleasure of familiarity in it. The water suggests innocence and simplicity; beyond that, it links with the sap of affection and contrasts with the withering that were mentioned at the beginning of the paragraph. The unremarkable brown pot contains, then, the universal symbol of fertility. The incident of its breaking is recorded in language dramatised by alliteration and consonance ('stumbled . . . step . . . stile . . . stones . . . stuck', 'falling with force', 'overarched . . . ditch', 'pot . . . picked . . . pieces . . . propped . . . place'), and thus by its position and the manner of its telling appears climactic.

When the pot is broken and repaired, it becomes a complex symbol. Broken in three and stuck together, it is transformed from 'precious utensil' and 'companion' of twelve years into a 'memorial' without practical use: Eliot thus openly invites us to consider its meaning, which is rather less clear than the water it once contained. From one point of view the pot expresses the nature of Silas's life. As his life is reduced to function without motive, the pot that cannot hold water is form without purpose; he looks like a man, but the flaws in his way of life leave him far short of full humanity. A related idea is that the pot expresses the emptiness of Silas's pursuit of gold, for it may be seen as an idol, propped in a place of honour but hopelessly broken, its three parts a parody of the trinity of the godhead. There is, however, a contrasting idea in the change in the nature of the pot after twelve years. The breaking of the pot may be seen as a harbinger of change in Silas's life. He is unwilling to give up his old familiar ways, but the pot will not be the same. Though there is 'grief in his heart' over the breakage, the grief itself betokens the stirrings of an emotional life long hidden. Grief links, through the implication of tears, with the sap, the fresh clear water that is capable of bringing renewal to the desert of Silas's meagre existence.

Which of these interpretations is closest to the truth? It is, of course, impossible to say, any more than it is possible to know how clear was Eliot's intention. The point is that the symbolism of the pot should stimulate thought and encourage sympathetic involvement in Silas's situation. If the interpretations suggested above appear contradictory, they reflect a turning-point in Silas's life: he is anxious to cling to the bare comfort of the known, yet is about to experience a radical change in his circumstances; and in the same way that the pot is broken, that change begins with a barely supportable loss as the necessary prelude to reconstitution; specifically, Silas must lose his gold before he can understand the value of human contact. Silas's fondness for the pot is ambiguous, too: it shows his capacity for affection, but this is after all only a pot, and he clings to it merely because it is something familiar to him as an alien in a hostile world. If Silas is to change, his slavery to gold and his love for the pot must likewise end. On one level, we may say that the routines on which he is dependent must be broken down. At a deeper level, the sap of affection is about to rise again in Silas's heart, but first it must be released from bondage to his lonely idolatry. The symbolism of the broken pot is not simple, but it is evidently crucial. The significance of the incident is emphasised at the end of the chapter when, having developed the imagery of water and barrenness and its relation to Silas's monomania at length, Eliot speaks of 'a second great change' (p. 22) in his life. And at that point, of course, Eliot breaks off to turn her attention to the Cass family.

The portrait of Silas Marner is a rich passage that touches on a variety of themes, including the conflict between love and money, the nature of work and its effect on character, the links between different levels of society, the place of the individual in society and the requirements of a satisfying life. Marner, however, is not sophisticated or articulate, and these resonances are introduced by the voice of the author who comments on character and event, pointing out the parallels between Marner and 'wiser' men, describing the relationship between Marner and the children of the neighbourhood, using imagery to portray Silas's nature, and developing a complex vein of symbolism to bring out different facets of an important and revealing incident. The first effect is to portray Silas as a convincing character; beyond that, however, he is presented as a key element in the complex moral frame of reference of the novel as a whole.

(iii) *Middlemarch*

The following extract from Chapter 1, in which Celia and Dorothea
look through their mother's jewellery, shows how character emerges
from dialogue and from contrast between different personalities:

Celia had unclasped the necklace and drawn it off. 'It would be a little
tight for your neck; something to lie down and hang would suit you
better,' she said, with some satisfaction. The complete unfitness of the
necklace from all points of view for Dorothea, made Celia happier in
taking it. She was opening some ring-boxes, which disclosed a fine
emerald with diamonds, and just then the sun passing beyond a cloud
sent a bright gleam over the table.

'How very beautiful these gems are!' said Dorothea, under a new
current of feeling, as sudden as the gleam. 'It is strange how deeply
colours seem to penetrate one, like scent. I suppose that is the reason
why gems are used as spiritual emblems in the Revelation of St John.
They look like fragments of heaven. I think that emerald is more
beautiful than any of them.'

'And there is a bracelet to match it,' said Celia. 'We did not notice
this at first.'

'They are lovely,' said Dorothea, slipping the ring and bracelet on her
finely turned finger and wrist, and holding them towards the window
on a level with her eyes. All the while her thought was trying to justify
her delight in the colours by merging them in her mystic religious joy.

'You *would* like those, Dorothea,' said Celia, rather falteringly, beginning to think with wonder that her sister showed some weakness, and
also that emeralds would suit her own complexion even better than
purple amethysts. 'You must keep that ring and bracelet – if nothing
else. But see, these agates are very pretty – and quiet.'

'Yes! I will keep these – this ring and bracelet,' said Dorothea. Then,
letting her hand fall on the table, she said in another tone – 'Yet what
miserable men find such things, and work at them, and sell them!' She
paused again, and Celia thought that her sister was going to renounce
the ornaments, as in consistency she ought to do.

'Yes, dear, I will keep these,' said Dorothea, decidedly. 'But take all
the rest away, and the casket.'

She took up her pencil without removing the jewels, and still looking
at them. She thought of often having them by her, to feed her eye at
these little fountains of pure colour.

'Shall you wear them in company?' said Celia, who was watching her with real curiosity as to what she would do.

Dorothea glanced quickly at her sister. Across all her imaginative adornment of those whom she loved, there darted now and then a keen discernment, which was not without a scorching quality. If Miss Brooke ever attained perfect meekness, it would not be for lack of inward fire.

'Perhaps,' she said, rather haughtily. 'I cannot tell to what level I may sink.'

Celia blushed, and was unhappy: she saw that she had offended her sister, and dared not say even anything pretty about the gift of the ornaments which she put back into the box and carried away. Dorothea too was unhappy, as she went on with her plan-drawing, questioning the purity of her own feeling and speech in the scene which had ended with that little explosion.

Celia's consciousness told her that she had not been at all in the wrong: it was quite natural and justifiable that she should have asked that question, and she repeated to herself that Dorothea was inconsistent: either she should have taken her full share of the jewels, or, after what she had said, she should have renounced them altogether.

'I am sure – at least, I trust,' thought Celia, 'that the wearing of a necklace will not interfere with my prayers. And I do not see that I should be bound by Dorothea's opinions now we are going into society, though of course she herself ought to be bound by them. But Dorothea is not always consistent.'

(pp. 13–14)

The most important source of character definition in this passage is contrast. In the course of discussing their mother's jewellery, the Brooke sisters reveal much about themselves. Their behaviour and speech express their attitudes to the jewels, and thence to some degree to life. The conflict between them, mild though it is, serves to highlight the disparity in spiritual outlook.

Differences between the sisters emerge gradually during the passage, rather as new facets of jewels may appear when they are viewed in a different light and from a different angle. As Eliot develops the dialogue and the characters engaged in it, previously unsuspected ironies develop. Ultimately, she comments openly on Dorothea's nature.

At the beginning of the passage, the contrast between the sisters seems simple. A hint of greater practicality, or perhaps less other-worldliness, is apparent from the narrative origin of the scene. The idea to sort through the jewels in the first place is Celia's: she has carefully calculated that it is six months to the day since their mother died – time enough has elapsed, in her view, for the daughters to look on the trivialities of personal adornment without risk of impropriety. Dorothea's acceptance of the suggestion is marked by resignation rather than enthusiasm: as the elder sister, it is her right to determine how they should proceed, and though she herself spends much of the novel in mourning, she has no desire to thwart her younger sister's harmless eagerness. At the outset, then, there is difference, but not conflict, between the sisters.

The initial distinction between the sisters is developed in the early part of the extract into a diametrical opposition in their attitudes to life. Celia has a very practical view of the jewellery, and considers only its fitness for their personal adornment. Her attitude is treated with mild irony: though she has no wish to seem overly greedy, she is relieved to be able to find that the necklace she picks up would be 'a little tight' for her sister's neck. Dorothea's feelings reveal a contrasting impracticality. Her response to the beauty of the jewels is idealistic; for her they are 'spiritual emblems . . . fragments of heaven'. As the sunlight suddenly gleams on the table, she is moved to exclaim on the beauty of the gems. Celia, too, thinks they are beautiful, but only as personal adornment. This contrast develops later in the passage towards the brink of conflict when Celia asks Dorothea, who has decided to keep the emerald bracelet and ring, whether she will wear them in company. Dorothea looks sharply at her sister, and reacts 'rather haughtily' to the implication that she may harbour any satisfaction in glorifying herself with such things. Ironically, this sharpness of Dorothea in protecting her aura of integrity is the only indication in this part of the extract that there may be a merely worldly tincture in her nature.

Eliot develops the contrast carefully in the remainder of the extract until the sisters appear rather divided by nature than united by blood. When Celia finds the bracelet which 'we did not notice at first' she seems to speak for herself alone, for Dorothea is so deeply entranced in looking at the jewels she has on her hand against the light from the window that it does not occur to her to search for others. Dorothea's absorption suggests that her delight in the jewels is instinctive: that is why she tries to find some religious way to 'justify her delight'. She loves them in a sensuous way – dazzled by their brilliant colours, she wants to 'feed' her eyes on them, and the alliteration with 'fountain' reinforces the power of her feelings. Her admiration of the jewels is a different thing from the acquisitive interest of Celia, who is a little dismayed at Dorothea's liking for them, as appears from her plaintive emphasis in 'You *would* like those'; she thinks that they would suit her own complexion very well. Celia's inquiry about wearing the jewels in company shows how little she understands her sister's feelings. Dorothea loves the jewels for their beauty: her sister loves them for their capacity to adorn her own appearance. That they are on Dorothea's hand as she admires them serves only to emphasise her innocence of lust to own them.

Unlike the jewels, the sisters are perceived to be flawed. When Celia's hunger for adornment is finally revealed in her question about wearing the jewels in company, Dorothea is at once indignant, and casts a 'scorching' glance at her. Celia's blushing, however, is not from a sense of being at fault, but from having given offence. She perhaps shows here a limited grasp, compared with Dorothea's, of human nature, and she awaits with 'real curiosity' the reactions of a sister who seems unpredictable because she is fathoms deeper. Yet she is sharply conscious of the flaws in Dorothea. She expects her older and more ascetic sister to 'renounce' the jewels. The word is used twice, and has the religious connotation of the renouncing of weaknesses, which is enshrined in baptismal vows. Yet, strangely, Celia perceives 'some weakness' in her sister's failure to give up the jewels. As Celia sees it, keeping two of the jewels and rejecting the rest of her share is inconsistent – forms of the word are used three times of Dorothea. There is a deeper dimension in Dorothea's inconsistency, of course, than Celia is aware of: keeping jewels reveals basic flaws in Dorothea's asceticism.

These flaws in the sisters are explored in the ironies that pervade the passage. Celia's capacity for self-deception is clear in the exaggerations of her opening advice to Dorothea, which allows her to feel 'happier' in taking a necklace because of its 'complete unfitness . . . from all points of view' for her sister. Later, her perception of Dorothea's weakness is mixed up with her own cupidity: Dorothea should renounce the jewels to satisfy the demands of a puritanical conscience, but also, conveniently, to make them available to Celia. Celia, too, has a conscience, but it is the kind which 'told her that she had not been at all in the wrong' – and indeed her sin is not great.

Dorothea, a more complex character, is examined at a more perilous level. Like her sister, she has a capacity for self-deception, but of a different order. She is captivated by the gleam of the jewels. As they stir a 'new current of feeling' in her, she strives desperately to explain their effect as religious inspiration. She refers to the 'spiritual emblems' in the Revelation of St John, speaks of them as 'fragments of heaven'. As she holds them towards the window for the delight of her eyes, another part of her – Eliot calls it 'her thought' – is trying to find in them the justification of 'mystic religious joy'. However, the jewels are described more vividly in Dorothea's eyes than in Celia's; she exclaims 'How very beautiful . . . !' and repeats 'beautiful', 'lovely'; even when she picks up her pencil again, after thinking of the 'miserable creatures' involved in the production of the jewels, she is still distracted by looking at them. Here, then, is a personality dangerously at odds with herself. Her admiration of the jewels operates at a deeper level than her sister's, and at the same time she has a horror her sister would not recognise of giving herself up to their sensuous appeal. Her persistence in self-deception is suddenly checked by Celia's question about wearing the jewels in company, and her keen look is occasioned by recognition as much of her own flaw as of her sister's. The effect is to throw her back upon her highest puritanical horse as she answers, with implausible uncertainty, that she 'cannot tell to what level [she] may sink'. Here in miniature is Dorothea's basal conflict in the novel: the conflict of duty and inclination.

The author's comments step beyond irony to direct statement in the tenth paragraph of the extract. She tells us that though Dorothea values her loved ones highly, she yet perceives them accurately in all their imperfection, and that her critical capacity is sharp. She suggests too, with a rather arch reference to 'Miss Brooke' suggestive of a similar clear-sightedness about her heroine, that her attainment of 'perfect meekness' would not be for 'lack of inward fire'. This is an interesting way to put it, for it suggests the inverse: that Dorothea's fieriness will prove an impediment to her achieving the state of meekness her idealism suggests for a goal. Though the author's voice is evident here, it is not intrusive, for it is enmeshed with the subject matter of the extract. There is an implicit contrast in the reference to Dorothea's 'imaginative adornment of those whom she loved' with the lesser adornment Celia seeks from jewellery. Similarly, the 'inward fire' Eliot indicates in Dorothea recalls the fire that gleams from jewels caught in sunlight. Thus even where the author speaks directly, what she says rests on the secure foundation of a dramatically realised scene in which the jewels have both a narrative and a symbolic function.

What emerges of the characters from the scene is necessarily partial. In such a vast structure as *Middlemarch*, character is a mosaic of many pieces. On the naturalistic level, changing moods are reflected in subtle modulations in the dialogue, for example in Dorothea's speaking 'under a new current of feeling' or 'in another tone' or 'haughtily', or in glances (lingering or darting), or movements such as the picking up of a pencil or the holding of a jewel in the light, or in Celia's faltering or blushing – still more, shortly after the conclusion of the extract, in a momentary caress. Yet central stable features of the characters emerge clearly beyond mood. In the mood of the moment, Celia's enthusiasm is quelled by a tiff with Dorothea about how the jewels should be dealt with. Behind that, however, the sisters are essentially well-meaning. They make allowances for each other's flaws, and they are both unhappy at their minor falling out. In a moment Dorothea invites Celia to look at her plans, and this gesture is received as an acknowledgement of error and a request for pardon which is freely given. There is nothing encapsulated about these characters. Dramatising the shifting moods of the moment, Eliot suggests the incessant modulations of relationships and the evolutionary potential of character. Her approach here is typical of the novel. Few indeed among the significant characters are fixed; most are shown in the process of forging their path through a terrain of broad mingled choice and chance.

Among the other major characters, Will Ladislaw is hardly the deepest. Yet he, too, is treated with considerable complexity. Consider this paragraph from the beginning of Chapter 10, where Eliot discusses his decision to travel in Europe. Subject and treatment are different, yet there is a comparable subtlety of perspective, and a comparable irony of tone:

> Young Ladislaw did not pay that visit to which Mr Brooke had invited him, and only six days afterwards Mr Casaubon mentioned that his young relative had started for the Continent, seeming by this cold vagueness to waive inquiry. Indeed, Will had declined to fix on any more precise destination than the entire area of Europe. Genius, he held, is necessarily intolerant of fetters: on the one hand it must have the utmost play for its spontaneity; on the other, it may confidently await those messages from the universe which summon it to its peculiar work, only placing itself in an attitude of receptivity towards all sublime chances. The attitudes of receptivity are various, and Will had sincerely tried many of them. He was not excessively fond of wine, but he had several times taken too much, simply as an experiment in that form of ecstasy; he had fasted till he was faint, and then supped on lobster; he had made himself ill with doses of opium. Nothing greatly original had resulted from these measures; and the effects of the opium had convinced him that there was an entire dissimilarity between his constitution and De Quincey's. The superadded circumstance which would evolve the genius had not yet come; the universe had not yet beckoned. Even Caesar's fortune at one time was, but a grand presentiment. We know what a masquerade all development is, and what effective shapes may be disguised in helpless embryos. – In fact, the world is full of hopeful analogies and handsome dubious eggs called possibilities. Will saw clearly enough the pitiable instances of long incubation producing no chick, and but for gratitude would have laughed at Casaubon, whose plodding application, rows of note-books, and small taper of learned theory exploring the tossed ruins of the world, seemed to enforce a moral entirely encouraging to Will's generous reliance on the intentions of the universe with regard to himself. He held that reliance to be a mark of genius; and certainly it is no mark to the contrary; genius consisting neither in self-conceit nor in humility, but in a power to make or do, not anything in general, but something in particular. Let him start for the Continent, then, without our pronouncing on his future. Among all forms of mistake, prophecy is the most gratuitous.
>
> (pp. 83–4)

Eliot's ironic intention in this paragraph appears to be to illustrate the gap between Will Ladislaw's view of life and the reality of the world. General views about the need for genius to be free from fetters and its need to have faith in the universe are presented from his limited perspective in the repeated phrase 'He held'. His aspirations are diminished by mock-epic allusions to De Quincy and Caesar. For Ladislaw, greatness has failed to materialise: it is not only from his experimenting with drugs that 'Nothing greatly original had resulted'. His lack of realism is implied in a ludicrous personification: 'the universe had not yet beckoned'. The irony of this portrait is so incisive as to colour every sentence. Eliot's portrait of the young man experimenting with wine, lobster and opium, supremely confident of his genius, and secure in the will of the universe to promote it, suggests an utterly feckless personality. Naturally he fails to visit Mr Brooke as he has been invited to do. Inevitably it is 'the entire area of Europe' that he proposes to visit: anything more precise would demand a discipline and decision quite beyond him. In this context the opening reference to 'Young Ladislaw' implies immaturity. Repeatedly employing the word 'held' for Ladislaw's beliefs suggests a superficial stance adopted for its convenience.

However, Ladislaw is presented in a more generous light than the ironic tone of the passage at first suggests. There is, for example, his awareness of the pitfalls of confidence: his consciousness of those 'hopeful analogies and handsome dubious eggs called possibilities'; he is not, therefore, entirely without the capacity to see his own situation objectively, and the sustained metaphor of embryo, egg, incubation and chick suggests Ladislaw's own satirical eye. Then there is the comparison with Casaubon. Beside that portrait of 'plodding application', Ladislaw's adventurism seems attractive; at the same time, gratitude forbids Ladislaw to mock the older man's efforts. Finally there are the closing sentences, in which Eliot refuses to 'pronounc[e] on his future', implying that something worthwhile may actually arise from him despite the facile irrationality of his expectation that he is chosen for some great purpose.

As with the dialogue of Celia and Dorothea, then, Eliot sets up a range of conflicting possibilities and interpretations which enrich the character and help to develop the sense of a world much broader than the novel focuses on directly. There is, as it were, a broad peripheral vision: there are many characters, and many of them are presented as having an indeterminate future. Thus, Will goes off to Europe to return we know not when, and Dorothea is 'not consistent'. Fictional complexity of different kinds is common to all the major characters of the novel.

This is in accordance with Eliot's preference for naturalism in her writing. The conclusion of the extract supposes that Ladislaw's career is not predetermined: his departure for Europe purports to have no outcome known to the author, who will not presume to issue any 'prophecy' that may turn out to be mistaken. At the same time, her discussion moves at will between the real and fictional worlds. The sentences about the egg metaphor, beginning 'We know', may be supposed to voice the ideas of Will Ladislaw; but the final sentence, which has much the same tone of voice, can only be the author's. Eliot's complex view of the author's role derives partly from Henry Fielding, whom Eliot refers to more than once as a model. Like him, Eliot sets her characters in a greater ethical and social environment than the characters can in themselves support.

Conclusions

The extracts studied above illustrate something of the range of characters in the novels, and something of the techniques Eliot uses in presenting character. Silas Marner, neither articulate nor sophisticated, stands at one extreme, and Dorothea, sensitive and allusive, at the other. The Tulliver family, in its various manifestations, occupies an area between these extremes. There is, obviously, a much larger variety of characters left unrepresented here, but the selection indicates the breadth of the society Eliot deals with. The extracts show Eliot's skill in drawing character out of narrative in the portraits of Silas Marner and Will Ladislaw, and out of dialogue in the conversation of Maggie with Tom and Dorothea with Celia. Some of the features that emerge strongly are:

- Naturalism. There is a careful notation of the appearance of characters, particularly in the *Silas Marner* extract, and of the transient moods and gestures of the moment, particularly in the *Middlemarch* extract. Eliot clearly treats her characters, and expects us to consider them, as if they were real people. They are seen for the most part engaged in ordinary activities and everyday worries; she avoids the sensational. When characters are given dialogue, it sounds lifelike, and is often developed at length, as if it were recorded from life. The *Middlemarch* extract is the best example quoted here, but there are many instances in *The Mill on the Floss* in conversations among the Tulliver uncles and aunts.
- There is frequent use of symbolism. In the extracts quoted it appears in Maggie's hair, Silas's pot and the Brooke jewellery.
- Irony is a natural tone in Eliot's voice, and is particularly evident in the extracts from *Middlemarch*.
- The author's voice is often heard more or less overtly. It appears in the reference to the shears towards the end of the extract from *The Mill on the Floss*, in the reference to wiser men in the portrait of Silas Marner, in the reference to Dorothea's 'inward fire' in her conversation with Celia, and in the comments on prophecy in the portrait of Will Ladislaw.
- Character pairings appear in the contrasts between siblings in the extracts. Maggie is measured against Tom, and more fully Dorothea is measured against Celia. In the novels at large, parallelism frequently illuminates the individuality of characters. Maggie is set against Lucy, and Tom against Stephen and Philip. Aaron Winthrop compares with Dunsey Cass, while Silas compares with Godfrey. Dorothea compares not only with her sister, but also with Rosamond and Mary; Casaubon compares with Bulstrode and Caleb Garth, while Lydgate compares with Fred Vincy and Ladislaw.
- A related feature is Eliot's use of characters in a choric mode. There are characters with an almost wholly choric role in the novels, such as Mrs Winthrop in *Silas Marner* and Mrs Cadwallader in *Middlemarch*. Many characters are used in a

choric way, however, and in the quoted extracts there are examples in Tom's derision at Maggie's cropped appearance, in the comments of the children about Silas Marner, and in Celia's judgement of Dorothea as inconsistent.

Despite the naturalistic manner of much of Eliot's writing, the author's manner of controlling her material is apparent in several of these features. Characters are very deliberately set side by side or placed in parallel situations. Whether Eliot addresses her readers directly or uses irony, her voice is a strong one. In this she shows her debt to Fielding, to whom reference is made more than once in her writings. In *The Mill on the Floss* (p. 516), there is reference to Sophia Western, the heroine of *Tom Jones*. Fielding himself is mentioned in Chapter 15 of *Middlemarch* in the phrase 'A great historian, as he insisted on calling himself'. Eliot's form of words appears to dispute the propriety of the term 'historian'; yet a little later she refers to herself and other writers of her own time in the phrase 'We belated historians' (both p. 141). This is interesting, since Fielding's masterpiece is so evidently stage-managed: leaving the intricacy of the plot aside, the introductory chapters to each book set the story in a moral realm devised by the author's imagination, while he simultaneously argues the realism of his tale. Eliot follows a similar pattern, and persists in treating her characters as if they were independent beings whose fate she reports without controlling it – as at the end of the Ladislaw portrait. There are points, particularly in *The Mill on the Floss*, where she discusses her characters as if both their future and their personality were things outside her jurisdiction. In reality, however, the organisational strength of Eliot's novels is everywhere evident. The characters form parts of a social and ethical universe that will be the subject of our discussions later in this book.

The effect is that Eliot's characters have an engaging complexity and irreducibility. In all three of the extracts discussed, there is discernible an inner conflict that provides in part the engine for each novel. In Maggie it is the conflict between her rebellious instinct and her perception of the power of convention. In Silas it is the conflict between his habitual, mindless, spiritually fossilised pursuit of gold and the stirrings towards some form of human contact. For Dorothea, the conflict lies in her temptation to sensuous delight which is held in check by her sense of duty and her sense of her own dignity. An important effect of this dependence on conflict is that development becomes an essential part of character: Silas and, even more, Maggie and Dorothea modify their ideas and behaviour in response to their circumstances and experience. In this world, there are few simple moral distinctions: the problems that beset Maggie and Dorothea, even the dispute over ownership of Eppie at the climax of *Silas Marner*, are tortuous in their moral implications. At the beginning of this chapter I said that there are no heroes or villains in George Eliot. That was a superficial way of putting it: Eliot's characters operate at a level that makes such simple categorisations irrelevant. It is this depth that, beyond the careful notation of appearance, manner and speech, conveys the strong impression of actuality in Eliot's writing.

Methods of Analysis

The discussions above adopted three different approaches to the study of characterisation. The discussion of *The Mill on the Floss* focused directly on the way Maggie is depicted as, with Tom's help, she crops her hair. The analysis of *Silas Marner* adopted a structural approach, dealing with each paragraph separately and then the connections between them. The discussion of *Middlemarch* considered a contrast between characters in the conversation between Dorothea and her sister, and the comparatively straightforward portraiture of the extract dealing with Ladislaw. The difference in approach is not accidental. Sometimes the student has the option of selecting from several equally appropriate methods. Often, however, the organisation of the extract itself will strongly suggest which approach is best.

Within the general structure of each approach, similar features are taken into account:

- Direct comment on character by the author. Examples are mentioned in the Conclusions section above.
- Comment on character by other characters – Tom's and Celia's remarks, for example.

- The character's appearance. Is it appropriate that Dorothea should have a larger neck than Celia? What does the fossilisation of Marner's posture reveal of him?
- The character's words. Contrast the different manner of speech of Tom and Maggie.
- The character's actions – the cutting of hair, the stamping of a foot, a sharp glance, for example.
- The use of objects to express aspects of character – Marner's pot, the Brooke jewels, the scissors in *The Mill on the Floss*.
- Linguistic or stylistic features of the writing. This includes a great deal. In the passages discussed above some examples are the use of alliteration to suggest strong feeling, the use of simple or complex language to suit, or to contrast with, the character, the use of irony. As we have noticed, there is often in Eliot's writing a great deal more communicated by implication than is immediately apparent from the surface narration or dialogue. The balance between dialogue and narration is important, for the manner of speaking is as significant as what is said.
- Setting, or reference to setting can be important. The natural imagery in the passage from *The Mill on the Floss* relates to the primary symbolism of the novel and its expression of Maggie's character and situation, while in *Middlemarch* it reflects the sensitive and more volatile aspects of Dorothea.

Further Work

The Mill on the Floss
Two further passages dealing with Maggie's early life suggest themselves as suitable for study. From Book One, Chapter 11, consider the opening paragraph which deals with Maggie's decision to run away, 'Maggie's intentions . . . always loved him very much' (p. 168), or else study Maggie's return home at the end of the chapter, 'Not Leonore . . . too wicked to be alluded to' (pp. 178–80). A more ambitious plan would be to compare the two passages.

Silas Marner

You may wish to develop the study of Silas himself by analysing a passage that deals with his disillusionment in Chapter 2: 'And what could be more unlike that Lantern Yard . . . had fallen on its keenest nerves' (pp. 16–17). Alternatively you may prefer to deal with different characters and study the argument between Godfrey and Dunsey in Chapter 3, 'Dunstan was moving off . . . rap the window-seat with the handle of his whip' (pp. 27–8).

Middlemarch

There are many possibilities. For an interesting passage of dialogue study Sir James's attempts to flatter Dorothea towards the end of Chapter 3, 'Miss Brooke was annoyed at the interruption . . . from whom we expect duties and affections' (pp. 30–1). Instead, or in addition, consider either the discussion of Mr Casaubon in Chapter 10, 'But at present this caution . . . claims some of our pity' (pp. 84–5), or the portrait of Mr Bulstrode in Chapter 13, 'In consequence of what he had heard . . . little enjoyment of tangible things' (pp. 123–4).

3

Relationships

Relationships are the lifeblood of Eliot's novels. They are an essential part of her method of developing character, and it will have become evident in the last chapter that discussion of character and characterisation inevitably strays into the domain of relationships. Through recognition of the expectations of others, and through acceptance or avoidance of responsibilities to others, her characters define themselves. Furthermore, the behaviour of characters involved in relationships allows Eliot to organise and develop the moral problems and moral choices over which her novels work; these will be the subject of later chapters.

Eliot felt the difficulties of personal relationships sharply in her own life. The reasons for this are discussed in Part 2 of this book in the chapter entitled 'George Eliot's Life and Work'. At present it will suffice to point to the complex of sibling and sexual relationships that dominates *The Mill on the Floss* in the various triangles formed by Tom, Maggie, Philip, Lucy and Stephen, and to the conflicts of personal feeling and social and personal responsibility in the other two novels.

(i) *The Mill on the Floss*

Any discussion of relationships in the novel must consider Maggie as the pivotal character. Since the novel shows a marked tendency to present its major characters in duets, passages treating relationships tend to include Maggie with one other character such as Tom or Stephen or Philip, to mention only the most obvious. Maggie's relationships with her mother, her father, Lucy and Dr Fenn are only a little less important in the structure of the novel and might equally usefully be selected for study. However, the development of sexual relationships in the process of Maggie's maturation is the central drive in the book, and crystallises in the first instance in her relationship with Philip. The following passage is the conclusion of the declaration of love between Maggie and Philip Wakem at the end of Chapter 4 of Book Five:

'Come, Maggie, say one kind word, or else you were better to me at Lorton. You asked me if I should like you to kiss me. Don't you remember? And you promised to kiss me when you met me again. You never kept the promise.'

The recollection of that childish time came as a sweet relief to Maggie. It made the present moment less strange to her. She kissed him almost as simply and quietly as she had done when she was twelve years old. Philip's eyes flashed with delight, but his next words were words of discontent.

'You don't seem happy enough, Maggie: you are forcing yourself to say you love me, out of pity.'

'No, Philip,' said Maggie, shaking her head, in her old childish way. 'I'm telling you the truth. It is all new and strange to me; but I don't think I could love any one better than I love you. I should like always to live with you – to make you happy. I have always been happy when I have been with you. There is only one thing I will not do for your sake – I will never do anything to wound my father. You must never ask that from me.'

'No, Maggie: I will ask nothing – I will bear everything – I'll wait another year only for a kiss, if you will only give me the first place in your heart.'

'No,' said Maggie, smiling, 'I won't make you wait so long as that.' But then, looking serious again, she added, as she rose from her seat, 'But what would your own father say, Philip? O, it is quite impossible we can ever be more than friends – brother and sister in secret – as we have been. Let us give up thinking of everything else.'

'No, Maggie, I can't give you up – unless you are deceiving me – unless you really only care for me as if I were your brother. Tell me the truth.'

'Indeed I do, Philip. What happiness have I ever had so great as being with you? – since I was a little girl – the days Tom was good to me. And your mind is a sort of world to me – You can tell me all I want to know. I think I should never be tired of being with you.'

They were walking hand in hand, looking at each other – Maggie indeed was hurrying along, for she felt it time to be gone. But the sense that their parting was near, made her more anxious lest she should have unintentionally left some painful impression on Philip's mind. It was one of those dangerous moments when speech is at once sincere and deceptive – when feeling, rising high above its average depth, leaves flood-marks which are never reached again.

They stopped to part among the Scotch firs.

'Then my life will be filled with hope, Maggie – and I shall be happier than other men, in spite of all? We do belong to each other – for always – whether we are apart or together?'

'Yes, Philip: I should like never to part: I should like to make your life very happy.'

'I am waiting for something else – I wonder whether it will come.'

Maggie smiled, with glistening tears, and then stooped her tall head to kiss the low pale face that was full of pleading, timid love – like a woman's.

She had a moment of real happiness then – a moment of belief that if there were sacrifice in this love – it was all the richer and more satisfying.

She turned away and hurried home, feeling that in the hour since she had trodden this road before, a new era had begun for her. The tissue of vague dreams must now get narrower and narrower, and all the threads of thought and emotion be gradually absorbed in the woof of her actual daily life.

(pp. 437–8)

This passage dramatises a key moment in the novel. It marks the transition in Maggie between childhood and adulthood, and is a moment Maggie recalls often, not least in the penultimate chapter. The scene is marked by its emotional intensity. This, after all, is the first experience these virginal characters have of passionate love. There is no doubt of the power of their feeling, for though she works within the confines of a reticent Victorian manner, Eliot uses all the elements of the scene to express sexual passion: Maggie and Philip both specifi-

cally differentiate their relationship from that of brother and sister;
their behaviour expresses psychological torment; the setting is known
by a name blatantly suggestive of passion, the Red Deeps.

Though this moment is treasured by Maggie as a time of promise
and happiness, and indeed forms of the word 'happy' appear six times
in the extract, the scene holds a delicate balance of delight and pain.
Overtly, the mood is tinged with something approaching ecstasy. The
talk is all of kissing, love and devotion. Philip is willing to wait a year
for a kiss if only he can have 'first place in [her] heart'; Maggie for
her part would like to live with Philip, to make him happy, thinks of
his mind as 'a sort of world' to her, and feels that she 'should never
be tired of being with [him]'. However, Philip's mood is equally one
of 'discontent', and what Maggie experiences is a moment of 'sweet
relief' from the burdens of her mind. Things seem strange to her, she
fears to leave some 'painful impression' on Philip. It is Philip who sets
the key for the scene when he uses the first of those six 'happy'
instances in a negative sense, telling Maggie that she doesn't 'seem
happy enough'. Much of what he says takes the form of complaint:
Maggie failed to keep her promise, she is kind to him only out of
pity; and he fears – or pretends to fear – that she is deceiving him.

The action of the scene supports its emotional complexity. Maggie
kisses Philip, and though his eyes 'flashed with delight', his words
show discontent. Maggie shakes her head to deny his doubts, smiles,
then looks serious again as she rises from her seat. They walk a little
'hand in hand, looking at each other', but Maggie is hurrying to be
gone. They stop only to part. Maggie smiles 'with glistening tears' as
she stoops to kiss Philip again, before turning away and hurrying
home.

It is, of course, this very complexity of mood that gives the scene
its poignant depth. Tension lies at its centre: these are moments of
passionate love snatched from a hostile world. Maggie insists that she
will never do anything to wound her father, and reminds Philip of
his own father's reactions, concluding that it is impossible that she
and Philip can be more than friends. Her comparison of their hereto-
fore platonic relationship with that of brother and sister, Philip's
response questioning whether she cares for him as a brother, and her
reference to 'the days when Tom was good to [her]', point emphati-

cally to the other, and the most obdurate, obstacle to their union – Tom. Love here, then, is rendered more intense by opposition – by the questioning of its chance of enduring, by the consciousness of its fragility, by the fear of misconception between the pair, by the sense of time's wingéd chariot hurrying near. For Maggie this is 'a moment of real happiness' all the more valuable for its rarity. The conclusion is a bleak resolve – even this questioned by Philip's hesitant tone – that 'We do belong to each other – for always – whether we are apart or together?' Maggie's acquiescence employs a pointed parallelism – 'I should like never to part: I should like to make your life very happy' – that implies reservation; she is already used to finding that she cannot do as she would like.

The characters have equal shares in the dialogue in the scene, but a most unequal weighting. Philip has, to be sure, his own independent personality. He seems wholly devoted in his promise to 'ask nothing . . . bear everything . . . wait' but much of what he says here is lover's complaint and lover's demand. He appears sincere in declaring his inability to give Maggie up and in his feeling that if he can but be assured of Maggie's love, his life 'will be filled with hope', yet his feelings are not dealt with in depth. Maggie, in contrast, is the focal figure in the scene as she is in the novel, and her side of the relationship is explored in much greater subtlety than Philip's.

Both durable and developmental qualities of character emerge from Maggie's response to this relationship. Initially, it is the transition from childhood to adulthood that is stressed. Maggie is tense, overcome with a situation 'new and strange' to her ('strange' appears twice near the beginning of the extract) until Philip reminds her of their time at Lorton, and 'The recollection of that childish time came as a sweet relief'. Only then is she able to kiss Philip, and she does so 'as simply and quietly as she had done when she was twelve years old'. Now, however, she can only look back on the time when she was 'a little girl'. By the end of the extract, 'a new era ha[s] begun for her': the ideas of childhood are now a 'tissue of vague dreams' that must diminish, to be replaced by 'the woof of her actual daily life'; the love of Philip is part of both eras, and even in the new era, a dream set aside – 'absorbed' – by the demands of practicality. Though Maggie is shown here adjusting to the demands of her life, her naivety is stressed in her expression of her faith in Philip, when she says to him, 'You can tell me all I want to know'. This is a turning-point, at which Maggie is both old and young at once, and sometimes in conflict with herself. So while on one level she feels herself to be Philip's inferior, on another, more significant level she controls the relationship. Anxious not to leave Philip in doubt or despair, she protects him from her knowledge in saying she should like never to part from him, to make him happy, and keeping silence over the impossibilities that loom in her mind. The alteration is rendered physically when she 'stoop[s] her tall head to kiss [his] low pale face'; and, in a reversal of conventional roles, his face is described as 'full of pleading, timid love – like a woman's'.

Underlying that reversal of roles there is the enduring feature that Eliot consistently picks out in Maggie: her sense of duty. Philip senses it in her when he accuses her, no matter how playfully, of forcing love out of pity. She expresses it baldly when she declares that she will do nothing to wound her father, and warns Philip never to ask such a thing of her. The moment when she reassures Philip follows from her sense of duty, but her sense of duty betrays her. Eliot prepares the moment with a metaphorical reference that looks forward to the conclusion of the novel. It deserves to be quoted again:

> It was one of those dangerous moments when speech is at once sincere and deceptive – when feeling, rising high above its average depth, leaves flood-marks which are never reached again.

Here Eliot hints, in language stressing the natural flow of feeling, how Maggie's reassurances are to be interpreted. When she tells Philip that she 'should like' to live a happy life in union with him, she means it but knows it will not happen – and since her words are intended to deceive she is insincere. She disguises this insincerity to herself as a kind of duty. Her 'moment of real happiness' derives not from love itself, but from the sense of 'sacrifice in this love' that makes her feeling 'all the richer and more satisfying'. As Eliot's use of the water metaphor suggests, this is no facile insincerity: Maggie's words are not spoken for convenience, but out of genuine fondness and a desire to protect: she is at this point willing to sacrifice anything, even truth, for Philip.

Eliot's stern doctrine of duty and service is a steady current in the novel, seeping into every part of its structure. Here it is clear that she is thinking of duty not in terms of cold pulpit precepts, but as a strong tugging of emotional gravity that appeals most powerfully to a sensitive and intelligent nature. The scene illustrates the sad irony that duty, mutating into the will to self-sacrifice, can betray itself through sheer intensity. Maggie is presented as an innocent victim of the call to duty: it is Eliot, not Maggie, who is fully aware of the depth of the flaw in her moral ideas and the behaviour they elicit from her. In the course of the novel Maggie learns much, however, and the complex discussions near the close of the novel show her, too, confronting the problem of duty.

In this scene Eliot deals with the relationship between Philip and Maggie with a skill and depth characteristic of her best writing. On the surface of faithful realism, she notes the modulations of mood from moment to moment between Philip and Maggie. She also shows the interaction between the two individuals and their social environment as represented by their fathers and her brother. At a deeper level, she shows how the individuals are tested by the demands of their relationship: particularly how Maggie is tested beyond her capacities at this stage in her development.

The scene is a significant one. The dream of a relationship with Philip remains always for Maggie a promise of an impossible paradise, and, like paradise, her dream contains an inherent flaw. The dream is 'vague', a fragile 'tissue', that must give way to the demands of the workaday world which is aptly suggested here in the 'woof' that recalls the aunts' obsession with materiality in both senses. Furthermore, there is a primal level not yet fully understood by Maggie herself, on which she cannot yield herself to Philip. The symbolism touched on here – the fir trees associated with Maggie herself, the pathways that represent moral development, the water imagery, the metaphor of life as the threads of a cloth – runs through the whole novel. The past here wears two faces: the happy face of childhood innocence and the grim face of parental prohibition. The scene looks forward to the conclusion of the novel in its reference to the leitmotif of the river. Equally, the conclusion looks back to this scene; one of the last things Maggie sees is the old Scotch firs referred to here. The flood that ends her life is a development of the current that carries her through the scene with Philip: thus the conclusion actualises the betrayal in this love-scene.

(ii) *Silas Marner*

Sexual or romantic relationships are less prominent in *Silas Marner* than in the earlier novel, though Godfrey Cass's past marital escapades have a crucial influence in the present. In this novel, relationships between parent and child, in different registers, take precedence. The following scene, which occurs soon after the beginning of Chapter 13, describes what happens when Silas brings the child he has discovered to the Red House:

> 'It's a woman,' said Silas, speaking low, and half-breathlessly, just as Godfrey came up. 'She's dead, I think – dead in the snow at the Stone-pits – not far from my door.'
>
> Godfrey felt a great throb: there was one terror in his mind at that moment: it was, that the woman might *not* be dead. That was an evil terror – an ugly inmate to have found a nestling-place in Godfrey's kindly disposition; but no disposition is a security from evil wishes to a man whose happiness hangs on duplicity.
>
> 'Hush, hush!' said Mr Crackenthorp. 'Go out into the hall there. I'll fetch the doctor to you. Found a woman in the snow and thinks she's dead,' he added, speaking low to the Squire. 'Better say as little about it as possible: it will shock the ladies. Just tell them a poor woman is ill from cold and hunger. I'll go and fetch Kimble.'
>
> By this time, however, the ladies had pressed forward, curious to know what could have brought the solitary linen-weaver there under such strange circumstances, and interested in the pretty child, who, half alarmed and half attracted by the brightness and the numerous company, now frowned and hid her face, now lifted up her head again and looked round placably, until a touch or a coaxing word brought back the frown, and made her bury her face with new determination.
>
> 'What child is it?' said several ladies at once, and, among the rest, Nancy Lammeter, addressing Godfrey.
>
> 'I don't know – some poor woman's who has been found in the snow, I believe,' was the answer Godfrey wrung from himself with a terrible

effort. ('After all, *am* I certain?' he hastened to add, silently, in antici-pation of his own conscience.)

'Why, you'd better leave the child here, then, Master Marner,' said good-natured Mrs Kimble, hesitating, however, to take those dingy clothes into contact with her own ornamented satin bodice. 'I'll tell one o' the girls to fetch it.'

'No – no – I can't part with it, I can't let it go,' said Silas, abruptly. 'It's come to me – I've a right to keep it.'

The proposition to take the child from him had come to Silas quite unexpectedly, and his speech, uttered under a strong sudden impulse, was almost like a revelation to himself: a minute before, he had no dis-tinct intention about the child.

'Did you ever hear the like?' said Mrs Kimble, in mild surprise, to her neighbour.

'Now, ladies, I must trouble you to stand aside,' said Mr Kimble, coming from the card-room, in some bitterness at the interruption, but drilled by the long habit of his profession into obedience to unpleas-ant calls, even when he was hardly sober.

'It's a nasty business turning out now, eh, Kimble?' said the Squire. 'He might ha' gone for your young fellow – the 'prentice, there – what's his name?'

'Might? Aye – what's the use of talking about might?' growled uncle Kimble, hastening out with Marner, and followed by Mr Crackenthorp and Godfrey. 'Get me a pair of thick boots, Godfrey, will you? And stay, let somebody run to Winthrop's and fetch Dolly – she's the best woman to get. Ben was here himself before supper; is he gone?'

'Yes, sir, I met him,' said Marner; 'but I couldn't stop to tell him anything, only I said I was going for the doctor, and he said the doctor was at the Squire's. And I made haste and ran, and there was nobody to be seen at the back o' the house, and so I went in to where the company was.'

The child, no longer distracted by the bright light and the smiling women's faces, began to cry and call for 'mammy', though always cling-ing to Marner, who had apparently won her thorough confidence. Godfrey had come back with the boots, and felt the cry as if some fibre were drawn tight within him.

'I'll go,' he said, hastily, eager for some movement; 'I'll go and fetch the woman – Mrs Winthrop.'

'Oh, pooh – send somebody else,' said uncle Kimble, hurrying away with Marner.

'You'll let me know if I can be of any use, Kimble,' said Mr Crackenthorp. But the doctor was out of hearing.

Godfrey, too, had disappeared: he was gone to snatch his hat and coat, having just reflection enough to remember that he must not look like a madman; but he rushed out of the house into the snow without heeding his thin shoes.

(pp. 114–16)

The most prominent relationship here is between Silas and the new-found child. There are several others of different kinds, however, including personal and structural relationships – that is, relationships of which the parties are at this stage unaware but which become significant in the course of the action of the novel. Among these other relationships are Godfrey's relationships with the dead woman, Nancy, the child and Silas. All of these are set against a social backdrop that serves by its normality to heighten the extraordinary nature of the foreground relationships, and thus a third kind of relationship is suggested that obtains between individuals and society.

Silas's relationship with the child is marked by its public acknowledgement and its private strength, and by the influence of chance, which is so strong as to suggest some extraordinary meaning. He feels an instinctive bond with the child he has discovered, yet at the outset is scarcely aware of it. He comes to the Red House about the child's mother, the woman dead in the snow at the fateful Stone-pits, rather than about the child itself, but has no thought of giving the child up to anyone else. He is thus surprised by Mrs Kimble's assumption that he has brought the child with the purpose of disposing of it; he responds 'abruptly' to her, asserts his refusal emphatically in a repeated 'no' and the parallelism of 'I can't part with it . . . let it go'. The following words, 'It's come to me – I've a right to keep it', have no more than the bare semblance of reasoning. They emerge from will and instinct, from 'a strong sudden impulse' that comes upon him 'like a revelation to himself'. The word 'revelation' recalls the powerful religious feeling in Silas and thus links the present event with his past – a link symbolised in the dual significance of gold in the novel. Silas's will is irrational – he has 'no distinct intention' – but powerful. His is a simple but strong personality moved, as his history shows, by superstition rather than reason, and his feeling for the child is characteristic. The desire to keep the child inhabits the same magical universe of signs and portents as his desire to preserve a broken pot in the episode studied in Chapter 2. For a man like Silas, it is natural, indeed imperative, to act in obedience to a miraculous event such as this manifestation of the golden child. Likewise his relationship with the child, once forged in the stars or heavens, will not easily be sundered: the idea of giving up this gift has for Silas the aspect of sin. The child, in reciprocation, 'cling[s] to' Marner, who has 'won her confidence'. Here, then, Eliot represents a relationship that lies deeper than reason: Marner and the child are strongly drawn to each other, and he is not much more able to express the origin of the attraction than is the child.

Set against this public, instinctive declaration of mutual need there is the very different cast of Godfrey's hidden relationship with the child's mother. Whereas Silas is determined to own, Godfrey is desperate to disown. He, like Silas, has a strong sense of sin, though he fights against it with all his will and reason. More sophisticated and articulate than Silas, he finds persuasive reasons for ignoring what his instincts tell him, yet he cannot quell the powerful reaction events stir in him. Thus at Silas's quiet news of the woman lying in the snow at the Stone-pits, Godfrey feels 'a great throb' as he recognises that his 'one terror' is of the woman's survival and thus of his own unmasking. His denial of her as 'some poor woman' he doesn't know demands 'a terrible effort', but he can nevertheless lull his conscience by sophistry ('After all, *am* I certain?') aimed at deceiving only himself. Later, when the child calls for its mother, Godfrey feels the cry 'as if some fibre were drawn tight within him', yet he restrains himself from acknowledging her as his. Finally, when he rushes into the snow, his concern is overwhelmingly to preserve the semblance of normality, detachment and thus guiltlessness. Eliot describes Godfrey's sensations, using religious language that Silas would understand, as 'an evil terror', an 'ugly inmate' in his 'kindly disposition'; it is as though he were possessed by a devil that distorts his behaviour with the appearance of rationality. However, Eliot utters no condemnation; rather, her attitude is one of compassion for a man, good at heart, betrayed into 'duplicity' by his desire for what appears to him to constitute 'happiness'.

The contrasting of Godfrey's denial of relationship and Silas's need for relationship receives considerable stress and amounts to a third, structural relationship that emerges fully into the light only in the later stages of the novel when Godfrey tries to take Eppie from Silas. While Silas speaks of the woman as lying 'not far from [his] door', Godfrey is busily keeping her as far from his own door as possible. This deceit is the 'ugly inmate' that finds 'a nestling-place' in Godfrey's essentially well-meaning soul, in contrast with the innocent inmate, the infant and as yet unnamed Eppie, in Silas's house and heart. It is worth noting here that Eliot says 'nestling' and not 'nesting': the word suggests a fledgling or child finding a cosy, warm and nourishing place to live and grow. Thus a deeper irony emerges, contrasting Godfrey's dark speculation with Silas's golden visitant, a destructive with a beneficent impulse. Both men are moved by deep feeling (a 'great throb' in Godfrey parallels Silas's 'sudden impulse'), but while Silas wants to discharge his overwrought emotion by revealing and explaining (as when he details his search for the doctor), Godfrey desires desperately to hide his true feelings. Here Eliot portrays two men at opposite extremes of the their social spectrum. Silas has none of Godfrey's advantages. What money he had is lost. He is not articulate. He has no friends, nor education, nor position. What he does possess in spite of his past and his lonely isolation – and Eliot appears to suggest that it is more important than Godfrey's advantages – is peace of mind. The child clinging to Silas's unlikely frame feels trust in, and thus represents, his simplicity and honesty.

Despite their antithetical quality, these relationships affecting Silas and Godfrey are exceptional. Eliot stresses their extraordinary nature by setting them against a backdrop of normality. The scene takes place in the Red House after supper-time as the company mellows. It is a social gathering of people well known to each other. Several members of the company are mentioned by name – Mr Crackenthorp the rector, Kimble the doctor, Mrs Kimble, Nancy Lammeter – and Dolly and Ben Winthrop are named in their absence. Behind these move unidentified characters of 'a numerous company' – too many to be sure whether Ben, who was present earlier, has left. When Silas appears, the women are described as 'press[ing] forward', suggesting something of a crush. Nancy is one of 'several ladies at once' who demand to know the identity of the child. Mr Kimble emerges from the card-room, where presumably another unseen group lurks, and has to ask the crowd of ladies to make way for him. Eliot invites us to imagine, then, a scene of people milling in slightly alcoholic social intercourse, at their ease, as a contrast to the protagonists in the scene. She emphasises the essential normality, even goodness of the society. Mrs Kimble is 'good-natured'; Mr Kimble, though irritated to be disturbed in his game of cards, nevertheless responds to the demands of duty, 'drilled by the long habit of his profession into obedience to unpleasant calls'; Dolly is sent for as 'the best woman to get'. Eliot treats them, at the same time, with gentle irony. Crackenthorp is anxious to protect the ladies present from the knowledge of the dead woman, but equally anxious, it seems, to protect himself, for he waits until Kimble hurries away to ask him to 'let me know if I can be of any use'. Mrs Kimble, good-natured though she may be and concerned for the welfare of the child, nevertheless declines to touch it with 'her own ornamented satin bodice' and sends for 'one of the girls' to fetch it. The conscientious Kimble, though a respected member of the community, growls in ill temper as he struggles into his boots and is, it seems, often somewhat drunk. What Eliot describes so economically here is a company of ordinary men and women, neither very good nor very bad, intent upon a pleasant evening, and unexpectedly confronted with a problem that must be dealt with.

Against this backdrop of the Red House and its normal, comfortable society with its virtues and failings, the protagonists, Silas and to some extent Godfrey, are both set apart superficially: Silas by his self-chosen isolation, Godfrey by his exalted social position as the Squire's son. Silas and Godfrey inhabit opposite ends of the social spectrum. Squire Cass stands at the top of a social group propped up by such as Silas Marner, who goes to the back of the Squire's house even on an urgent errand, and only on finding no one there returns to the front 'where the company was'. At a deeper level Silas and Godfrey stand out as shocking, set apart by their odd behaviour and the secrets that dictate it. Crackenthorp wishes to conceal the probability of the death of the unknown woman because 'it will shock the ladies'; thus he acts as an indicator of how far beyond the pale of convention Godfrey's troubled soul has travelled. When Silas insists on keeping the child, Mrs Kimble demands 'in mild surprise' of her neighbour, 'Did you ever hear the like?' At the end of the extract Godfrey has just enough presence of mind to realise that he 'must not look like a madman' as he hastens out into the snow with only thin shoes on his feet.

What this passage presents, then, is not a relationship but a complex of relationships in which Silas and the child contrast with Godfrey and the woman, and both stand apart from what the society they inhabit perceives as normal. This web of relationships is important from the thematic point of view. In the novel as a whole Silas is more successful than Godfrey on the personal level, and this appears to suggest that honesty and simplicity are more useful and more desirable than property and influence. Appropriately, the shape of the extract strangely reflects that of the novel. In the course of describing his search for the doctor, Silas reveals his instinct that, as a lowly man, his proper place is at the rear of the house of the great Squire Cass. However, his bringing the child to the company at the Red House prefigures his reintegration into society in the hitherto alien environment of Raveloe under the influence of Eppie's presence. Godfrey's behaviour at the end of the extract prefigures the end of the novel for him, too. His precipitate exit from the warmth of the Red House into the snow looks forward to the damage his reputation suffers in the later stages of the novel and to his self-exclusion from its final scene. Those thin shoes are as useless against the wintry conditions as his feeble effort to protect his fragile social status will be against the evidence of his wickedness. What Eliot does in this extract is much more than to present two isolated relationships: rather, she shows, through the exploration of two contrasting situations, how the nature of those relationships may influence the social destiny of the protagonists.

(iii) *Middlemarch*

In *Middlemarch* romantic and sexual relationships again predominate in multiple layers. The structure of the novel invites comparisons among a series of relationships: Dorothea with Casaubon, Lydgate and Ladislaw; Celia with Sir James; Rosamond with Lydgate and Ladislaw; Fred with Mary; Caleb Garth with his wife; Bulstrode with his wife. Around these grows a multitude of less important relationships and parallels taking in Farebrother, the Cadwalladers, Celia and Sir James among other characters. In their similarities and differences as well as in the presentation of the changes in these relationships Eliot finds it possible to distinguish minute gradations of feeling. The relationship between Lydgate and Rosamond is perhaps the most dangerously fraught with the tensions of incompatibility and misunderstanding. In this extract from the middle of Chapter 27, Eliot describes their mutual attraction:

> Certainly her thoughts were much occupied with Lydgate himself; he seemed to her almost perfect: if he had known his notes so that his enchantment under her music had been less like an emotional elephant's, and if he had been able to discriminate better the refinements of her taste in dress, she could hardly have mentioned a deficiency in him. How different he was from young Plymdale or Mr Caius Larcher! Those young men had not a notion of French, and could speak on no subject with striking knowledge, except perhaps the dyeing and carrying trades, which of course they were ashamed to mention; they were Middlemarch gentry, elated with their silver-headed whips and satin stocks, but embarrassed in their manners, and timidly jocose: even Fred was above them, having at least the accent and manner of a university man. Whereas Lydgate was always listened to, bore himself with the careless politeness of conscious superiority, and seemed to have the right clothes on by a certain natural affinity, without ever having to think about them. Rosamond was proud when he entered the room, and when he approached her with a distinguishing smile, she had a delicious sense that she was the object of enviable homage. If Lydgate had been aware of all the pride he excited in that delicate bosom, he might have been just as well pleased as any other man, even the most densely ignorant of humoral pathology or fibrous tissue: he held it one of the prettiest attitudes of the feminine mind to adore a man's pre-eminence without too precise a knowledge of what it consisted in.
>
> But Rosamond was not one of those helpless girls who betray themselves unawares, and whose behaviour is awkwardly driven by their

impulses, instead of being steered by wary grace and propriety. Do you imagine that her rapid forecast and rumination concerning house-furniture and society were ever discernible in her conversation, even with her mamma? On the contrary, she would have expressed the prettiest surprise and disapprobation if she had heard that another young lady had been detected in that immodest prematureness – indeed, would probably have disbelieved in its possibility. For Rosamond never showed any unbecoming knowledge, and was always that combination of correct sentiments, music, dancing, drawing, elegant note-writing, private album for extracted verse, and perfect blond loveliness, which made the irresistible woman for the doomed man of that date. Think no unfair evil of her, pray: she had no wicked plots, nothing sordid or mercenary; in fact, she never thought of money except as something necessary which other people would always provide. She was not in the habit of devising falsehoods, and if her statements were no direct clue to fact, why, they were not intended in that light – they were among her elegant accomplishments, intended to please. Nature had inspired many arts in finishing Mrs Lemon's favourite pupil, who by general consent (Fred's excepted) was a rare compound of beauty, cleverness, and amiability.

Lydgate found it more and more agreeable to be with her, and there was no constraint now, there was a delightful interchange of influence in their eyes, and what they said had that superfluity of meaning for them, which is observable with some sense of flatness by a third person; still they had no interviews or asides from which a third person need have been excluded. In fact, they flirted; and Lydgate was secure in the belief that they did nothing else. If a man could not love and be wise, surely he could flirt and be wise at the same time? Really, the men in Middlemarch, except Mr Farebrother, were great bores, and Lydgate did not care about commercial politics or cards: what was he to do for relaxation? He was often invited to the Bulstrodes'; but the girls there were hardly out of the schoolroom; and Mrs Bulstrode's naive way of conciliating piety and worldliness, the nothingness of this life and the desirability of cut glass, the consciousness at once of filthy rags and the best damask, was not a sufficient relief from the weight of her husband's invariable seriousness. The Vincys' house, with all its faults, was the pleasanter by contrast; besides, it nourished Rosamond – sweet to look at as a half-opened blush-rose, and adorned with accomplishments for the refined amusement of man.

(pp. 267–9)

At least three distinct voices are heard in this passage, though all belong, however directly or indirectly, unmistakably to George Eliot. First Eliot appears mainly in the guise of Rosamond. Then, in the second half of the first paragraph (the passage beginning 'If Lydgate had been aware . . .') Eliot as author discusses Lydgate and Rosamond with her readers. In the second paragraph Eliot wears the personality of Lydgate. All three voices are dedicated to the aim of showing how it may be possible for a relationship such as that of Rosamond and Lydgate to come about and develop to the point of marriage. Eliot treats the relationship as if it were a three-dimensional object such as a piece of sculpture which she can walk round and view from different perspectives. As she does so, the flaws in the object become ever more obtrusive. The tool used to discover these flaws is the irony that dominates the passage.

The first section of the extract begins with Rosamond's feeling that Lydgate is 'almost perfect', and all that follows grows from those two words. She admires Lydgate and feels proud when he enters the room, comparing him advantageously to Plymdale and Larcher who are from the successful trading families that represent the gentry of Middlemarch. It is clear from the absence of depth and its emphasis on superficialities that Rosamond's response to Lydgate is shallow. She is critical of Plymdale and Larcher for knowing no French, but her contempt for their empty pride in 'silver-headed whips and satin stocks' reflects on her own more subtle frivolity. She acknowledges her brother's superiority to them in possessing at least 'the accent and manner' of a university man, but fails, however, to consider his intellectual abilities or quality of character. Similarly, she fails to consider the nature of Lydgate beyond noticing that he behaves 'with the careless politeness of conscious superiority'. Her approbation of Lydgate is encapsulated in her perception that he seems to 'have the right clothes on by a certain natural affinity, without ever having to think about it'. The quasi-scientific phrase used here, 'natural affinity', hints at much that Rosamond misses about the nature of Lydgate, as well as at something that is missing from the relationship.

So much for Lydgate's imperfect approach to what Rosamond thinks of as 'perfection'. What of the shortcomings that lead to his being labelled 'an emotional elephant'? These turn out to be limited to his ignorance of music (not knowing 'his notes') and inability to 'discriminate the refinements of her taste in dress'. The irony here is that Lydgate's 'deficienc[ies]' illuminate Rosamond's rather more tellingly: her admiration of Lydgate and her judgement of his faults both stem from self-regard. He is insufficiently aware of Rosamond's music as he is of her dress. Her pride when he enters the room derives from her conviction of his smile 'distinguishing' her, so that she has the 'delicious sense' that he loves her. Eliot's grandiose phrase, 'enviable homage', suggests both the importance to her of being perceived by her society as elevated and the regal status she wishes to accede to. Her feeling for Lydgate, that is, is motivated by a need for social recognition and by simple vanity; she needs him because he can support her sense of her own importance.

Thus far, implication has been Eliot's method of indicating judgement. In the next section of the first paragraph she changes tack, turning to open discussion first, briefly, of Lydgate, then of Rosamond. Irony remains, however, her weapon. Though it is clearly Eliot discussing Rosamond here, she nevertheless adopts the voice of Middlemarch society. Thus she admires Rosamond for her careful approach to Lydgate and control of her amorous feelings, contrasting her 'wary grace and propriety' with the self-betrayal of 'helpless girls' who are driven by 'impulses'. In the rhetorical question beginning 'Do you imagine . . . ?' and the exhortation 'pray' Eliot compliments Rosamond on her reticence in avoiding speaking prematurely, even to her mother, of furnishings and guests, on her avoiding displays of knowledge beyond that conventionally expected of elegant young ladies, on her openness, on her lack of interest in money and on her honesty. Every phrase, however, carries irony. That there is no premature thought of married life 'discernible' in Rosamond's behaviour suggests that it exists freely in her mind. She never lies, but views speech as an accomplishment to be deployed as seems to suit her company: thus what she says offers 'no direct clue' to truth. She is not mercenary because money is beneath her consideration. Each statement made by Eliot is double-edged. Much of this is amusing, using a variety of comic devices: they include hyperbole ('immodest prematureness') and circumlocution ('the habit of devising falsehoods') mixed with cliché ('the irresistible woman for the doomed man of that date') and bathos ('Fred's excepted'). The whole, however, adds up to a damning and serious denunciation. The passage is packed with negations that offer only a semblance of picking out Rosamond's virtues. Consider for, example, 'not one of those help- less girls . . . never showed any unbecoming knowledge . . . Think no unfair evil of her . . . no wicked plots, nothing sordid . . . never thought of money . . . not in the habit . . . not intended'. The stream of negatives is capped by a final grand positive climax in the encap- sulation of Rosamond as 'a rare compound of beauty, cleverness, and amiability' – but at this point, such a judgement sounds utterly hollow. Beauty she undoubtedly has. The 'cleverness' of Rosamond, however, is instinctive: it is one of the arts which 'Nature had inspired . . . in finishing' this pupil of polite society; she knows how to attract Lydgate, how to impress society with her accomplishments, and how to deceive and lie without turning a pretty hair. As to her 'amiabil- ity', it will be hard to reconcile with the glaring faults that Lydgate later discovers in her behaviour.

Beginning, then, with Rosamond's perception of minor flaws in Lydgate's near-perfection, the first paragraph develops towards a por- trait of the essential vices in Rosamond's own character. Her feelings towards Lydgate are shown to be shallow, and it is already clear that their relationship will be based on the shaky foundations of misun- derstanding and false expectation. Relationships are not independent of character: they depend on it.

Lydgate is a deeper character, but not more discerning when it comes to love. Intelligence and expertise such as his are no better immunisation against the insidious assault of love than any lesser man has, 'even the most densely ignorant of humoral pathology or fibrous tissue'. As with Rosamond, his idea of relationships depends on char- acter. The sentence that deals with him in the first paragraph offers a negative facet of the 'conscious superiority' that Rosamond admires, for Lydgate feels himself to be superior – superior, in particular, to women. The feminine mind is in his estimation an extension of the 'prettiness' of the feminine body: its function is 'to adore a man's pre- eminence without too precise a knowledge of what it consist[s] in'. The second paragraph of the extract develops this simple idea, con- cluding with a description of Rosamond as 'a half-opened blush-rose

... adorned with accomplishments for the refined amusement of man'. Here 'man' clearly excludes women, who are considered merely as ornaments. Of course, it is as an ornament, as we have seen, that Rosamond wishes to present herself; but the innocence implied in the comparison with the rose is grandly inconsistent with the subtle vices of her nature and ironically points to Lydgate's, not Rosamond's, naivety.

Nevertheless, Lydgate is not blameless in bringing the relationship to its dismal conclusion. The earlier part of the last paragraph describes his pleasure in the company of Rosamond and his sense of security in a harmless flirtation. They are never alone with each other; nothing is said implying a deep relationship. Lydgate is satisfied with the limits of this association: he intends to 'flirt and be wise'. His pleasure in it lies, however, in a source as self-regarding as Rosamond's different motives. Having sampled the nature of Middlemarch society in general, Lydgate is unenthused: the men are mostly 'great bores' interested only in commercial rivalries or playing cards; he needs diversion, 'relaxation' from the stresses of his absorbing professional work. Rosamond, in short, is a convenient solution to his boredom. Flirtation, harmless though it may be, contains just sufficient danger and excitement to entertain him but requires no commitment to detract from his work. It is, then, not merely Rosamond that Lydgate holds in cheerful, admiring contempt, but sexual relationships in general.

The reference to Mrs Bulstrode is particularly interesting. She is described as 'naive' and indeed there is nothing subtle about her confusion of standards. The point is that Lydgate is more than capable of discerning the unresolved conflict in her of idealism and materialism, yet is apparently unconscious at this stage of the comparable conflict in Rosamond. The conclusion must be that Lydgate, despite his capacity for insight, is dazzled more than he understands by Rosamond so that he fails to perceive in her what he clearly sees in Mrs Bulstrode. Eliot presents here a portrait of a man who is rendered more than usually gullible by the subtle blandishments of a girl who does not know what an unscrupulous adventuress she is. In her world the man of science knows nothing – whether about her or about himself.

The seeds of the destruction of this relationship are already present. Indeed, they are specifically referred to. Now Rosamond 'never [thinks] of money except as something necessary which other people would always provide'; soon she will reveal an impermeable, even resolute, failure to recognise monetary necessity. Where here 'her statements [are] no direct clue to fact', though she does not think of herself as lying, soon her relationship with Lydgate will be irredeemably compromised by her incorrigible readiness to deal behind his back. Their relationship reaches its nadir in Chapter 65 (pp. 665–7) when Lydgate confronts Rosamond with the consequences of her writing to Sir Godwin. There he accuses her of 'delud[ing him] with a false assent', presents himself as 'at the mercy of [her] devices' and lays at her door 'a want of openness and confidence' between them (all pp. 665–6). Rosamond's defence is that her actions are justified by her desire to 'avert some of the hardships which [their] marriage has brought on [her]' (p. 666), to avoid 'wretchedness', by which she means the 'miserable way' (p. 667) that results from impecuniosity. Feeling deeply wronged she weeps at being unjustly taken to task by her cruel husband.

Rosamond clearly has no firm grasp on the realities of her situation. But then neither, earlier, did Lydgate. Both harboured false expectations of their relationship, and both are disappointed. The result is unhappy for both of them, but it is far from haphazard, for Eliot analyses here a central evil that colours many of the relationships in the novel: the deep-rooted evil of egoism. What Eliot means by egoism (a term she uses from time to time in the novel) is not a philosophical system, nor self-interest, nor simple selfishness: rather it is the habit of seeing the world as revolving around one's own existence. It is defined more precisely in Rosamond and Lydgate than in any other relationship in the novel. There is a double irony in her name, derived as it is from *rosa mundi*, rose of the world: she appears for a time to be the most beautiful rose of Lydgate's world; more truly she herself is the centre of her own world. Neither she nor Lydgate is wicked, and neither is unreasonable; their relationship fails because they are neither of them capable of seeing what the other requires from the relationship, and because they do not perceive the partiality of their own points of view. Lydgate and

Rosamond do not speak each other's moral language; but it is a long time before they understand that fact. Lydgate wants a wife who will support him in his scientific endeavours and provide him with relaxation from them; Rosamond wants security, a comfortable life and social status. Initially it is not apparent even that their aims are in conflict, for they spend no time determining what their aims are. Why, after all, need they do so? It is obvious to each of them that everyone else's aims can only be identical with his or her own.

The relationship between Dorothea and Casaubon illustrates another aspect of the same basic failure. Casaubon illustrates egoism in being absorbed so wholly in the interminable scholarly oeuvre to which he has dedicated his existence. Dorothea illustrates it, ironically, in being so immoderately dedicated to service. So romantically desperate is she to sacrifice herself that she fails to consider whether the kind of sacrifice she has in mind is acceptable to the recipient. Casaubon and Dorothea have little of the kind of analysis by discussion that Rosamond and Lydgate provide. Instead, Eliot uses more indirect methods. Consider the implications of the scene towards the end of Chapter 42 in which Dorothea comes into the garden to support Casaubon after he has been told of his impending death by Lydgate:

> Dorothea had been aware when Lydgate had ridden away, and she had stepped into the garden, with the impulse to go at once to her husband. But she hesitated, fearing to offend him by obtruding herself; for her ardour, continually repulsed, served, with her intense memory, to heighten her dread, as thwarted energy subsides into a shudder; and she wandered slowly round the nearer clumps of trees until she saw him advancing. Then she went towards him, and might have represented a heaven-sent angel coming with a promise that the short hours remaining should yet be filled with that faithful love which clings the closer to a comprehended grief. His glance in reply to hers was so chill that she felt her timidity increased; yet she turned and passed her hand through his arm.
>
> Mr Casaubon kept his hands behind him and allowed her pliant arm to cling with difficulty against his rigid arm.
>
> (p. 425)

Dorothea's submission to Casaubon's will is ironically emphasised in her feeling it necessary to discipline her natural feelings for fear of offending him. The oppositions in 'impulse . . . hesitated' and 'ardour . . . repulsed' narrow to 'thwarted energy' as, restraining her spontaneous desire to go to his side, she waits for him to appear. Characteristically, it is Casaubon's glance, censorious and envious as a knife, that first expresses his hostility to her sympathy. Eliot, describing him at this point as a 'poor man' (p. 424), sees him as an object of pity because he cannot help the rigidity pictured so vividly in the final sentence of the extract. With his hands kept resolutely to himself, incapable of responding to the 'heaven-sent angel' who can comfort his last days, he is the saddest victim of his own egoism. As Casaubon's rigidity is symbolised in his arm, Dorothea's adaptability is represented in her 'pliant arm'. As the vignette suggests, her failure is not to recognise that the object of her will to service is incapable of availing himself of what she has to offer. Like Rosamond, though in a finer way, she misreads her husband in the light of her own ego.

In contrast, Fred Vincy comes to a clear understanding of his place in the world and what is demanded of him by the world – the world is, of course, represented by Mary – when he resolves to compensate for the errors of his past by working for Caleb Garth. In announcing his decision to his parents, however, he meets an unexpected rebuff when his father resentfully accuses him of having 'thrown away [his education], and gone down a step in life' (p. 568). Here Eliot reveals the flaws beneath the plausible appearance of parental love which in Mr Vincy's case 'had had a great deal of pride, inconsiderateness, and egoistic folly in them' (p. 568). At the same time, she shows how egoism can accompany good decisions as well as bad: Fred is shocked by his father's response because, although he expected his father's disappointment, he failed to anticipate its depth and significance.

There are, then, gradations of egoism affecting different kinds of relationship. The effects range from the lightest comedy to the darkest tragedy, and there will be opportunity to study the extremes in the recommendations for further work at the end of the chapter.

Conclusions

Rather than attempting to survey all the varieties of sexual and platonic relationship that appear in Eliot's novels, this chapter endeavours to consider Eliot's way of looking at relationships in general. Of
the three examples of sexual relationship discussed in detail above,
one – that of Philip and Maggie – is clearly more romantic than the
others; one, that of Godfrey with his dead wife, is marked by guilt;
the third, Lydgate's with Rosamond, is characterised by misunderstanding. Eliot presents all three, however, as parts of a more complex
range of relationships. Thus Maggie feels not only her duty to Philip,
but also the demands of her relationship with Tom and the demands
of the relationships of both Philip and herself with their fathers. In
the extract from *Silas Marner* a dangerous web of sexual and parental
relationships links Godfrey, his wife, his child and Nancy – at this
point no more than a bystander – with Silas. Though in the extract
dealing with Lydgate and Rosamond no mention is made of other
individuals closely concerned in the relationship, awareness of the
general social context is much more powerfully presented: Rosamond
compares Lydgate with her brother and other young men of her
acquaintance, while Lydgate thinks of Rosamond as an attractive
alternative to the male society of Middlemarch or to the family life
of the Bulstrodes. In the earlier two novels, the focal relationship has
a social context; in *Middlemarch,* the relationship of Lydgate and
Rosamond is in effect a function of the social context of the town
they live in.

The extracts cover a broad range of feeling. The simplest feelings
are those of Philip, who is dominated by romantic love, and Silas,
whose sudden attachment to the child is unthinking though of
obscure origin. In *Middlemarch,* the simpler characters include
both the appallingly prepossessing Rosamond and Celia. The more
complex characters, such as the troubled Maggie, the haunted
Godfrey and the embittered Lydgate, however, are rather more interesting on the whole – though the novelist's art brings a degree of
fascination to Rosamond who would be insufferable, if imaginable at
all, as an actuality.

This simple division of characters throws up an interesting characteristic of Eliot's treatment of relationships: the parties to relationships have unequal weight. In the extract from *The Mill on the Floss*, Maggie evidently feels and understands a great deal more than Philip: she knows their love is doomed, but keeps the knowledge from him for fear of causing unnecessary hurt. Similarly, in *Middlemarch*, Lydgate is much exercised with the deep stupidity of Rosamond: his effort, however, is directed towards bringing her to understand and confront reality. Dorothea, though trapped in a very different kind of relationship, nevertheless understands more than the clever Casaubon. In each case, the deeper and more sensitive character is pushed into the position of protecting the other from himself.

Eliot's central relationships are, then, complicated and not especially happy. The simple and happy relationships occur on the periphery of the novels, though they are often very important: Dolly and Adam Winthrop and the Garth family are obvious examples. As the analyses indicate, Eliot charts the changing moods of dialogue and feeling between Maggie and Philip and between Lydgate and Rosamond in detail, bringing out the inherent difficulty of relationship itself. These characters constantly try but fail to achieve a stable understanding. Their relationships are as fleeting and variable as their feelings.

There are widely differing reasons for the difficulties that beset these relationships. One of the reasons for the complexity of Eliot's perspective is that emotional relationships never exist independently of the wider web of family and social relationships that impose stresses, often insuperable stresses, on relationships between two individuals. This social web is the subject of the next chapter. However, Eliot also shows the individuals themselves failing to develop sound relationships because of their false or ill-considered expectations. Love betrays as often as it offers hope or support or delight.

Difficult, flawed and imperfect as they are, emotional relationships are always crucial in Eliot's novels, and their thematic importance will emerge more fully in later chapters of this study. Before we leave the subject here, it will be well to note briefly some examples of the consistency with which Eliot stresses the virtue of sympathetic relationships. In *The Mill on the Floss* Eliot refers to Maggie's strong will to act rightly after her return to St Ogg's and speaks of 'the faith and sympathy that were the best organs of her soul' (p. 582). Her decision to face St Ogg's grows from her consciousness that there lies the essential web of her feelings, her sense of the past, and the familial and communal associations most dear to her. A little later, as Dr Kenn considers Maggie's situation, Eliot contrasts 'the men of maxims' – those who live by the rule, by principle or precept over-rigidly applied – with those whose emotional life is 'vivid and intense enough to have created a wide fellow-feeling with all that is human' (both p. 628). In the extract from *Silas Marner* analysed above Eliot stresses the purely spontaneous, instinctive attraction of Marner towards the child. He offers no rational justification for his desire to keep her: the demand comes from his heart. Under her influence, his life expands. Neighbours begin to smile upon him. When Dolly Winthrop, good-hearted as she is, counsels Silas, who is puzzled by 'the incompatible demands of love' to shut Eppie in the coal-hole to teach her to behave properly, he delays doing so 'not only because it was painful to him to hurt Eppie, but because he trembled at a moment's contention with her, lest she should love him the less for it'. When his token gesture towards discipline fails before Eppie's undaunted sense of fun, it 'shook Silas's belief in the efficacy of punishment' and she is thereafter 'reared without punishment, the burden of her misdeeds being borne vicariously by father Silas' (all pp. 126–9). And, of course, as we shall see in the extract that is to be analysed in Chapter 5, the dispute over Eppie between Silas and Godfrey dramatises a conflict of emotions of differing intensity and validity. *Middlemarch* focuses constantly in all its complexities on the significance of spontaneous feeling. Dorothea above all others expresses Eliot's ideas: through all the vicissitudes of her story, having 'early begun to emerge from that stupidity' of 'taking the world as an udder to feed our supreme selves' (both p. 211), she strives to be true to the highest impulses of her own nature. She is 'alive to anything that gave her an opportunity for active sympathy' (p. 204), and this includes charitable works and personal responsiveness. Even towards Rosamond, she feels 'a great outgoing of her heart' (p. 798). Similar ideas appear in the context of other plots. All are embraced in the general reference made by the narrator's voice to 'the deep-seated habit of direct fellow-feeling with individual fellow-men' (p. 619).

Further discussion of the moral implications of Eliot's point of view will find a place in Chapter 5.

Methods of Analysis

The extracts discussed above are different kinds of writing and demand different kinds of response. The content and structure of each show how it should be approached.

In the extract from *The Mill on the Floss* the movements and physical appearance of Philip and Maggie are important. In addition to what they say, the inflection of Maggie's words demands analysis, and references to the natural background deepen the meaning of the scene. The social environment appears only in references to other characters.

The social environment is more prominent in the *Silas Marner* extract. Here the analysis must focus on the contrast between the protagonists, Silas and Godfrey, and the relatively normal society they inhabit. The words and actions of the actors in the scene are, of course, important. The heart of the meaning of the scene lies partly in the way those words and actions express the minds of Silas and Godfrey, and partly in the implied structural relationship between the protagonists.

Action and its symbolic meaning are significant in the brief quotation from *Middlemarch* about the relationship of Dorothea and Casaubon. In the major extract, however, Eliot's method is ironic analysis of the feelings of first Rosamond, then Lydgate. Study of that extract therefore demands identification of the voices adopted by Eliot, and analysis of the operation and target of the irony.

Criticism of these extracts, then, depends on analysis of the words spoken, the actions performed, the feelings expressed and the language used. The social, physical or natural background is often important too in deepening, by parallel or by contrast, the foreground scene. Finally, the complexity of Eliot's approach to relationships needs to be recognised: she uses a variety of conflicting signals to ensure that the relationships of characters – such as Philip's with Maggie, and Lydgate's with Rosamond – cannot be interpreted as simple, idealised romantic love.

Further Work

The Mill on the Floss

Several passages suggest themselves. You may wish to look at a later stage in the relationship between Philip and Maggie when he visits her after her disgrace (Book Six, Chapter 10, pp. 563–4: 'We can just catch the tips of the Scotch firs . . . the subtlest fold of the heart'). If you wish to explore a different relationship from the one discussed in this chapter, you might consider the dialogue between Tom and Maggie after confronting Philip in the Red Deeps (Book Five, Chapter 5, pp. 449–51: 'He seized Maggie's right wrist . . . Let us remember that in future and be silent'). Another fruitful idea is to deal with the relationship between Stephen and Maggie. Look, for example, at the crucial episode in which he kisses her for the first time (Book Six, Chapter 10, pp. 561–3: 'Stephen was mute . . . that gentle, unsuspicious sister').

Silas Marner

As a sequel to the extract analysed above you might look at the passage in which Silas attends to the child in Chapter 14 ('Anybody' ud think . . . Baby's gymnastics', pp. 121–2). Another possibility is to deal with the sibling relationship between Dunsey and Godfrey in Chapter 3 ('The door opened . . . though I'm sorry to part', pp. 25–6). A final alternative is to look at the passage dealing with Nancy's feelings towards Godfrey in Chapter 17 ('There was one main thread of painful experience . . . the mode in which Nancy's life was regulated', pp. 154–6) or at Godfrey's confession of his wrong-doings to Nancy in Chapter 18 ('He was silent . . . Can you forgive me ever?', pp. 162–3).

Middlemarch

If you would like to analyse the outcome of the relationship of Rosamond and Lydgate, a useful passage to deal with is their conversation

after the sale of the house in Chapter 69 ('Forgive me for this misery
. . . a great deal worse for her', pp. 701–2). You may prefer to examine
a sibling relationship in Celia's announcement of her engagement to
Dorothea in Chapter 28 ('Do you think it nice to go to Rome . . .
saturate a neighbouring body', p. 277). A darker episode is the impact
of Bulstrode's disgrace on his marriage in Chapter 74 ('She locked
herself in her room . . . I am innocent', pp. 749–51).

4

Society

This chapter deals with the carefully detailed social structure that provides the backdrop of the novels and considers Eliot's effort to create the illusion of historical reality within which her characters exist. Though the social worlds of the novels are distinct from each other, they all share something of the quality of the conceit that dominates *Middlemarch* – the web. This chapter does not attempt to sum up Eliot's thinking about society, nor does it try to explore the social worlds of the novels fully. Rather, a few strands are selected that suggest the range and tendency of Eliot's social concerns. Among the most prominent topics she deals specifically with the position of women in society, the gap between rich and poor, and the importance, social and personal, of work.

Society at large is given a voice in each novel. In *The Mill on the Floss* it is partly the Tulliver uncles and aunts who express the outlook of the wider community, and Dr Kenn's congregation has a voice strong enough to control his behaviour towards Maggie. In *Silas Marner* there is a double voice too: Mrs Winthrop's straightforward kindness and simple beliefs naturally reflect the community from which she has sprung, and she represents its attitude towards Silas; the men at the Rainbow show how the community behaves and how it adapts to, and at length absorbs, Silas. In *Middlemarch*, society has many voices: Mrs Cadwallader has a major choric role; the members of the medical committee at which Bulstrode is denounced have a formal choric voice, while the Tankard in Slaughter Lane and the

Green Dragon, like the Rainbow in *Silas Marner*, provide an informal forum where local affairs are discussed.

Middlemarch is exceptional in placing society in an environment of wealthier detail and greater historical accuracy. Here the web embraces politics, transport, health, marriage and scientific discourse as well as simple gossip.

(i)   *The Mill on the Floss*

Maggie's moral world is defined by a widening succession of communities extending from her family to St Ogg's. Eliot, of course, realises that the world she describes is restrictive, and so describes it in speaking of the 'oppressive narrowness' of Maggie's social environment with its 'conventional worldly notions and habits without instruction and without polish' (both p. 362). It is nevertheless the world that determines the lives of the Tullivers. At the beginning of the second chapter of Book Seven, Eliot records the judgement of St Ogg's on Maggie's escapade with Stephen Guest. The passage is rather long, but is particularly interesting because it presents the attitude of society towards different outcomes of Maggie's behaviour and thus reveals a great deal about Eliot's vision of the nature of the society itself:

> It was soon known throughout St Ogg's that Miss Tulliver was come back: she had not, then, eloped in order to be married to Mr Stephen Guest – at all events, Mr Stephen Guest had not married her – which came to the same thing, so far as her culpability was concerned. We judge others according to results; how else? – not knowing the process by which results are arrived at. If Miss Tulliver, after a few months of well-chosen travel, had returned as Mrs Stephen Guest – with a post-marital *trousseau* and all the advantages possessed even by the most unwelcome wife of an only son, public opinion, which at St Ogg's, as elsewhere, always knew what to think, would have judged in strict consistency with those results. Public opinion, in these cases, is always of the feminine gender – not the world, but the world's wife: and she would have seen, that two handsome young people – the gentleman of quite the first family in St Ogg's – having found themselves in a false

position, had been led into a course, which, to say the least of it, was highly injudicious, and productive of sad pain and disappointment, especially to that sweet young thing, Miss Deane. Mr Stephen Guest had certainly not behaved well; but then, young men were liable to those sudden infatuated attachments – and bad as it might seem in Mrs Stephen Guest to admit the faintest advances from her cousin's lover (indeed it *had* been said that she was actually engaged to young Wakem – old Wakem himself had mentioned it) still she was very young – 'and a deformed young man, you know! – and young Guest so very fascinating, and, they say, he positively worshipped her (to be sure, that can't last!) and he ran away with her in the boat quite against her will – and what could she do? She couldn't come back then: no one would have spoken to her. And how very well that maize-coloured satinette becomes her complexion – it seems as if the folds in front were quite come in – several of her dresses are made so – they say, he thinks nothing too handsome to buy for her. Poor Miss Deane! She is very pitiable – but then, there was no positive engagement – and the air at the coast will do her good. After all, if young Guest felt no more for her than that, it was better for her not to marry him. What a wonderful marriage for a girl like Miss Tulliver – quite romantic! Why – young Guest will put up for the borough at the next election. Nothing like commerce nowadays! That young Wakem nearly went out of his mind – he always was rather queer; but he's gone abroad again to be out of the way – quite the best thing for a deformed young man. Miss Unit declares she will never visit Mr and Mrs Stephen Guest – such nonsense! pretending to be better than other people. Society couldn't be carried on if we inquired into private conduct in that way – and Christianity tells us to think no evil – and my belief is, that Miss Unit had no cards sent her.'

But the results, we know, were not of a kind to warrant this extenuation of the past. Maggie had returned without a *trousseau*, without a husband – in that degraded and outcast condition to which error is well known to lead; and the world's wife, with that fine instinct which is given her for the preservation of society, saw at once that Miss Tulliver's conduct had been of the most aggravated kind. Could anything be more detestable? – A girl so much indebted to her friends – whose mother as well as herself had received so much kindness from the Deanes – to lay the design of winning a young man's affections away from her own cousin who had behaved like a sister to her? Winning his affections? That was not the phrase for such a girl as Miss

Tulliver: it would have been more correct to say that she had been actu-
ated by mere unwomanly boldness and unbridled passion. There was
always something questionable about her. That connection with young
Wakem, which, they said, had been carried on for years, looked very
ill: disgusting, in fact! But with a girl of that disposition! – to the world's
wife there had always been something in Miss Tulliver's very physique
that a refined instinct felt to be prophetic of harm. As for poor Mr
Stephen Guest, he was rather pitiable than otherwise: a young man of
five and twenty is not to be too severely judged in these cases – he is
really very much at the mercy of a designing bold girl. And it was clear
that he had given way in spite of himself – he had shaken her off as
soon as he could: indeed, their having parted so soon looked very black
indeed – for her. To be sure he had written a letter, laying all the blame
on himself, and telling the story in a romantic fashion so as to try and
make her appear quite innocent: of course he could do that! But the
refined instinct of the world's wife was not to be deceived: providen-
tially! – else what would become of society? Why – her own brother
had turned her from his door – he had seen enough, you might be
sure, before he would do that. A truly respectable young man – Mr
Tom Tulliver – quite likely to rise in the world! His sister's disgrace was
naturally a heavy blow to him. It was to be hoped that she would go
out of the neighbourhood – to America, or anywhere – so as to purify
the air of St Ogg's from the taint of her presence – extremely dangerous to daughters there! No good could happen to her: – it was only to
be hoped she would repent, and that God would have mercy on her:
He had not the care of society on His hands as the world's wife had.

(pp. 619–21)

Here Eliot engages in a characteristic one-sided discussion with the
reader. In the course of it she adopts the voice of St Ogg's – or rather
its wife – to offer judgements about two different outcomes of
Maggie's story. Of course, only one of these outcomes is valid, but
the differences in the way St Ogg's judges them throws a spotlight on
the standards of the community rather than on Maggie. The ideas
are echoed in the structure of the extract. In the first, after noting the
public knowledge of Maggie's return, Eliot alludes to the natural inclination to judge people by results and considers what might have been
the result had Maggie returned as the wife of Stephen Guest; she
imagines the response of St Ogg's to such an event and mid-way

through the paragraph she modulates into a hybrid of direct and reported speech enclosed in quotations marks to express St Ogg's in its own words. The second paragraph reverts to the actuality of the novel in which Maggie returns unmarried; here, though no quotation marks are necessary, the same voice of St Ogg's as in the first paragraph is heard venting its opinions on this alternative event.

At the outset Eliot focuses on the essential object of moral judgement: the assessment of 'culpability'. Speedily, however, culpability comes to appear an effect, and not a cause, of events. Depending on whether or not there is a marriage, all the protagonists are judged differently. After the hypothetical marriage, Stephen, though recognised as having behaved badly, is excused as a young man 'liable to those sudden infatuated attachments' and what has happened will not impede his progress to the borough election; Maggie is 'very young' and may well be excused for succumbing to her 'fascinating' lover; the course of their love seems 'quite romantic'. Unmarried, the young people suffer a very different judgement: Stephen is 'pitiable', Maggie a 'designing bold girl' guilty of 'unwomanly boldness and unbridled passion' whom Stephen had 'shaken off' as soon as possible. The other characters affected alter their colour too. It is Miss Deane who is 'pitiable' in the first paragraph: 'Poor Miss Deane' is regarded as 'a sweet young thing', and it is assumed that she will no doubt return from her visit to the seaside much strengthened; in the second paragraph, she is seen as the victim of a cousin towards whom she had behaved 'as a sister'. Philip Wakem is conveniently dismissed in the first paragraph, despite 'nearly [going] out of his mind', as 'always . . . rather queer'; twice referred to as 'a deformed young man', he is sent 'abroad . . . out of the way' as 'quite the best thing'. In the second paragraph, the relationship between Philip and Maggie has degenerated from an actual engagement to 'That connection' which had been 'carried on for years' and looked 'very ill: disgusting'. The word 'romantic' appears again, but in the second paragraph only to describe the superficial illusion of innocence that Stephen has tried to weave in his letter to exonerate Maggie. In short, all the characters are judged by whether or not a marriage has taken place. That 'wonderful marriage' would have cast a glow of romance on all the circumstances surrounding it; without it – 'without a *trousseau*, without a husband' in perhaps that order of material importance – Maggie is reduced to a 'degraded and outcast condition'.

Eliot voices no overt condemnation of the misconceptions on which such judgements are based. St Ogg's stands in for the real world, and Eliot accepts that 'We judge others according to results': how else should we judge, having no access to what underlies them? But the tone of the extract conveys a very thorough perception of the absurd confidence such judgements carry with them. Eliot notes ironically that 'public opinion . . . always knew what to think'; cascades of exclamations and rhetorical questions extenuate the circumstances of the relationship of Maggie and Stephen in the first paragraph under the kindly light of marriage, while a briefer series expresses disgust in the second. Opinion bolsters itself, repeating 'to be sure' three times. It reassures itself that it is speaking on behalf of objective values 'for the preservation of society', expressing its will repeatedly in an impersonal 'it was [only] to be hoped'. In actuality opinion is informed by nothing more than the unthinking prejudice underlined in the ironies of the extract. There is an incremental irony, in particular, in the repeated reference to the instinct that guides opinion – once a 'fine instinct' and twice a 'refined instinct'. These references match ill with the unrefined lack of discrimination apparent everywhere in the extract. Consider, for example, the equation of trousseau and husband already mentioned; or the mingling of comments on Maggie's moral behaviour with remarks on how well the 'maize-coloured satinette becomes her complexion'; or the complacent security of conviction that 'error is well known to lead' to exclusion from society; or the absurdity of the discussion of visiting cards, Christianity and Miss Unit with which the first paragraph concludes.

No condemnation is pronounced, then, but certainly a very satirical eye is cast on this society. The first error of St Ogg's is in misjudging its own importance. Eliot speaks of public opinion as 'always of the feminine gender – not the world, but the world's wife'. In fact, though it is only the wife of St Ogg's, it persists in viewing itself as universal and inclusive while in practice it behaves very exclusively. It wishes to protect its own interests, and first the status quo that preserves it. Banishment is the harshest punishment it can mete out. Miss Deane goes to the coast; Philip Wakem goes abroad. Maggie's greatest error, perhaps, is in returning to St Ogg's, which heartily hopes that she will go 'out of the neighbourhood – to America, or anywhere', for her presence is an embarrassment. St Ogg's thinks of itself as the world's wife, but it is aware that there is a much wider world less respectable than St Ogg's. The idea of banishment has a more serious side too. Although 'Christianity tells us to think no evil', and St Ogg's must be Christian in tradition as well as in name, the town clearly can think no good of an unmarried Maggie, and can only hope that, given repentance, 'God would have mercy on her' – for the wife of St Ogg's certainly won't.

The voice of St Ogg's is a powerful one in the novel. The Tulliver uncles and aunts have a share in it, and so has Dr Kenn's congregation which effects the removal of Maggie. It applies different standards to men and women, and informs Mr Wakem's remark, in the course of his argument with Philip about Maggie, that 'We don't ask what a woman does – we ask whom she belongs to' (pp. 542–3). It is an ancient voice, echoing through the generations, so that whatever a child does must be done by reference to the voice of the past represented chiefly by its own parents. It protects those of its children who listen to it and rejects those who don't. Its watchword is respectability. Thus St Ogg's sees as the major victim of Maggie's 'disgrace' her brother, Tom, 'a truly respectable young man . . . quite likely to rise in the world'. Thus, also, when she turns to him, Tom rejects her with a countenance as hard as the hardest in St Ogg's:

> But Tom's face, as he stood in the hot still sunshine of that summer afternoon, had no gladness, no triumph in it. His mouth wore its bitterest expression, his severe brow its hardest and deepest fold, as he drew down his hat farther over his eyes to shelter them from the sun, and thrusting his hands deep into his pockets, began to walk up and down the gravel. No news of his sister had been heard since Bob Jakin had come back in the steamer from Mudport and put an end to all improbable suppositions of an accident on the water by stating that he had seen her land from a vessel with Mr Stephen Guest. Would the next news be that she was married – or what? Probably that she was not married: Tom's mind was set to the expectation of the worst that could happen – not death, but disgrace.
>
> (p. 611)

Here the set of Tom's hat and the hiding of his hands match the expression on Tom's face. All betoken rejection. And when he is forced to address his sister a little later, it is with a word harsher than the harshest spoken by the world's wife: 'I wash my hands of you. You don't belong to me' (p. 612). It is in its effect on Tom, therefore, that the world of St Ogg's is seen at its most noxious. He is unable to behave otherwise towards Maggie, because he has absorbed the standards of his society. Equally, earlier in the novel, he cannot countenance the relationship between Maggie and Philip because he is 'bound by his duty to his father's memory, and by every manly feeling' (p. 579). Here 'bound' means a moral obligation, but it also implies lack of freedom. Tom does not choose to be as he is: St Ogg's has made him in its own image. Ironically, the index of the sickness of St Ogg's lies in its very success with Tom. Eliot's condemnation of St Ogg's thus emerges most forcefully not in direct statement nor even in irony, but in the action of the novel.

St Ogg's may not be the world, but it stands for it, or at least for the part of the world that Eliot grew up in. The oppression that overbears Maggie is of much the same kind that Eliot fought against; Maggie's brother is the counterpart of Eliot's brother, Isaac. In *The Mill on the Floss* Eliot may be seen as trying to exorcise the vestiges of the power her background still exercises in her. It is her own world as much as St Ogg's that she characterises in the extract and attempts to diminish by revealing its limitations. This society is not the world but behaves as if it is and thus reveals its narrowness.

(ii) *Silas Marner*

With its stronger tone of folk lore and myth, *Silas Marner* may appear at first sight to have less to say about society than the other novels. closer inspection quickly reveals, however, a carefully detailed social world, less commonplace perhaps than in the other novels but nevertheless convincing. Silas's very isolation throws into relief the different social worlds of the novel: Lantern Yard, the Rainbow and the Cass family. To a degree the society of Raveloe is defined by the character of its leading members. In Chapter 3, Eliot turns from Silas himself for the first time to consider the family at the pinnacle of Raveloe society and introduce the other main strand of her story:

It was still that glorious war-time which was felt to be a peculiar favour of Providence towards the landed interest, and the fall of prices had not yet come to carry the race of small squires and yeomen down that road to ruin for which extravagant habits and bad husbandry were plentifully anointing their wheels. I am speaking now in relation to Raveloe and the parishes that resembled it; for our old-fashioned country life had many different aspects, as all life must have when it is spread over a various surface, and breathed on variously by multitudinous currents, from the winds of heaven to the thoughts of men, which are for ever moving and crossing each other with incalculable results. Raveloe lay low among the bushy trees and the rutted lanes, aloof from the currents of industrial energy and Puritan earnestness: the rich ate and drank freely, accepting gout and apoplexy as things that ran mysteriously in respectable families, and the poor thought that the rich were entirely in the right of it to lead a jolly life; besides, their feasting caused a multiplication of orts, which were the heirlooms of the poor. Betty Jay scented the boiling of Squire Cass's hams, but her longing was arrested by the unctuous liquor in which they were boiled; and when the seasons brought round the great merry-makings, they were regarded on all hands as a fine thing for the poor. For the Raveloe feasts were like the rounds of beef and the barrels of ale – they were on a large scale, and lasted a good while, especially in the winter-time. After ladies had packed up their best gowns and top-knots in bandboxes, and had incurred the risk of fording streams on pillions with the precious burden in rainy or snowy weather, when there was no knowing how high the water would rise, it was not to be supposed that they looked forward to a brief pleasure. On this ground it was always contrived in the dark seasons, when there was little work to be done, and the hours were long, that several neighbours should keep open house in succession. So soon as Squire Cass's standing dishes diminished in plenty and freshness, his guests had nothing to do but to walk a little higher up the village to Mr Osgood's, at the Orchards, and they found hams and chines uncut, pork-pies with the scent of the fire in them, spun butter in all its freshness – everything, in fact, that appetites at leisure could desire, in perhaps greater perfection, though not in greater abundance, than at Squire Cass's.

(pp. 23–4)

Eliot here deals with Raveloe and its leading family, headed by Squire Cass, as a feudal society characterised by a popular myth of jollity and an opposed underlying actuality. The only earlier reference to the Squire is incidental, and now Eliot approaches her subject in a general way, giving no specific hint of the ignoble, rending feud between the brothers, Dunstan and Godfrey, which is shortly to be dramatised with unsavoury precision. Such detail as there is in this opening paragraph seems extraneous: Betty Jay appears nowhere else in the novel, and her name makes an appearance here to develop the note of homeliness – of the familiar, ordinary and unthreatening – that characterises one aspect of the extract.

The jolly-rural-England thread appears mainly in the second half of the extract. Its smell emanates from the boiling hams and their 'unctuous liquor', from the Raveloe feasts with their beef and ale, from Mr Osgood's hams, chines and singed pork pies; its prettiness is that of finely dressed ladies with top-knots in their bandboxes; its mood is one of leisure, abundance and perfection; it tastes of plenty and the richness of spun butter. A similar mood appears earlier too in the idea of Raveloe as something of a backwater, a haven of peace affected neither by the commercial and religious ferments of the day – 'aloof from the currents of industrial energy and Puritan earnestness' – nor by its political crises. The paragraph as a whole is sandwiched between phrases dominated by positive moods – between 'glorious . . . favour of Providence' and 'greater perfection . . . greater abundance'. Given a lantern or two and a coach and horses this scene would not fall far short of a certain kind of Christmas card. Nothing could be further from the narrow haunted world of the recluse Silas Marner.

This picture does a considerable disservice to what Eliot has written: she is more subtle, underpinning the jolly images with spiky ironies. The dichotomous nature of the paragraph is hinted at in the first line where the scene is placed in the past of the Napoleonic wars, an era described as 'glorious war-time'. While we cannot say that the phrase is inherently oxymoronic, so much depends on the perception of the reader as to load the meaning of 'glorious' with ambiguity. The tendency of the writing becomes firmer later in the sentence with the association between Providence and the profligate and inefficient small farmers ('yeomen') and landowners. Clearly Eliot treats this group, which includes the Cass family, with grim irony: 'anointing their wheels' develops the religious reference of 'Providence' and suggests a well-oiled, fat life; thus while the 'small squires and yeomen' bask in the confidence of the protection of Providence, enjoying the benefits of their privileged position, their extravagance speeds their unwitting journey to impoverishment. Eliot depicts this group as insulated from reality. Theirs is a complex world of change, of new ideas both political and religious, of scientific progress and economic development: Eliot speaks of 'currents' twice, stressing the evolutionary nature of their world, and recognises its complexity in 'multitudinous' and 'incalculable'. But folk like the gentry of Raveloe are oblivious of all this. Indeed, they are unaware even of the link between their bad habits and bad health, thinking of illnesses like gout and apoplexy as 'mysteriously' prevalent in 'respectable' families. The word Eliot chooses to describe their oblivion, 'aloof', normally suggests a sense of superiority, and indeed the rural gentry of Raveloe think of the tempests of the world beyond their own precinct, when they think of them at all, as irrelevant to their own welfare; here, however, the word evidently implies ignorance or wilful disregard. They need not, and will not, look beyond their own fur-lined comfort.

Far from presenting a pleasant picture of rural England, then, Eliot depicts a society ruled by fat parasites for their own benefit. Their rule goes unquestioned by those whom they hold in subjection: Eliot reveals her own point of view when she says that the poor 'think that the rich were entirely in the right of it to lead a jolly life'; clearly, she regards the poor as deluded in their views. Not only do the poor collude with the rich, they are actively grateful for the 'orts' (leftovers) that fall from the rich men's tables. The bitterness in Eliot's ironic description of these orts as 'the heirlooms of the poor' provides the key to the whole paragraph. While ostensibly recounting winter festivities, she paints a thumbnail sketch of a rural England divided against itself. On the one hand are the poor subsisting on scraps. On the other, a life of fine clothes, gowns and top-knots, feasting and finery in plenty, and no doubt valuable heirlooms too: the gentry eat and drink 'freely' in 'great merry-makings . . . on a large scale' with everything in 'abundance'; the good things pile up in terraces of beef and ale, hams, chines and pies. They have 'everything . . . that appetites at leisure could desire'.

The paragraph as a whole suggests a series of violent but latent oppositions. The rich parasitise the poor but have yet to be found out. This 'glorious' era of the Napoleonic wars shows rural England ailing, with a deep-seated social sickness that has developed from the days of feudalism, but unaware of it. The extravagant life lived by the squires and yeomen is moribund, but they do not yet know it: they happily eat and drink their way to their own demise. As for the poor, they exist in a state approaching serfdom in this period, nearly half a century before the publication of the *Communist Manifesto*, unaware of their chains and with no thought of uniting against their oppressors.

There is a closer connection between this paragraph and the preceding account of the life and habits of Silas Marner than at first appears. He is, admittedly, not poor, for he has hoarded his gold in sufficient quantity to offer temptation to the son of the first family in the neighbourhood, Dunsey Cass. Yet, bent as he is in the shape of his labour he presents something of the aspect of the slave chained to his oar and to that extent stands representative of the poor ordinary folk of Raveloe. The novel reaches its climax when Godfrey Cass, offering to take Eppie, moves to deprive Silas of the dearest thing in his life and thus to make Silas twice the victim of the Cass family. *Silas Marner* is far from a Marxist pamphlet. Rather, the novel deals with the individual development of two individuals. Nevertheless, there is in it a powerful sense of the social inequality and injustice that pervade Raveloe and communities like it. In the immediate sequel Eliot presents, in Dunsey's viciousness and greed, a particularly appalling example of the moral quality of the rulers of this small world.

This paragraph shows that, although the novel has the quality of myth or legend, there is also a significant element of realism in it. Primarily the story of the personal development of Silas and Godfrey, the novel nevertheless shows a strong consciousness of what lies beyond them. They are part of a Raveloe that stands for other rural communities. Beyond them lie towns and cities and countries with concerns much wider than those of Raveloe. Though the extract looks back to the past, there is only a superficial note of nostalgia. The ironic tones build to a denunciation of the social disunity that persisted into Eliot's own time.

The novel touches on two of the traditional organs of social life in portraying the community at the Rainbow and recounting the process of integration of Silas into the church. The Rainbow is well-named, for it acts as host to a cross-section of the community, as well as providing a good-humoured forum for discussion. The church, equally, may be a home for all colours of Christian faith, and the traditional ceremony of marriage brings the novel to a happy conclusion. Yet both these centres of social life are darkened by the guilt, dishonesty and division that the narrative turns on.

(iii) *Middlemarch*

Society itself is the subject of this 'Study of Provincial Life'. Eliot uses a broad canvas, intertwining a number of individual stories to build a picture of middle England – the middle classes in the midlands. In the course of the novel she touches on many aspects of the structure of the society, including work, class and religion, but it is on marriage as a defining social instrument that she spends most of her energy. Much of the novel is concerned with the marriages that occur within its span: Celia's with Sir James, Dorothea's with Casaubon and Will Ladislaw, Lydgate's with Rosamond, Fred's with Mary. Other marriages that originate prior to the action are important too, such as the Bulstrodes' and the Garths'. The first paragraph of Chapter 1 comments on the marriageability of the Brooke sisters and the Finale reviews in traditional style the outcome of the marriages that have taken place. This rich and complex topic is explored in a variety of strands in the novel. A good example of Eliot's treatment of marriage occurs in Chapter 74. It takes for its epigraph a quotation from the Marriage Prayer from the Book of Tobit, 'Mercifully grant that we may grow old together', and begins with a discussion of the reputation of the Bulstrodes:

In Middlemarch a wife could not long remain ignorant that the town held a bad opinion of her husband. No feminine intimate might carry her friendship so far as to make a plain statement to the wife of the unpleasant fact known or believed about her husband; but when a woman with her thoughts much at leisure got them suddenly employed on something grievously disadvantageous to her neighbours, various moral impulses were called into play which tended to stimulate utterance. Candour was one. To be candid, in Middlemarch phraseology, meant, to use an early opportunity of letting your friends know that you did not take a cheerful view of their capacity, their conduct, or their position; and a robust candour never waited to be asked for its opinion. Then, again, there was the love of truth – a wide phrase, but meaning in this relation, a lively objection to seeing a wife look happier than her husband's character warranted, or manifest too much satisfaction in her lot: the poor thing should have some hint given her that if she knew the truth she would have less complacency in her bonnet, and in light dishes for a supper-party. Stronger than all, there was the regard for a friend's moral improvement, sometimes called her soul, which was likely to be benefited by remarks tending to gloom, uttered with the accompaniment of pensive staring at the furniture and a manner implying that the speaker would not tell what was on her mind, from regard to the feelings of her hearer. On the whole, one might say that an ardent charity was at work setting the virtuous mind to make a neighbour unhappy for her good.

There were hardly any wives in Middlemarch whose matrimonial misfortunes would in different ways be likely to call forth more of this moral activity than Rosamond and her aunt Bulstrode. Mrs Bulstrode was not an object of dislike, and had never consciously injured any human being. Men had always thought her a handsome comfortable woman, and had reckoned it among the signs of Bulstrode's hypocrisy that he had chosen a red-blooded Vincy, instead of a ghastly and melancholy person suited to his low esteem for earthly pleasure. When the scandal about her husband was disclosed they remarked of her – 'Ah, poor woman! She's as honest as the day – *she* never suspected anything wrong in him, you may depend on it.' Women, who were intimate with her, talked together much of 'poor Harriet', imagined what her feelings must be when she came to know everything, and conjectured how much she had already come to know. There was no spiteful disposition towards her; rather, there was a busy benevolence anxious to ascertain what it would be well for her to feel and do under the circumstances, which of course kept the imagination occupied with her character and history from the times when she was Harriet Vincy till now. With the review of Mrs Bulstrode and her position it was inevitable to associate Rosamond, whose prospects were under the same blight with her aunt's. Rosamond was more severely criticised and less pitied, though she too, as one of the good old Vincy family who had always been known in Middlemarch, was regarded as a victim to marriage with an interloper. The Vincys had their weaknesses, but then they lay on the surface: there was never anything bad to be 'found out' concerning them. Mrs Bulstrode was vindicated from any resemblance to her husband. Harriet's faults were her own.

(pp. 741–2)

The subject here is, typically, not marriage alone, nor indeed is it marriage primarily. Rather it is marriage as a part of general social intercourse. The first paragraph considers in general the notion of reputation as a function of the status of one's spouse: it deals with how people perceive each other. The second focuses more specifically on Harriet Bulstrode; but still the emphasis rests on other people's opinion of her. Thus the impact on Harriet of the revelation of her husband's skulduggery becomes not so much a personal drama as the stuff of social comedy. Her marriage is treated here as a means to analyse the community of which she is a member.

After a relatively plain statement, the first paragraph strikes a predominantly comic tone. Masquerading as a semi-academic dissertation on the motives of Middlemarch women in spreading bad news, it deals in logical order with candour, love of truth and 'regard for a friend's moral improvement', summing up the whole in the phrase 'ardent charity'. The mock-academic tone derives from style as well as from formal structure. The paragraph relies heavily on periphrasis: 'to use an early opportunity of letting your friends know that you did not take a cheerful view of their capacity, their conduct, or their position' is the most extravagant example, purporting to be a quasi-lexical definition of 'candour' according to Middlemarch usage, but beginning with business-speak ('use an early opportunity') and concluding with understatement ('did not take a cheerful view'). Other definitions follow: 'love of truth [is] a lively objection to seeing a wife look happier than her husband's character warranted'; 'a friend's moral

improvement' is 'sometimes called her soul'. The effect of this aggran-
disement is, of course, ironic. The 'robust candour' with which
Middlemarch women express their opinions means no more than
bluntness. Concern for a friend's soul is in fact nothing more than
the will to make her unhappier. The 'love of truth' that prompts
speech or look is actually a delight in spreading gossip. The complexity this simple device can develop appears early in the extract in
the reference to a 'feminine intimate'. The phrase clearly carries, in
its context, more than its surface meaning: in itself, it might perhaps
be thought to mean simply a female friend, but here it means a
woman who matches the phrase only in claiming as friendship a
rather mean-minded acquaintanceship; with such friends, a Harriet
Bulstrode would need no enemies. The phrase carries violent irony:
see, in contrast, the second paragraph, where 'Women, who were
intimate with her' means no more than it says. In the paragraph as a
whole, Eliot's use of definitions serves to focus attention on the range
of meanings of the words she uses and the ironies implicit therein.

Irony, indeed, colours the whole of the first paragraph. Eliot repeatedly presents vicious motive as moral purpose. An idle woman ('a
woman with her thoughts much at leisure') is prey to 'various moral
impulses . . . which tended to stimulate utterance', and therefore is
likely to want to spread defamation at the first opportunity. Of
course, directness is impossible. Instead, she hints what she knows
and would speak but may not. The ironies reach a climax in the final
sentence. The introductory 'one may say' recalls the academic tone
and definitions earlier; the ardent charity Eliot mentions is actually a
burning desire to know the satisfaction of making a friend miserable;
the 'virtuous mind' is actually a thoroughly nasty intelligence, and
her purpose, far from tending for her neighbour's good, is really intent
upon her own satisfaction in being instrumental in seeing a neighbour cast down in disgrace. The ironies reveal that what moves
Middlemarch is not high moral purpose but hypocrisy. Hypocrisy is
not restricted to individuals: as in the rest of the novel, Eliot focuses
on society rather than on any one individual. The extract opens with
a personification that makes the point clear: it is 'the town', behav-
ing like a organism, that 'held a bad opinion'. The effect is to depict
hypocrisy as woven into the fabric of Middlemarch life: sanctimony

is the weave, and calumny the woof; its bilious colours are those of envy.

This environment is a nest of scorpions for anyone unlucky enough to fall into disrepute. The second paragraph turns its attention to Harriet Bulstrode as a particularly vulnerable victim. It is not that her intimates turn against her, or that Middlemarch has fault to find with her. On the contrary, people speak of her with sympathy and approbation. She is 'not an object of dislike' but is considered 'a handsome comfortable woman'; she is thought to be 'honest as the day'; there is 'no spiteful disposition towards her'. Instead, people occupy themselves with the more insidiously damning posture of feeling sorry for her: she is 'poor Harriet'. There is in Middlemarch what masquerades as an earnest good will towards her – a 'busy benevolence' that explores, unfolds and discusses every aspect of her life and inquires in imagination into her private feelings. Thus far, the attitude of Middlemarch – it is heterogeneous but behaves like a single organism – towards Harriet appears, though undesirable, less virulent than the kind of hypocritical vindictiveness outlined in the first paragraph of the extract. The scorpion's sting, however, is in its tail. Middlemarch, having 'vindicated' Harriet from association with her husband's errors, turns its attention to the 'faults [which] were her own'. The sequel discovers a variety of evils in Harriet, including being 'showy' and trying to 'hold her head up above Middlemarch' (both p. 742) – than which no greater crime is imaginable. This paragraph, then, appearing at first milder than its predecessor, actually reinforces and develops it. Beginning with superficial benevolence towards Harriet, who at this stage is innocent of any knowledge of, as well as of any hand in, her husband's crimes, it proceeds after the benign prelude to a detailed dissection of her character. The structure of the paragraph reflects the character of the society it describes: Middlemarch uses the appearance of benevolence to mask its savagery. This is a society not to be trusted with the care of its members. Harriet need not expect from her community the mercy for which the ironic epigraph to the chapter earnestly prays.

This is not to say that the benevolence is wholly dishonest. One of the distinguishing features of Middlemarch is its conservatism and there is a real respect for the Vincys as a 'good old . . . family'. Though the family has its faults, they are known: 'their weaknesses . . . lay on the surface'; there are no secret crimes to be discovered. Gossip, however, though ready to make fine judgements as to culpability, is indiscriminate in its range. Harriet may not be implicated in Bulstrode's disgrace other than by marriage, but the situation invites a thorough analysis of her as an individual. Equally, it is 'inevitable to associate Rosamond' with the censure of her aunt, and to view her prospects as suffering the same 'blight'. Like Harriet, she is spoken of with superficial sympathy as 'a victim of marriage with an inter-loper', for Lydgate is much less well known to Middlemarch than Bulstrode; but she is 'more severely criticised and less pitied', and given the nature of Middlemarch gossip it is hard to say whether the criticism or the pity is the more cutting. There is, in the end, nothing personal about the disparagement of reputations. It is as much a defensive as an aggressive behaviour. What is happening here is that Middlemarch is protecting itself – or its notion of itself – by working busily over a troublesome situation: criticism and benevolence, pity and contempt, analysis and rumour are all part of an organic process.

Furthermore, though Eliot's irony is biting, the process of social readjustment is seen as natural. Indeed, there is a vivid realisation of the minute detail of social life in these paragraphs. The first concludes with a comic dramatisation of the demeanour of the friend who stares meaningfully at the furniture and makes general gloomy remarks to show that she knows more than she is willing to say. The second sets the discussion of Harriet Bulstrode in the context of colloquial speech in, for example, 'honest as the day', 'you may depend on it' and 'found out'. Thus her story, like Rosamond's, is presented as part of the common currency of social intercourse. A degree of casual malevo-lence is a natural part of Middlemarch.

Eliot uses a number of different parallels to describe the workings of social life. She refers to society as a web in Chapter 15, where she speaks of her role in 'unravelling certain human lots, and seeing how they were woven and interwoven' (p. 141). She uses the image of bees distributing pollen to suggest the way in which news – here meaning gossip or rumour as much as news – spreads through a community:

News is often dispersed as thoughtlessly and effectively as that pollen which the bees carry off (having no idea how powdery they are) when they are buzzing in search of their particular nectar.

(p. 599)

Here nectar suggests the insidious delight of gossip, at its sweetest when its target is richest. Most apposite in view of the nature of the community's behaviour towards Harriet and Rosamond is the contrasting image of disease: gossip spreads like cholera.

Middlemarch is, of course, a microcosm that represents a more general social pattern. Though in some ways this study of provincial life reveals a remarkably narrow society, Eliot succeeds in bringing out its connection with much wider movements in politics, communications and science. She sets the novel in a specific historical context (see, for example, the opening of Chapter 37), and in particular refers more than once to the first Reform Bill. The use of motifs to do with the web, or epidemic, plays a significant part in broadening the reference of the novel. There is, too, Lydgate's interest in scientific advances: like Middlemarch society, science is seen as part of a process of communication; even Casaubon's research, dead-end though it is, forms part of the web of academic intercourse. In slow replication of the progress of disease or rumour, the railway comes to link Middlemarch with a greater outside world. All these features are fully integrated in the structure of the novel: the advent of the railway, for example, has a direct effect on the life of Fred Vincy. Middlemarch then is restricted but microcosmic. Provincial life reflects the wider world.

Marriage, as one of the foundations on which society rests, links with every aspect of Middlemarch life as in the wider regional and national society. Caleb Garth voices the view of the honest folk of Middlemarch when he speaks of the importance of 'true love for a good woman' in 'shap[ing] many a rough fellow' (p. 564), and of marriage as 'a taming thing' (p. 691). In the event, by the agency of marriage with Mary, Fred Vincy is saved from his own weaker nature. For Dorothea marriage and work are inextricably linked. Hoping through marriage with Casaubon to devote herself to a worthwhile project she finds herself instead condemned to support him in his delusion: 'She longed for work which would be directly beneficent like the sunshine and the rain, and now it appeared that she was to live more and more in a virtual tomb' (p. 475). Though she feels entombed, Dorothea does not question the duty that lies upon her as Mrs Casaubon. Her husband's death changes her circumstances but not her attitudes. In an interesting passage at the end of Chapter 72, when she has been released by his death from Casaubon's chill repression, Dorothea disputes with Celia over the right of women to determine their own lives:

> 'Now, Dodo, do listen to what James says,' said Celia, 'else you will be getting into a scrape. You always did, and you always will, when you set about doing as you please. And I think it is a mercy now after all that you have got James to think for you. He lets you have your plans, only he hinders you from being taken in. And that is the good of having a brother instead of a husband. A husband would not let you have your plans.'
>
> 'As if I wanted a husband!' said Dorothea. 'I only want not to have my feelings checked at every turn.' Mrs Casaubon was still undisciplined enough to burst into angry tears.
>
> 'Now, really, Dodo,' said Celia, with rather a deeper guttural than usual, 'you *are* contradictory: first one thing and then another. You used to submit to Mr Casaubon quite shamefully: I think you would have given up ever coming to see me if he had asked you.'
>
> 'Of course I submitted to him, because it was my duty; it was my feeling for him,' said Dorothea, looking through the prism of her tears.
>
> 'Then why can't you think it your duty to submit a little to what James wishes?' said Celia, with a sense of stringency in her argument. 'Because he only wishes what is for your own good. And, of course, men know best about everything, except what women know better.'
>
> Dorothea laughed and forgot her tears.
>
> 'Well, I mean about babies and those things,' explained Celia. 'I should not give up to James when I knew he was wrong, as you used to do to Mr Casaubon.'
>
> (pp. 735–6)

Here Celia's mixture of common sense and naivety casts a richly comic light on Dorothea's serious concerns. Her touching faith in Sir

James of course depends for its comedy on earlier scenes in which Sir James has been shown to be short of the intellectual capacity to meet Dorothea's mind, and thus unlikely to be able to 'think for' her. There is, nevertheless, a serious point made about the responsibility of men towards women and the reciprocal duty of women towards men. The fact of her lacking a husband places Dorothea in a difficult position in Celia's eyes, and it thus seems natural to Celia that her husband should become her sister's mentor. After all, he will be a benevolent despot, allowing to her to have her plans. This will be a harmless freedom, for the form of words presumes that such plans will never have a practical outcome, and indeed that they are unlikely to have significance in themselves. Celia's view is that Dorothea needs guidance, and, having escaped subjection to Casaubon, should voluntarily submit to another master in the interest of steering a just course through her life. In the end, however, Celia's instinct serves her well in the idea that 'men know best about everything, except what women know better' – an unwitting paradox that upholds realism and common sense against social convention.

There is a further serious point in Dorothea's attitude towards duty. She submitted to Casaubon 'because it was [her] duty; it was [her] feeling for him'. The two parts of her justification are mutually dependent. Her duty was one she had elected to take upon her through the formal medium of marriage. Celia's rejoinder, asking why she will not 'submit a little' to Sir James, shows her missing the significance of her sister's statement. Thus, wishing not to have her feelings thwarted at every turn, Dorothea scorns the prospect of a second husband. She respects the duty enshrined in marriage, and therefore will at this stage have nothing to do with it.

This brief interchange outlines the limits of Dorothea's ambition. Though she follows her own code, Dorothea is far from revolutionary. Indeed, she is in many respects as conservative as Middlemarch. From this perspective, her final disappearance as Will Ladislaw's wife into the ranks of the unknown Teresas is unsurprising.

Dorothea's disappearance has the important effect of underlining the general theme of the novel: no matter how absorbing her story or the stories of other individuals may be, the novel deals with provincial life rather than this or that individual character. Lydgate plays a part in a process of scientific inquiry, restricted by his social, economic and personal circumstances. Casaubon endeavours to contribute to an academic discussion. The worlds of Caleb Garth and Fred Vincy intersect with the development of the railway. Romantic relationships and marriage form the cornerstones of the novel, yet are strands in a social order. Eliot deals with the individual stories and the feelings of the partners with insight and sympathy, yet stresses the broader social dimensions of the relationships: the Casaubons, Ladislaws, Vincys, Bulstrodes and Garths are all affected by a web of controls including social reputation, social expectation, moral imperative and economic necessity.

Conclusions

The novels deal with society in very different ways. *The Mill on the Floss* places Maggie's behaviour under the spotlight of social disapprobation. St Ogg's, or its wife, judges her and she is found wanting: Tom's rejection of her expresses his subscription to the standards of the society in which he has made himself a success. At the same time, Eliot indicates the distinction between St Ogg's and the world, thus suggesting that the standards of St Ogg's are far from absolute, but admitting by the course of the story that they have practical power over the sons and daughters of the town. Nevertheless, the discussions of Maggie's relationships with Stephen and Philip in the latter part of the novel broaden the ethical landscape far beyond what St Ogg's will countenance. This is one reason for the dissatisfaction that many readers feel with the conclusion of the novel: the moral dimensions of the discussion overflow the social dimensions of the action. *Silas Marner* is by comparison more controlled and less ambitious. It takes for its subject a much more restricted society than that of the earlier novel. Its social world is dominated by the gap between the rich and the poor, and the imperfect allocation of moral qualities between them. It shows the slow absorption of Silas into a close community and leads to an assertion of his rights over Eppie against the expectations of a wealthy, powerful but corrupt gentry. *Silas Marner* confines itself neatly within the moral parameters of its action. There is none of the reaching into the unknown that occurs in *The Mill on the Floss*. *Middlemarch*, however, is a bigger concept altogether, and the provincial life that provides the material is of a more sophisticated kind. Social perspective is crucial as in the story of Maggie Tulliver, but the field of vision is much greater, dealing with characters at more diverse social levels. There is, however, no suggestion of the material outstripping the author's control.

Certain common features emerge despite the differences among the books. Work is important in all three novels. Tom devotes himself to his work as a means of restoring the dignity of his family, lost in his father's unsuccessful feud with Wakem: he commands respect but also makes personal sacrifices; and Maggie's rejection suggests that those sacrifices may be too great. Silas Marner's physical aspect suggests the presence of an invisible spinning wheel, but Aaron Winthrop is a much more straightforward expression of the dignity of labour, contrasting sharply with the dissolute Dunsey Cass. *Middlemarch* deals with this subject more fully. Fred Vincy, who might have turned into someone a little like Dunsey Cass, becomes instead rather more like Aaron Winthrop as he begins work for Caleb Garth. Caleb himself is a rock of workmanlike steadiness and good sense, contrasting notably with Bulstrode. Lydgate is pushed into lowlier work than he is capable of or wishes for by the expectations of an insensitive wife. Dorothea demands to be useful. In all the novels, work is thought of as generally useful and ennobling; correspondingly, those who do not do it and do not need it are not highly regarded.

The concept of duty in its social context is closely linked with work. Maggie and Dorothea are both deeply concerned to do what they conceive to be required of them socially and morally. Maggie must return to her own people to be held accountable for her mistakes: escape is not an option for her. Dorothea submits to the demands of her marriage with Casaubon even as she acknowledges the delusions that led her into it. Lydgate, too, accepts the burden that his ill-judgement in marrying Rosamond has brought upon him. Conversely, the effects of attempting to escape one's duty are all too evident in the fate of Godfrey Cass and Nicholas Bulstrode. Eliot's is a conservative world in which wrongdoing always emerges and is always appropriately punished.

In all three novels, sexual, romantic and marital relationships are essential to social structure. In *The Mill on the Floss*, Tom perceives that Maggie's errors have direct, and destructive, bearing on the standing of his family in the community; behind whatever else is involved in moral or personal spheres, his objection to her behaviour expresses social fear. One of the strands of *Silas Marner* is based in large part on the two marriages of Godfrey Cass, one of which he disavows because it is socially destructive, while the second, a socially acceptable marriage, might be destroyed by the first; the other strand in the action of the novel depends partly on the product of the earlier marriage, Eppie. The world of *Middlemarch* is more complex and subtle. Eliot explores more fully the relationship between individuals, their partners and their society. Dorothea shows a strong consciousness of the expectations of society in jealously protecting the propriety of her behaviour towards Casaubon and Ladislaw; she is equally strongly conscious of the extent to which Rosamond and Ladislaw fall short of propriety. Lydgate's relationship with Rosamond forms a web of pressures involving their economic situation, Lydgate's relationship with Bulstrode, his day-to-day work, his scientific ambitions and Rosamond's expectations of standing in society. Rosamond's brother contrasts with her in accepting a lesser social prestige in the interests of attaining personal dignity through work and the economic stability that follows from it; Mary is both goal and assistant in the process. These characters' fictional lives have the complexity of reality; their world, with its multi-threaded structure, resembles the multiplicity of actual society.

Despite the comic or satirical mood of parts of the extracts analysed here, Eliot's portrayal of society is a serious attempt to represent it as it really was. She had studied the writings of Auguste Comte and adopted or adapted those elements of his ideas that she found useful. Thus the beginning of *Silas Marner* shows a society in the earliest stages of Comtian development; *The Mill on the Floss* may be thought of as showing the conflict between the theological and metaphysical stages; and *Middlemarch* reflects the conflict of both these and the emerging positive stage. Eliot was also aware of the ideas underlying the development of sociology, which treated the social organism as biology treated the biological organism. Thus she sees society not as a static pattern, but as subject to change and open to many influences; even Raveloe responds to Silas eventually; and Dorothea is seen as part of an evolutionary process at work in Middlemarch. The influence of the Romantic writers was significant too. Eliot enjoyed the work of Scott, and was much influenced by Wordsworth, who is discussed by Mr Brooke in Chapter 2 of *Middlemarch*, and whose poems provide the epigraph to *Silas Marner* and epigraphs to Chapters 2, 52 and 80 of *Middlemarch* (this last, significantly, from the 'Ode to Duty') – there are also several references in *Daniel Deronda*. What these writers have in common, among other things, is an interest in the ordinary and commonplace that finds expression in descriptions of nature and ordinary people. In Wordsworth's own words in the Preface to the 1800 edition of *Lyrical Ballads*, his purpose was 'to make the incidents of common life interesting by tracing in them, truly though not ostentatiously, the primary laws of our nature'. This aim is echoed everywhere in Eliot's novels. Most directly it appears in *Adam Bede* in Eliot's praise for 'the faithful representing of commonplace things' (Chapter XVII, p. 174). It appears also in Eliot's discussion of the lives of the Tullivers and Dodsons in *The Mill on the Floss*, Book Four, Chapter 1, where she remarks, of 'this old-fashioned family life on the banks of the Floss' with its 'sense of oppressive narrowness', that 'there is nothing petty to the mind that has a large vision of relations' (all pp. 362–3); repeatedly Eliot stresses the ordinariness of the shaken lives she is describing, the 'still, sad monotony' (p. 367) of a world without prospect of an outlet for a vivid imagination, the frustrations of 'cherishing very large hopes in very small lodgings' (p. 506). *Silas Marner* as a whole, of course, is dedicated partly to illustrating the process of integration of an alien individual into a rigid, unsophisticated rural community. The target of *Middlemarch* is precisely stated in its subtitle, 'A Study of Provincial Life', and Eliot speaks of the nature of her subject from time to time, as in her ironic discourse on 'elevating a low subject' at the end of Chapter 35 (p. 341); later she refers to 'low people by whose interference . . . the course of the world is very much determined' (p. 412). Towards the end of the novel, when Dorothea experiences a heightened perception of the social organism of which she is a part, it is through the stimulus of ordinary people – a man with a bundle and a woman with a baby – that 'she felt the largeness of the world and the manifold wakings of men to labour and endurance' (p. 788).

Eliot's social vision was by no means restricted to her interpretation of Comte: the many thinkers who influenced her are discussed in Chapter 8 of this study; here, let it suffice to refer to the influence of Darwin and the pioneers of the theory of evolution as applied to social development. Nor are her novels expressions simply of a social vision. But her perception of society as a living, developing organism underlies the way she presents the social environment of her characters. The very different social worlds of her novels are characterised by variety of point of view, by conflict and by error. The process according to which characters interact with their social groups is the engine of social evolution.

Methods of Analysis

In this chapter, as in others, the process of analysis grows from the subject. The focus of analysis in this chapter is therefore to consider the linking of individual stories with Eliot's vision of society as a whole. All three major extracts take a general view of society: St Ogg's judges Maggie, the people of Raveloe enjoy the generosity of the Cass and Osgood landowners, and Middlemarch judges Harriet Bulstrode. In all three Eliot speaks with the voice of the community: it is by means of irony that she establishes her distance from the community she is discussing. In all three irony emerges from contrasting the universal with the microcosm of the story: St Ogg's is not the world, and public opinion appears to emerge from the mouths of the wives of the town, but the effect is to place St Ogg's in a wider social framework; Raveloe is a little aside from the great currents of the world, but nevertheless picks out elements still at work in wider society; the wives of Middlemarch dignify their petty gossip as moral rectitude, and in so doing reveal the limitations of provincial morality. Picking out these ironies requires close attention to the characteristic features of Eliot's writing that have been noticed in the analysis: circumlocution, displacement of meanings, the contrasting of local speech patterns with moralistic abstraction.

In the complex metalanguage of the major extracts the voice of the author is often audible. It simultaneously represents and suggests judgements about the communities it discusses. Eliot speaks to us directly in the extract from *The Mill on the Floss* and offers a view of recent history in the extract from *Silas Marner*. Much of the time, however, she appears to be speaking with the voice of the community, referring for example to 'the good old Vincy family'; yet again, as when she voices a general comment beginning 'one might say', she prefers to occupy a middle ground. The variety and subtlety of these changes of tone ask for sensitive appreciation from the reader.

The additional, briefer extracts have been chosen to show how the general social background emerges in relation to individual characters. Analysis demands attention to different aspects of Eliot's writing, such as the symbolism and mood of description, and the ironic clashing of points of view in dialogue. The vivid description of Tom's face and behaviour as he awaits Maggie reflects his view of society and the way it influences him. Dorothea's dialogue with Celia looks back to the effects of her marriage with Casaubon and forwards to the demands of her relationship with Ladislaw. It is important to notice in Eliot's work the remarkable organisation of scene as part of a structure: these episodes do not stand alone, but grow out of and reflect upon other elements in the novels.

Further Work

The Mill on the Floss
An interesting passage that develops the ideas in the analysis above appears at the beginning of Book Seven, Chapter 4. The attitudes of the ladies of St Ogg's towards Maggie are again discussed, but now there is the additional complication of Dr Kenn's role to consider. Study the passage from 'By the end of the week . . .' to '. . . not to be interfered with in their treatment of each other' (pp. 636–7), and try to arrive at an assessment of how Eliot sees Dr Kenn in relation to the community.

Silas Marner

An interesting choice for this topic is the discussion of Silas's position in the community in Chapter 2 ('Gradually the guineas . . . dubious as a balloon journey', pp. 19–20), which suggests ideas about work and about the limitations of the community he works in, and about the contrast between Silas and the people of Raveloe. Alternatively, consider Aaron's attitude to work in Chapter 16, from 'That good-looking young fellow . . .' to '. . . sheltered lane' (pp. 138–40).

Middlemarch

Caleb Garth's discussion of Fred Vincy, his relationship with Mary and work in Chapter 56 ('After we'd done our work . . . Caleb's ardent generosity?', pp. 564–5) touches on several social themes in the novel. Another interesting passage that combines comedy with serious ideas is the discussion of mourning in Chapter 55 ('One day she went to Freshitt . . . Suppose we change it', pp. 548–9)

5

Morality

The subject of this chapter is large. It will have been apparent in the earlier chapters that Eliot's novels adopt a consistently moral perspective. The nature of the moral vision is not always easy to assess, however, because of the varying tone of Eliot's narrative style. The analyses of *The Mill on the Floss*, for example, have considered the cutting of Maggie's hair as an expression of rebellion against the constraints of her family life, and the possible effect on her family of her relationship with Philip Wakem; she is judged morally by the standards of St Ogg's, but those standards are in turn treated ironically by Eliot. The opening of *Silas Marner* deals with the sense of evil in rural communities, and the whole novel hinges on the falsely assigned crime in Silas's past, his eventual overcoming of the oppression of Lantern Yard and the inhumanity of Godfrey's treatment of his first wife. The extracts in this novel, too, have a moral aspect, focusing on Godfrey's sense of guilt, or at least anxiety at the discovery of the woman in the snow, and the nature of the position of the Cass family in the community of Raveloe. *Middlemarch* establishes its moral perspective at once by opening with a discussion of St Teresa. Another extract, in which Celia and Dorothea consider their mother's jewels, considers the propriety of wearing them. The relationship between Rosamond and Lydgate focuses on the nature of relationships and the expectations individuals place in them. Like St Ogg's, Middlemarch makes moral judgements about its members and Harriet Bulstrode must submit, like Maggie, to moral dissection under the microscope of communal gossip. There are here evidently many perspectives embracing both superficial and temporal social judgements on the one hand, and absolute distinctions on the other. Of the moral seriousness of Eliot's intentions there can be no doubt.

Certain specific moral concerns have emerged clearly already. The importance of the concept of duty is particularly prominent. Eliot associates it specifically with respect for one's parents in *The Mill on the Floss*, and with propriety in social behaviour in *Middlemarch*. The consciousness of duty forms a part also of romantic or marital relationships between, for example, Maggie and Philip, Godfrey Cass and his wives, or Rosamond and Lydgate. Her characters experience many kinds of conflicts, but they often take the form of religious or quasi-religious oppositions between natural inclination and consciousness of absolute values, between duty and passion, between individual and community, or between self and service. Though Eliot was a humanist who had actively rejected Christianity in her early years, her novels show a strong awareness of both the power and the value of Christian religious belief; admittedly, they show, too, an equally strong awareness of its limitations.

This chapter seeks to explore more fully the ways in which these moral questions are raised and explored in the novels. Morality is thematically central to Eliot's work. Analysis of the extracts from this point of view will touch on every aspect of the novels, including the significance of the past as a repository of values or as a tool for moral evolution, the importance of family and tradition, the moral dimensions of relationships, and the basic elements of characterisation.

(i)   *The Mill on the Floss*

The following passage is from Book six, Chapter 14, which recounts what takes place at Mudport after Maggie's return with Stephen Guest from their ill-fated boat trip. The title of the chapter, 'Waking', links Maggie's desire to withdraw from the situation her passions have led her into with earlier scenes, such as her cutting of her hair and her running away to the gipsies, in which timid retreat follows on a surge of rash confidence: it is as if an illusion is destroyed, or a dream shattered. Here, confronted with Maggie's flat denial of the possibility of their future relationship, Stephen pleads with Maggie to recognise the demands of passion:

'Maggie! Dearest! If you love me, you are mine. Who can have so great a claim on you as I have? My life is bound up in your love. There is nothing in the past that can annul our right to each other – it is the first time we have either of us loved with our whole heart and soul.'

Maggie was still silent for a little while – looking down. Stephen was in a flutter of new hope – he was going to triumph. But she raised her eyes and met his with a glance that was filled with the anguish of regret – not with yielding.

'No – not with my whole heart and soul, Stephen,' she said, with timid resolution, 'I have never consented to it with my whole mind. There are memories, and affections, and longing after perfect goodness, that have such a strong hold on me – they would never quit me for long – they would come back and be pain to me – repentance. I couldn't live in peace if I put the shadow of a wilful sin between myself and God. I have caused sorrow already – I know – I feel it – but I have never deliberately consented to it – I have never said, "They shall suffer, that I may have joy." It has never been my will to marry you – if you were to win consent from the momentary triumph of my feeling for you, you would not have my whole soul. If I could wake back again into the time before yesterday, I would choose to be true to my calmer affections and live without the joy of love.'

Stephen loosed her hand and, rising impatiently, walked up and down the room in suppressed rage.

'Good God!' he burst out, at last, 'what a miserable thing a woman's love is to a man's. I could commit crimes for you – and you can balance and choose in that way. But you don't love me – if you had a tithe of the feeling for me that I have for you, – it would be impossible to you to think for a moment of sacrificing me. But it weighs nothing with you that you are robbing me of my life's happiness.'

Maggie pressed her fingers together almost convulsively as she held them clasped on her lap. A great terror was upon her – as if she were ever and anon seeing where she stood by great flashes of lightning, and then again stretched forth her hands in the darkness.

'No – I don't sacrifice you – I couldn't sacrifice you,' she said, as soon as she could speak again, 'but I can't believe in a good for you, that I feel – that we both feel is a wrong towards others. We can't choose happiness either for ourselves or for another – we can't tell where that will lie. We can only choose whether we will indulge ourselves in the present moment or whether we will renounce that for the sake of obeying the divine voice within us – for the sake of being true to all the motives that sanctify our lives. I know that belief is hard – it has slipped away from me again and again; but I have felt that if I let it go for ever, I should have no light through the darkness of this life.'

(pp. 603–4)

The scene is vividly realised. Stephen's exclamations 'burst out' as he rises to his feet 'impatiently', loosing Maggie's hand so that he can walk to and fro to relieve 'suppressed rage'. In contrast Maggie punctuates his restlessness with lacunae of silent inner torment, pressing her fingers together 'convulsively' in her lap. She feels not rage but 'the anguish of regret'. While he storms about, she remains seated, raising her eyes to his to meet his will with her own quiet but unyielding conviction. Her posture and speech express the mixed diffidence and confidence evoked in the oxymoron 'timid resolution'.

What is dramatised here is a moral conflict. At the beginning of the extract Stephen presents a simple case for their love: 'If you love me, you are mine'. He believes that they have a 'right' to each other based on the peremptory demand of their passion. In the preceding paragraphs of the chapter, he has dismissed Maggie's sense of guilt about their betrayal of Lucy and Philip as irrelevant: the harm that has been done to them cannot be undone, and thus 'there is nothing in the past that can annul' the claim he and Maggie have upon each other. Maggie, however, cannot ignore the guilt of the past. Their relationship is poisoned because it is rooted in 'a wrong towards others' and, indeed, Maggie has at no time formulated the 'will to marry' Stephen.

Stephen's feeling for Maggie is not presented as trivial. Fond as he is of Lucy, he feels a stronger sexual attraction for Maggie, and one that he has limited control over. He declares a love of 'our whole heart and soul', and there is no need to try to diminish the power and sincerity of his feelings. His phrase includes sexuality, emotion and passion; he speaks for Maggie to the extent that what she feels for him is patently more inclusive than her regard for Philip Wakem, the limitation of which is equally clear in the extract discussed in Chapter

3. Maggie, however, contending with Stephen that she does not love him with her whole heart and soul, introduces a new element when she says that she never 'consented' to their love with her 'whole mind'. She insists that Stephen might conceivably play upon 'the momentary triumph of my feeling for [him]' but could nevertheless not thereby win her entirely.

Heart, soul and mind are often nebulous entities yet the context here makes clear what is meant. Acknowledging the power of her feelings, Maggie speaks of the stronger claims of 'memories and affections' that are inescapable – they would return and 'be pain' to her no matter what her circumstances otherwise. She insists that she has never consented to make others suffer for the sake of her own 'joy'. Eliot resorts to religious language to characterise the demand of 'mind'. A past wrong would place 'the shadow of a wilful sin between [Maggie] and God': instead of achieving the 'perfect goodness' she strives for, she would be condemned to a life of 'repentance'. In the last paragraph of the extract Maggie refers to 'the divine voice within us' as if she is referring to the conventional religious concept of conscience, yet despite the religious language it appears that 'mind' is associated with something less specific than the voice of conscience in its conventional guise. The reference to the 'shadow' of the sin she wishes to avoid committing looks forward to the 'darkness of this life' at the end of the extract, and correspondingly the 'peace' of the second paragraph looks forward to the 'light'. The breadth of these terms points not to a particular religious code, but to the instinctive emotional springs that underlie such codes. Maggie's sense of sin derives from the fear of betraying her relationship with those with whom she has cultivated love, and not from religious doctrine.

There are many clues in the novel to the origins of Maggie's feelings. Her desire to 'wake back again into the time before yesterday' reflects and partly explains the title of the chapter: she wishes to recover the world of innocence that her earlier life now seems to have inhabited. That world is the repository of the 'memories and affections, and longing after perfect goodness, that have such a strong hold on [her]': it is hallowed by time and experience; it consists of all of that experience and not simply the people who belong to it; and it is the birthplace of 'all the motives that sanctify our lives'. Again, the language is religious; but again, it is so only at the deepest level and in the most general sense. The concluding paragraphs of Chapter 5 of Book One of the novel introduce the theme by referring to the natural environment – flowers, birds, hedgerows, trees, the sky itself and earth – as 'the mother tongue of our imaginations' (p. 94). During the novel Maggie expresses the attraction of that time repeatedly: her constant withdrawal from the unknown into the womb of the family, her respect for the will of her parents, her subjection to Tom as well as her fondness for Lucy and Philip derive from the same source; and thus, despite her creative impulse towards new, exciting or forbidden experience, she is repeatedly drawn back into the safety of the known and traditional. After her adventure with Stephen the choice that has been instinctive becomes conscious. Here Maggie expresses it in the doctrine of renunciation: she refuses to 'indulge [herself] in the present moment' and renounces passion in favour of the inner voice counselling the harder path.

Though the voice that tells Maggie the difference between right and wrong is not specifically Christian, it concurs with the views of the Christian Dr Kenn. After Maggie's confession to him, in which she stresses the feelings that have drawn her back to her family, he is silent in inner communion for some minutes before at length pronouncing that '[her] prompting to go to [her] dearest friends – to remain where all the ties of [her] life have been formed – is right'. His reference to 'ties' is as non-specific as Eliot's references elsewhere and he speaks a little later of 'the adherence to obligation which has its roots in the past'; nevertheless, he sees in these ties the expression of Christian brotherhood. He also bewails in his own flock the loss of 'discipline and Christian fraternity' (all pp. 624–5). Thus he brings out the Christian dimension in a principle that is not intrinsically Christian in origin. As if to exemplify this distinction, Dr Kenn's flock fulfils his fears by driving out Maggie to whom he has sought to offer the protection of a Christian. The characteristic features of the feelings he and Maggie serve find expression in words like 'obligation', 'responsibility', 'discipline' and 'renunciation'. Dr Kenn's parishioners, as the extract in Chapter 4 illustrates, are not good at these; they are, however, good at backbiting and at defending their own more superficial standards of morality.

One of the more intriguing ironies of the novel is that apparently similar standards of judgement can have quite different effects in action. Dr Kenn and his congregation might claim to hold the same principles: as he himself points out, 'the Church ought to represent the feeling of the community' (p. 624). Equally, Tom banishes his sister because she has failed to abide by the principles he, as a loyal son of the Tulliver line, holds dear. Having no inkling of the depth or intensity of her self-analysis, he charges her with bowing to no principle – 'Not religion – not . . . natural feelings of gratitude and honour' (p. 613); meanwhile Mrs Tulliver stands paralysed in the doorway of their house, unable to be sure whether she is more appalled by her daughter or by her son.

Maggie pleases few by her actions. Stephen underestimates her as wildly as Tom does. He interprets Maggie's preference for 'calmer affections', even if that means to 'live without the joy of love', simply as an admission that she lacks passion. He inveighs against 'woman's love' as 'a miserable thing'. He accuses her of having only a fraction (a 'tithe' is a medieval word for a tenth) of his capacity for love. He sees her rejection of him as her making a 'sacrifice' of both of them. In fact, of course, the problem is that her view of their love is more complex than his. He sees heart and soul and thinks they are all: she sees 'mind' as well. In his blinkered incomprehension, Stephen illustrates perfectly the error of egoism that Eliot explores more fully in *Middlemarch*. His flaw is yet clearer in the letter he writes to Maggie later in the novel. There, in a 'passionate cry of reproach', he asks histrionically, 'whose pain can have been like mine? Whose injury is like mine?', and claims with all too little justification from the context, 'I have no motives: I am indifferent to everything' (all pp. 646–7).

Stephen's egoism ensures that he can have no understanding of the meaning of what happens in the extract. He condemns Maggie for 'robbing [him] of [his] life's happiness', apparently thoughtless of what she herself is losing. The structure of the extract makes clear, in fact, that the conflict between Stephen and Maggie is not the only conflict in progress in the scene, and perhaps not the bitterest. There is also Maggie's struggle with herself: 'she was undergoing an inward as well as an outward contest' (p. 602). Thus Stephen's point of view seems to come to reflect a side of Maggie's inner self. But it is only one side: the whole Maggie perceives much more, and here as in the dialogue with Philip that was discussed in Chapter 3, she has despite her doubts and diffidence greater command than her counterpart over the broad territory of the contest between them. It is a fine irony that Stephen's outburst against Maggie succeeds only in revealing his own inadequacy.

In contrast, Maggie's outward certainty and invincibility derive from her having already fought within herself the same battle she is engaged in with Stephen. The inner victory is not easy, but it is already won. Even so, the terror of the conflict and its aftermath are still with her. Eliot represents the violence of Maggie's inner conflict both in her convulsive flexing of her fingers, and in violent psychological imagery. She feels 'great terror . . . upon her' as she confronts a brutal reality. She senses herself stretching out her hands; whether in supplication or propitiation or in prayer to some pagan power is unclear. The darkness of her spiritual condition looks back to her reading of Thomas à Kempis. The intermittent 'great flashes of lightning' that illumine her situation have the power of preternatural revelation. The second sentence of the penultimate paragraph of the extract not only describes cryptically Maggie's spiritual crisis: it looks forward to the actual storm of the conclusion, in which she finally reaches out to her hitherto implacable brother.

(ii)   *Silas Marner*

The moral crisis of the novel places Silas Marner in direct confrontation with Godfrey Cass over the future of Eppie. The extract comes from the middle of Chapter 19, when Godfrey has explained his plan of taking charge of Eppie and Silas has refrained from objection, inviting Eppie to thank her benefactors. Up to this point, Silas having quelled his painful emotions, there seems no obstacle to Godfrey's intention. When Eppie unexpectedly rejects his offer – clearly an attractive one from the point of view of her status and wealth – on the grounds that she 'couldn't give up the folks [she has] been used to', the real meaning of Godfrey's plan emerges from his anger:

Godfrey felt an irritation inevitable to almost all of us when we encounter an unexpected obstacle. He had been full of his own penitence and resolution to retrieve his error as far as the time was left to him; he was possessed with all-important feelings, that were to lead to a predetermined course of action which he had fixed on as the right, and he was not prepared to enter with lively appreciation into other people's feelings counteracting his virtuous resolves. The agitation with which he spoke again was not quite unmixed with anger.

'But I've a claim on you, Eppie – the strongest of all claims. It's my duty, Marner, to own Eppie as my child, and provide for her. She is my own child – her mother was my wife. I've a natural claim on her that must stand before every other.'

Eppie had given a violent start, and turned quite pale. Silas, on the contrary, who had been relieved, by Eppie's answer, from the dread lest his mind should be in opposition to hers, felt the spirit of resistance in him set free, not without a touch of parental fierceness. 'Then, sir,' he answered, with an accent of bitterness that had been silent in him since the memorable day when his youthful hope had perished – 'then, sir, why didn't you say so sixteen year ago, and claim her before I'd come to love her, i'stead o' coming to take her from me now, when you might as well take the heart out o' my body? God gave her to me because you turned your back upon her, and He looks upon her as mine: you've no right to her! When a man turns a blessing from his door, it falls to them as take it in.'

'I know that, Marner. I was wrong. I've repented of my conduct in that matter,' said Godfrey, who could not help feeling the edge of Silas's words.

'I'm glad to hear it, sir,' said Marner, with gathering excitement; 'but repentance doesn't alter what's been going on for sixteen year. Your coming now and saying "I'm her father" doesn't alter the feelings inside us. It's me she's been calling her father ever since she could say the word.'

'But I think you might look at the thing more reasonably, Marner,' said Godfrey, unexpectedly awed by the weaver's direct truth-speaking. 'It isn't as if she was to be taken quite away from you, so that you'd never see her again. She'll be very near you, and come to see you very often. She'll feel just the same towards you.'

'Just the same?' said Marner, more bitterly than ever. 'How'll she feel just the same for me as she does now, when we eat o' the same bit, and drink o' the same cup, and think o' the same things from one day's end to another? Just the same? that's idle talk. You'd cut us i' two.'

Godfrey, unqualified by experience to discern the pregnancy of Marner's simple words, felt rather angry again. It seemed to him that the weaver was very selfish (a judgment readily passed by those who have never tested their own power of sacrifice) to oppose what was undoubtedly for Eppie's welfare; and he felt himself called upon, for her sake, to assert his authority.

'I should have thought, Marner,' he said, severely – 'I should have thought your affection for Eppie would make you rejoice in what was for her good, even if it did call upon you to give up something. You ought to remember your own life's uncertain, and she's at an age now when her lot may soon be fixed in a way very different from what it would be in her father's home: she may marry some low working-man, and then, whatever I might do for her, I couldn't make her well-off. You're putting yourself in the way of her welfare; and though I'm sorry to hurt you after what you've done, and what I've left undone, I feel now it's my duty to insist on taking care of my own daughter. I want to do my duty.'

(pp. 169–70)

Structurally this extract is simple. Godfrey presents his case for taking charge of Eppie and Marner disputes it. Eppie is mostly a bystander at this stage, though it is her rejection of Godfrey's offer that provokes this new, more violent stage in the conflict of their wills, and it is her statement that gives Silas the determination to contest Godfrey's claim.

The conflict presented here is dramatised by clashing of emotions as well as opposed arguments and contrasting personalities. Godfrey feels 'irritation' and 'agitation', he is 'angry'. Silas speaks 'with an accent of bitterness', with 'a touch of parental fiercenenss', 'with gathering excitement', 'more bitterly than ever'. Godfrey feels 'the edge' of Silas's words as of a sword; Silas speaks of himself and Eppie being cut in two. This language mirrors the seriousness of this climactic confrontation.

Difference in social rank accentuates the conflict. Silas calls Godfrey 'sir': Godfrey addresses Silas as 'Marner'. His superior social rank confers on Godfrey a delusion of superior right, and he sees Marner's opposition as a kind of rebellion. He urges Marner to 'look at the thing more reasonably'; he has the politician's fondness for annexing to himself the monopoly of plain common sense. He speaks 'severely' to Marner in an effort to 'assert his authority'; he underestimates Marner, thinking of him as 'selfish' for standing in the way of Eppie's betterment; he concludes that it is his 'duty to insist' on enforcing his claim on Eppie. The scene might be used as a definition of the cliché of the iron fist within velvet glove: the appearance of reasonableness that coloured Godfrey's earlier arguments has vanished to reveal his trust that social might will win the argument. At the end of the extract, Godfrey places his faith in blunt force to achieve his end. His dismissal of Marner as selfish serves to relieve him of the need to take serious account of Marner's rights or feelings. As a mere weaver, indeed, Marner has in this feudal world little right to feeling at all; naturally he may be expected to lack the finer sensibilities that might be considered innate in a squire's son.

Against the force of Godfrey's practical arguments – Eppie will be 'well-off' and may marry someone better than 'some low working-man' – Silas can offer in support of his own claim on Eppie only the power of custom and familiarity, and the naked need of love. To take her from him would be to 'take the heart out o' my body'. He is just as sure as Godfrey of the soundness of his claim, for he sincerely believes that Eppie is a gift from heaven – 'God gave her to me' – and that therefore no one has the right to put them asunder. He disputes Godfrey's claim to be her father because 'It's me she's been calling her father ever since she could say the word'. He treats with the contempt it deserves his opponent's suggestion that Eppie would come to visit him often, and would be 'just the same' towards him. 'That's idle talk', he says brutally. Their relationship could not be as now, when they drink the same drink, eat the same food, and 'think o' the same things from one day's end to another'. Silas is here making the same point that Eliot stressed in *The Mill on the Floss* in speaking of the 'subtle inextricable associations of the fleeting hours of our childhood' that she calls 'the mother tongue of our imagination' (p. 94): the language, even of Silas brought by powerful emotion to an unaccustomed pitch of eloquence, is necessarily simpler, but the faith in the touchstones of the known, familiar and trusted carries the same conviction.

There is no doubt where Eliot's sympathies lie. She makes pointed criticisms of Godfrey. He is 'unexpectedly awed by the weaver's direct truth-speaking' – the final ungainly phrase underlining the plainness of the unsophisticated man's manner of speech – and 'unqualified by experience to discern the pregnancy' of Silas's statements. The superficial point is that Godfrey is unused to plain speech; accustomed to the tones of comparatively sophisticated, educated ladies and gentlemen, his ear is not attuned to the plain weave of Silas's words from the heart. There is a deeper level, too, at which Godfrey, having betrayed his wife and denied his child, is unqualified by experience. Silas makes this point vigorously when he demands why Godfrey did not claim his daughter sixteen years earlier instead of turning his back on her. Though vigorous, his words are innocent: he cannot know the depth of guilt suppurating in Godfrey's soul.

Godfrey's guilt apparently goes unfelt by the man himself except as a spur to his actions here. He says briefly that he 'was wrong' but claims that he has 'repented'. What fills his being is not the knowledge of his perfidy, but faith in the justice of his claim. He uses the word 'duty' three times: once in his first statement in the extract, and twice at the end. It is not hard to see that this overpowering sense of duty is a delusion, if not a masquerade. His first statement, 'I've a claim on you, Eppie . . . It's my duty, Marner, to own Eppie as my child', mixes 'duty' and 'claim' – a selfless and a selfish impulse – as if they were identical. When at the end of the extract he declares, 'I want to do my duty', the emphasis lies on 'want' rather than 'duty'. When he speaks of his duty to 'own' Eppie as his child, the meaning is ambiguous: does he mean to acknowledge her, or to possess her?

These ambiguities throw light on essential flaws in Godfrey and his case. What presents as reason – doing the best thing for Eppie – turns out to be the expression of egoism. Godfrey thinks of Marner as selfish, and reproaches him for being unwilling to 'give up something' and 'putting [himself] in the way of [Eppie's] welfare'; but Eliot suggests that his is 'a judgement readily passed by those who have never tested their own power of sacrifice'. Throughout the extract Godfrey shows his inadequacy. The obstacle of Silas's and Eppie's resistance to his plan is unexpected because he is 'not prepared to enter with lively appreciation into other people's feelings': his is a closed mind. He has 'fixed on' a 'predetermined' plan which he sees as 'right' because it is 'undoubtedly for Eppie's welfare'. His claim, he says, is 'natural', and 'must stand' despite the objections of the others involved in it. Though surprised and impressed by Silas's straightforward simplicity of utterance he still fails to appreciate the truth in it. His failure in his attempts at bullying Silas into submission reveal a nature in which, despite his general agreeableness, there is an element of brutishness. When he claims at the end of the extract that he is 'sorry to hurt' he fails to convince: Eliot here portrays a foiled unconscious egoist who cannot understand why the world will not fall into the pattern most convenient to his own ends.

Godfrey is evidently not presented as unintelligent but there is a significant lack of discernment in him that the extract specifically brings out. It goes beyond his failure to see other people's point of view: he fails to see the significance of his own life. He acknowledges that he has done wrong and 'left undone' what was right, and he claims to have 'repented of [his] conduct'. Marner, the simple man, makes the telling riposte that 'repentance doesn't alter what's been going on for sixteen year'. Eliot calls this 'truth-speaking'. There are, indeed, two truths that emerge. One is that by his denial of his first wife, his deception of his second and his refusal to acknowledge his child for sixteen years, Godfrey has forfeited whatever rights he might otherwise have had. The other is that a man with such a history can hardly expect to be entrusted with the welfare of a daughter, regardless of what practical advantages his position in society might bring her. Seen in this light, Godfrey's assertion of 'a natural claim' is deeply ironic: his conduct has been most unnatural in the Shakespearian sense. Marner make the point strongly when he says that Godfrey's saying he is her father 'doesn't alter the feelings inside us': though his blood does not run in her veins, it is for all practical purposes Marner who is Eppie's 'natural' father.

This assertion of the power of 'nature' reflects Eliot's ideas in *The Mill on the Floss*. In both, she rejects superficial claims of rank or religion or convention and stresses rather the supreme importance of personal ties and common experience. This is not to say that she discounts convention: Silas's integration into the community of Raveloe is an important part of his regeneration. Nor does she discount religion: it fosters the probity we see in Silas and has a part to play in social evolution. Nor is she unaware of the advantages of rank:

but she is conscious of the irony in the unreasoning assumption of qualitative difference that permits such a man as Godfrey to disparage the idea of Eppie's marrying 'some low working-man'. Eliot places her faith not in spontaneous feeling, but in the instinctive feelings nurtured by habit and familiarity, and moderated by communal religious and social values.

Such feelings depend on experience, and here Silas and Godfrey differ significantly. Silas responds to Godfrey's claim on Eppie 'with an accent of bitterness that had been silent in him since the memorable day when his youthful hopes had perished'. The reference here is clearly to his banishment from the womb of Lantern Yard. That experience has determined his life. It has reduced him to the narrow existence of his earlier years in Raveloe and still influences his ideas and behaviour. The Silas who accepts Eppie as a gift from God has much the same habit of mind as the earlier Silas who accepted the drawing of lots as the expression of God's will. There is an incorrigible rigidity in Silas's nature. Yet that same quality leads to an honest and serious view of his experience, so that when in Chapter 7 Mr Macey objects to Silas's suspicion of Jem Rodney as 'accusing o' the innicent' (p. 57), Silas is at once struck by compunction, remembering the injustice done to him earlier. Eliot makes the point with a significant negation, saying that Silas's 'Memory was not so utterly torpid . . . that it could not be awakened by these words'. The past is not in Eliot's view ignorable. As long as Silas's past lies dormant in him, he is unable to build on it: recognising the parallel between himself and Jem, however, enables him to make a reasoned judgement and here admit that he is wrong to make an unfounded accusation. This is part of the point of his return at the end of the novel to the site of Lantern Yard: only by confronting it can he relegate it to its proper place in his past.

The past is equally important for Godfrey, who spends much of the novel trying to conceal the secrets of his past and worrying about the risk of their disclosure. Eliot describes his feelings in Chapter 3, referring to the 'ugly' secret of his marriage and his vain hope of 'deliverance from . . . the hateful consequences to which he had sold himself'. Here, however, as in the novel as a whole, he is portrayed more sympathetically than in the extract. Eliot presents Godfrey as

'fast becoming a bitter man, visited by cruel wishes . . . like demons',
but this is the effect of 'wrong-doing [that] will breed hate in the
kindliest nature' (all p. 32). He has as many hurdles to overcome as
Silas. His confession to Nancy shows him confronting his past as Silas
does, but that is by no means the end of his development. It is not
until the scene in the extract and its aftermath that Godfrey is brought
to understand fully the consequences of his actions in the past. Even
in the extract he is inclined to dismiss Silas's brutally direct criticism,
'you turned your back upon her', and its corollary, 'you've no right
to her'. He speaks precisely the same words as Silas to Mr Macey
in Chapter 7 (p. 58), 'I was wrong', but with very different effect.
Whereas Silas's admission leads him to reassess his view of his loss,
Godfrey uses the same form of words merely as a springboard to make
renewed claims. He makes a show of acknowledging his guilt merely
in order to set it aside, and is compelled finally to accept the consequence of what he has done only by Silas's persistence in stubborn
refusal.

The extract is not then, as it may first appear, a simple dialectic of
reason and feeling. It also opposes rank against lack of it, guilt against
innocence and sophistication against simplicity. Underlying these
oppositions, however, there is a more powerful common theme of
understanding the past in the effort to order the present.

(iii) *Middlemarch*

The moral influence of the past is less prominent in *Middlemarch*,
which contains many more strands than the earlier novel, but the
shadow of past misdeeds nevertheless dominates the career of Nicholas
Bulstrode. Like Godfrey Cass, Bulstrode nurses a guilty history that
remains secret until the arrival of Raffles in Middlemarch threatens to
destroy the virtuous reputation the banker has carefully nurtured for
so many years. Again like Cass, Bulstrode is moved rather by fear than
guilt. Unlike Cass, however, Bulstrode has a more than ordinary reputation to protect: he has his religious stature as well as his social standing. His dual superiority adds piquancy to the distress the threat of
unmasking causes in him. The following extract is from Chapter 61:

Bulstrode felt himself helpless. Neither threats nor coaxing could avail: he could not count on any persistent fear nor on any promise. On the contrary, he felt a cold certainty at his heart that Raffles – unless providence sent death to hinder him – would come back to Middlemarch before long. And that certainty was a terror.

It was not that he was in danger of legal punishment or of beggary: he was in danger only of seeing disclosed to the judgment of his neighbours and the mournful perception of his wife certain facts of his past life which would render him an object of scorn and an opprobrium of the religion with which he had diligently associated himself. The terror of being judged sharpens the memory: it sends an inevitable glare over that long-unvisited past which has been habitually recalled only in general phrases. Even without memory, the life is bound into one by a zone of dependence in growth and decay; but intense memory forces a man to own his blameworthy past. With memory set smarting like a reopened wound, a man's past is not simply a dead history, an outworn preparation of the present: it is not a repented error shaken loose from the life: it is a still quivering part of himself, bringing shudders and bitter flavours and the tinglings of a merited shame.

Into this second life Bulstrode's past had now risen, only the pleasures of it seeming to have lost their quality. Night and day, without interruption save of brief sleep which only wove retrospect and fear into a fantastic present, he felt the scenes of his earlier life coming between him and everything else, as obstinately as when we look through the window from a lighted room, the objects we turn our backs on are still before us, instead of the grass and the trees. The successive events inward and outward were there in one view: though each might be dwelt on in turn, the rest still kept their hold in the consciousness.

(pp. 614–15)

Though he is one of the least attractive characters in the novel, Bulstrode is presented with considerable sympathy. Here Eliot expresses the terror of his expectation of discovery vividly. It 'sharpens' his 'intense' memory of a time that has lain dormant in his mind; it 'smart[s] . . . like a reopened wound'; it works in his mind, 'quivering' with physical dread, 'bringing shudders' and 'tinglings'. The simile of the wound is perhaps not outstandingly original; nevertheless it conveys tellingly the mental actuality and physical symptoms of Bulstrode's torment. A more precise conceit in the third paragraph expresses the dominance of the past in his life: it obtrudes itself relentlessly between him and the external world of the present as reflections impose themselves on the scene outside a lighted window.

At the same time, there is no attempt to excuse Bulstrode. If he feels himself 'helpless', defenceless against whatever Raffles chooses to do, he has himself rather than Raffles to blame. It is not that he has been guilty of a crime punishable by law or bankruptcy. His error lies in attempting to conceal and indeed ignore the meanness of which he has been guilty and of which he must therefore be essentially capable. Eliot describes his past as 'blameworthy' – a word of neutral force, but significant when applied to a man whose effort is to present a blameless portrait to the world. The past is 'long-unvisited' – the phrasing glances at the biblical meaning of a visitation – in his memory, and thus returns to him with redoubled force. Of course, he is a religious man and repents the wrongs he has done in a general sense, but that does not redeem the specific wrong that comes before his mind. His wrong 'is not a repented error shaken loose from life': that is, it cannot be simply set aside, but must be confronted. At this point it is not the consciousness of having done wrong that frightens Bulstrode: rather, it is humiliation before his wife and disgrace before his religious and secular community that shake his mediocre soul.

Bulstrode's hypocrisy is refined. Eliot says a little later in the chapter that he is not one of those 'coarse hypocrites, who consciously affect beliefs and emotions for the sake of gulling the world' (p. 619); he is as much a believer in his own illusion as anyone else. He is, she says earlier, 'doctrinally convinced that there was a total absence of merit in himself' (p. 521), but this conviction and the ritual repentance associated with it do not lead inevitably to a sincere awareness of his own specific sins. Instead, Bulstrode has found ways of reaching accord between his sincere beliefs and the human desires which once conflicted with them. This, says Eliot, is a common human failing ('a process which shows itself occasionally in us all', p. 619); it is therefore a failing which we may acknowledge as wrong without holding in contempt others who may be guilty of it. Furthermore, in succumbing to it, Bulstrode represents what Eliot perceives to be a fundamental flaw in human nature.

The root of Bulstrode's error is explored thoroughly in Chapter 61. It lies not wholly in hypocrisy. A deeper cause is his egoism, for in all his doings, Bulstrode's primary article of faith is that he is the instrument of God; sinful and imperfect he may be, yet he is singled out for special labours in the vineyard of the Almighty. In the extract he considers the possibility that he may be saved from disgrace 'if providence sen[ds] death to hinder' Raffles – an idea wholly preposterous to anyone who lacks Bulstrode's exalted vision of himself as the agent of heaven. Of course, he is willing to give God a little help in the cosmic effort to preserve Nicholas Bulstrode and imagines 'a threatening Providence urg[ing] him to a kind of propitiation' (p. 620). Whatever his moral qualities, he thinks of himself as a servant of God's cause, and part of the meaning of his ambiguous fear of being 'an opprobrium of [his] religion' is not selfish: he strongly desires not to be the cause of disrepute to the faith he has diligently served. He does not hope to benefit in any material sense from his special relationship with Providence, but hopes that he may make it possible for God somehow to save him from the consequences of his actions; it is only reasonable that God should be anxious to preserve so loyal a servant. Thus, trying to think of 'some sacrifice [that] could stay the rod', Bulstrode distorts religious faith into a more primitive, even magical belief that humans can control their God by ritual. Eliot speaks of him as moved by 'a great dread' to seek 'a kind of propitiation'; language appropriately reminiscent of the Old Testament refers to repentance, restitution and sacrifice, and the reference to 'stay[ing] the rod' leads up to Eliot's summation of the soul of Bulstrode in the assertion that 'the religion of personal fear remains nearly at the level of the savage' (all p. 620).

In actuality, however, Bulstrode's torture has its source not in God, but in his own deeds. It is the past which is 'making a conscience within him' (p. 620). Time has, by slow erosion, made him what he is: his delusions are what 'the years had been perpetually spinning . . . into intricate thickness, like masses of spider-web, padding the moral sensibility' (p. 617). It is the power of the past that transforms his theoretical sense of sin – his conviction of his 'total absence of merit' – into a 'distinct shape in memory', stimulates 'the tingling of shame [and] the pang of remorse' and awakens the sharp dread of discovery (all p. 521). Time has dulled his moral perception but the past cannot be changed.

Bulstrode is not condemned, and he is not the only victim of egoism. Eliot takes a charitable view of him as 'simply a man whose desires had been stronger than his theoretic beliefs, and who had gradually explained the gratification of his desires into satisfactory agreement with those beliefs' (p. 619). Other characters illustrate other features of the general vice. Rosamond habitually judges the outside world simply according to whether it presents a face favourable or disagreeable to her; unexpectedly confronted with the need to moderate her habits, she becomes a 'poor thing [who] saw only that the world was not ordered to her liking' (p. 649). Her husband, despite his more subtle ideas, shows himself infected with a similar vice when he perceives in Rosamond a 'want of sensibility, which showed itself in disregard both of his specific wishes and of his general aims'; admittedly, he is shown to be right about Rosamond, but it is his egoism that draws him to Rosamond as someone who may possibly show 'the tender devotedness and docile adoration of the ideal wife' (both p. 52). Neither of these characters is capable of perceiving the other as an independent entity: indeed each is judged by how far he or she fails to match the preconceptions of the other. When Eliot compares the disillusionment of his marriage with 'a fracture in delicate crystal' (p. 52), the simile expresses Lydgate's misconception of both Rosamond and the nature of marriage. Of course, egoism is by no means the only standard of judgement applied to the ill-matched pair: Rosamond's blind materialism appears close to contemptible by comparison with Lydgate's dedication, no matter how self-interested it may be. The range of shades of egoism matches the multiplicity of characters. Casaubon in his monomania stands at one extreme, pigeonholed with uncanny accuracy by Mr Brooke as a man 'a little buried in books' (p. 39). One of the more superficial expressions of egoism appears in the scene where the possibility that others may find the behaviour of Celia's baby monotonous remains 'quite hidden' from its mother (p. 535). As Will Ladislaw sets out to engineer an encounter with Dorothea at Lowick Church the debate in his mind between Inclination and Objection is resolved by 'unreason' until 'Everything seemed to know that it was Sunday, and to approve of his going' (p. 470). Even Dorothea herself is not immune, for she marries Casaubon in the determination to serve his academic purposes, quite unconscious of the possibility that his expectations may differ from hers. Even idealism, then, can founder on the rock of egoism.

The theme of egoism lies at the heart of the novel and is vividly expressed in the much-discussed conceit of the pier-glass that opens Chapter 27:

> Your pier-glass or extensive surface of polished steel made to be rubbed by a housemaid, will be minutely and multitudinously scratched in all directions; but place now against it a lighted candle as a centre of illumination, and lo! the scratches will seem to arrange themselves in a fine series of concentric circles round that little sun. It is demonstrable that the scratches are going everywhere impartially and it is only your candle which produces the flattering illusion of a concentric arrangement, its light falling with an exclusive optical selection. These things are a parable. The scratches are events, and the candle is the egoism of any person now absent – of Miss Vincy, for example.
>
> (p. 264)

A pier-glass is a full-length mirror on a stand (the pier) and is thus capable of representing the whole person of the viewer. Eliot's point is that the image in the steel is distorted by the subjectivity of the viewer. The ego senses its own consciousness as the most lively reality in its experience; external or alien realities are inevitably subsidiary and necessarily follow the pattern determined by the observing consciousness. The conceit depends for its effect on the scratching of the metal surface: mirrors of modern glass do not exhibit the effect, though they share some other distortions of mirror images. The effect is, however, universal: whatever is examined by the light of the candle in the mirror will suffer the halo distortion which Eliot describes as 'the flattering illusion of a concentric arrangement'. Thus the conceit expresses the consciousness of 'any person', and Miss Vincy, though particularly apposite, is no more than an example.

Is no one then immune? Is the censure not too general to be meaningful? The Garths largely escape criticism, and Mr Farebrother, resolutely relinquishing Mary to Fred, stands out as an example of selflessness. But these are the exceptions. Eliot's vision of the general character of the world as of Middlemarch is encapsulated in several brief statements such as the following remark about Dorothea:

> We are all of us born in moral stupidity, taking the world as an udder to feed our supreme selves: Dorothea had early begun to emerge from that stupidity, but yet it had been easier to her to imagine how she would devote herself to Mr Casaubon, and become wise and strong in his strength and wisdom, than to conceive with that distinctness which is no longer reflection but feeling – an idea wrought back to the direct-ness of sense, like the solidity of objects – that he had an equivalent centre of self, whence the lights and shadows must always fall with a certain difference.
>
> (p. 211)

Dorothea thus expresses a universal evil – the 'moral stupidity' of egoism that sees itself as the centre of the perceived world. However, she herself also expresses the most refined kind of egoism. Her very idealism becomes the diabolical snare to betray her: desiring sincerely to serve, she omits to wonder whether her service is welcome. Fur-thermore, she fails to sense Casaubon as an entity wholly separate from herself and imagines his individuality reduced to a part of the pattern of her own mind. At this point, then, her selflessness reveals moral short-sightedness and her idealism is shown to be tainted by romantic delusion. Well intentioned and dutiful she certainly is, but she has yet to achieve the status of a Teresa. Rather than true self-lessness, she has achieved only devotion to its concept.

The antithesis of egoism finds a less than pellucid representation in the last quotation. Eliot refers uncomfortably to 'that directness which is no longer reflection but feeling . . . the directness of sense, like the solidity of objects'. Elsewhere Eliot denies the security of established religious beliefs, asserting that 'There is no general doc-trine which is not capable of eating out our morality' (p. 619). Instead of Christianity, or any other orthodox belief, Eliot looks to 'the deep-seated habit of direct fellow-feeling with individual fellow-men' (p. 619). Thus expressed, Eliot's view inevitably appears vague and shape-less. In action in the novel, however, it achieves sharp engagement with reality. Farebrother questions Mary Garth closely about the nature of her feelings before he rides out of her life. Fred Vincy has to assess himself with remorseless precision before he begins working for Mr Garth. As for Dorothea, she eventually comes to see that she is 'part of [the world's] involuntary, palpitating life, and could neither look out on it from her luxurious shelter as a mere spectator, nor hide her eyes in selfish complaining'; the scene takes place in an appropriate setting as she opens the curtains with 'light piercing into the room' (both p. 788). Eliot's ideas are thus represented in the meta-language of the novel, in its action and in its imagery. They are also represented antithetically. Casaubon, cut off in the cul-de-sac of his pointless research, stands at the opposite extreme from Dorothea who feels 'the largeness of the world and the manifold wakings of men to labour and endurance' (p. 788).

Conclusions

Eliot parted company with specifically Christian doctrine at an early date. She turned instead to Feuerbachian humanism which not only diverged from Christianity, but actively opposed it as a particularly insidious expression of egoism. Feuerbach's ideas underlie much of the moral texture of her novels: her translation of *The Essence of Christianity* was published in 1854, two years before she began writing fiction. The influence of Feuerbachian theory is most obvious in *Middlemarch*, but in all three of the novels discussed here there is a sharp distinction between characters who demonstrate a grasp of objective reality and those who are dominated by egoism.

Clearly Eliot's objection to Christian doctrine and practice did not extend to the principles enshrined therein. On the contrary, the more she divorced herself from Christianity, the more intensely moral she became. All the novels focus on sharp moral dilemmas involving individual relationships: Maggie must resist the temptation of Stephen Guest, Silas resists the pleas of Godfrey Cass and Dorothea resists her own inclination to Will Ladislaw. Such relationships stand out from a carefully depicted social background but are not independent of it: these characters make their decisions in relation to the established customs and values of their society.

Christian ideas are essential to the kind of society Eliot describes. They are closely linked (though not necessarily essential to) the principles of fidelity, loyalty and service that define the attitudes of characters such as Dorothea and Lydgate, Maggie Tulliver and her family, and the people of Raveloe. Clergymen have a crucial role to play in society and are often regarded as having special authority in the moral sphere. Dr Kenn's right to act as Maggie's moral mentor goes unquestioned, for example, and Mr Farebrother is peerless in self-abnegation when he concedes Mary to Fred Vincy. On the other hand, Eliot satirises the ungenerous impulses of supposedly Christian societies mercilessly in portraying the views of Dr Kenn's congregation about Maggie or of Middlemarch society about the faults in Lydgate and Bulstrode. *Silas Marner* offers many fascinating ideas about religion, from the attitudes of the farmers who think that over-frequent attendance at church is a sign of eschatological greed to the semantic difficulties of Mrs Winthrop and Silas over whether they have attended church or chapel. More seriously, opposed views emerge here: Silas's integration into the conventional religious life of Raveloe betokens his general acceptance and thence his regeneration, and Mrs Winthrop's kindness and good intentions are a natural outcome of her practice of Christian principles; at the same time, however, Silas's experience of Lantern Yard illustrates the potential for perversion in religious practice, while in his daily life the broken pot on its shelf is as potent as any god on its altar. *Silas Marner* provides an interesting parallel for the ambivalence of Eliot's views about Christianity, for in rather the same way that she supports morality as distinct from Christianity, Silas upholds the significance of his actual day-to-day relationship with Eppie against Godfrey's lesser claim of mere paternity *in absentia*. Eliot's outlook appears essentially to combine conservatism and pragmatism. What she upholds is what the development of society has shown to work, and if that includes more than a dash of Christian principle she, humanist though she is, remains undismayed.

Part of the power of the past is that it is the repository of values – traditional, natural, Christian, pagan or from whatever source – that having been passed down through generations are worthy of respect. *The Mill on the Floss* expresses this idea most powerfully in the idea of nature itself as 'the mother tongue of our imagination, the language that is laden with all the subtle inextricable associations the fleeting hours of our childhood left behind them' (p. 94). The passage is a personal one spoken in Eliot's own voice – it begins 'The wood I walk in' – that serves to bridge an interlude in the history of the Tulliver children, and carries all the more general force. In practice, the past assumes the human form of parental expectation. The power of the past thus makes a specific impact on the action of the novel later, when Maggie, seeking to find her way through the problems with which Philip confronts her, thinks first of her duty to her father. Her brother is moved by comparable motives in striving to better the lot of his family after Mr Tulliver's disgrace. In the later novels the past has as much power, though it takes different forms. Just as strongly as the past holds positive values in *The Mill on the Floss* it preserves the roots of evil in *Silas Marner* and *Middlemarch*. In all three novels the past functions as a key to the stable reality underlying the currents of passion, delusion and self-deception.

Moral action in the novels tends to resolve itself into conflicts which, essentially simple, are circumstantially complex and sometimes beyond the power of characters to resolve. Maggie has to determine a rational course of action while confused by the different blandishments of Philip Wakem and Stephen Guest; and in the background there is always the presence of Tom. She has done no wrong, yet is punished as if she has. Rather than a sinner, she is the victim of the unreasoning egoism of the male characters and of the composite irrationality of the ladies of St Ogg's. Dorothea has to deal with the error of her marriage to Casaubon and resist her attraction to Will. For her, as for Maggie, the conflict lies between duty and passion: in Eliot's world, despite her belief in direct fellow-feeling, the demands of duty are always overriding. For Godfrey Cass and Nicholas Bulstrode, the conflict is rather between their desire to preserve their social eminence and the necessity to confess their perfidy. Lydgate's is a particularly brutal dilemma: gifted and ambitious, he is brought face to face with the consequences of the egoism that earlier led him to the arms of Rosamond when at last he is compelled to place his uncomprehending wife before his profession; thus is his desire to serve thwarted and diminished.

Eliot's is not a comfortable morality. Hers is a world in which the potential for future action is limited by the effect of the past: the greatest error is to try to escape the responsibilities imposed by past choices. The highest virtue is to submit to duty, but it is a grim one. Duty does not reward; service does not ennoble. Maggie's fidelity to Tom results only in their death; Godfrey's absence from the wedding of his daughter symbolises both his achievement and his loss; Dorothea's highest achievement is likewise to disappear; Lydgate's victory over himself is a bitter one. The reward of service, then, is no more than the consciousness of having done one's duty – and perhaps to have developed an idea. The discussion of St Teresa that frames *Middlemarch* drives the point home painfully, for in Eliot's universe there is no place for the traditional religious reward, no personal glorification in a Christian heaven. Instead there is only the hope of having contributed to the evolution of a more wholesome society.

Methods of Analysis

It will have been apparent from the detailed analyses in this chapter that Eliot uses all the technical features characteristic of her writing to realise the moral questions that drive her work. The extract from *The Mill on the Floss* shows the dramatisation in action and dialogue of the conflict of passion and duty, includes psychological analysis of Maggie and concludes with a symbolic judgement of Maggie's situation. In the *Silas Marner* extract there is a similarly dramatic confrontation, realised in contrasting styles of speech, manner and class, and in physical description of Eppie's reactions. There is psychological analysis of both Silas and Godfrey. In both extracts Eliot makes characteristic use of irony. The *Middlemarch* extracts show different sides of Eliot's writing. In these she focuses on analysis of Nicholas Bulstrode's inner conflict, and, in the pier-glass passage, on an effort to render vivid by metaphor the nature of egoism. The third quotation from *Middlemarch* exemplifies the metalinguistic control that Eliot exerts over the disparate elements of both this and her earlier novels.

There are, however, features of her writing to be aware of that relate specifically to her moral concerns. Chief of these is her penchant for treating characters in conflicting pairs to represent different sides of a moral debate. Maggie's discussions with Tom, Philip and Stephen are of this kind, drawing her towards differing worlds of tradition, romanticism and passion. Particularly towards the conclusion of the novel, the moral dilemma of Maggie is drawn out with painstaking detail, until the book begins to sound more like a moral treatise than a work of fiction. In *Middlemarch* there are dialogues between Rosamond and Lydgate that, despite their very different subject matter, occupy much the same moral dimension. Like Maggie, Dorothea is drawn to different worlds by the contrasting personalities of Casaubon, Lydgate and Ladislaw. There are, of course, innumerable subsidiary polarities in all three novels. Despite their range and variety, however, these polarities tend to resolve themselves into oppositions of qualities such as duty and passion, or reality and dream. Maggie's grasp of reality and her sense of duty stand firm against Stephen's call to passion, which Maggie knows to be an illusory attraction. Lydgate insists on the realities of his life with Rosamond, and holds fast to the discipline it requires, despite Rosamond's failure to recognise that things have changed for both of them. At times Eliot allegorises this basic conflict, most obviously when inclination and objection fight for control of Will Ladislaw on his way to church to waylay Dorothea. Such polarities emerge clearly from the analysed extracts from *The Mill on the Floss* and *Silas Marner*.

Another feature, to which the extract from *The Mill on the Floss* draws specific attention, is the use of letters. Of course there are many uses for letters in novels, and in George Eliot's novels they often have potential for changing lives. The letter is an interesting mode of communication, however, in being addressed to another person and yet giving greater opportunity for self-expression than ordinary dialogue can: the writer of the letter places himself centre stage. Letters to Maggie from Philip and Stephen at the end of *The Mill on the Floss* reveal their egoism in a brutally clear light. Equally, Casaubon's letter of proposal to Dorothea reveals him all too clearly to us, and it is merely the measure of Dorothea's delusion that she fails to be alert to the hints of his inadequacy contained in it. Other examples from

Middlemarch are Casaubon's letter to Ladislaw and Sir Godwin's brief and brutal note to Lydgate. In all these instances, the writer reveals himself in a direct, unvarnished manner, as if in soliloquy.

A third situation that recurs commonly in the novels is that of accusation or confession. It is a feature, if not an especially prominent one, in all the extracts discussed in this chapter. Stephen accuses Maggie and Godfrey accuses Silas, and Maggie and Silas are thus compelled to defend themselves; Bulstrode's sense of guilt is a trap that must eventually express itself in a confession to his wife that is not the less painful for being silent and incomplete. There are many other examples in the novels. Tom accuses and disowns Maggie, who confesses herself to him and to Dr Kenn. *Silas Marner* hinges on the false accusation against Silas who echoes it unjustly in condemning Jem Rodney, while Godfrey Cass is driven by circumstances to make his confession to his wife. Fred's rehabilitation must be preceded by the humiliation of confessing what he has done to the Garths. Rosamond receives no pardon for her confession to Dorothea, despite their reconciliation.

The process of confession is linked closely with my final point. Confession is essential to redemption. Only when the past has been exorcised by honest confrontation are the characters free to develop. However, the plotting of the novels reaffirms the determinist element in Eliot's moral world. The past is inescapable, and there are correspondingly no easy routes to escape, or even to development or change, for her characters. Her moral code is inexorable, and its operation detailed minutely in the convincing picture she paints of the actual moral lives as well as the social lives of her characters. The past may be confronted, confessed and exorcised, but it can never be erased.

Further Work

The Mill on the Floss
Study Stephen's meeting with Maggie in the lane, from 'Not a word was spoken . . .' to 'that pleading beauty gained new power over him' (Book Six, Chapter 11, pp. 566–71). This makes an interesting

passage to analyse on its own, or to compare with the analysis in this chapter.

Silas Marner

Eppie's rejection of Godfrey's offer, 'Eppie, my dear . . . unable to say more' (Chapter 19, pp. 171–3) makes a useful comparison with the passage analysed in this chapter. A very different passage deals with Nancy's reception of Godfrey's confession in Chapter 18 ('"Nancy," said Godfrey, slowly . . . I doubt it can never be all made up for', pp. 162–4).

Middlemarch

A key stage in Lydgate's remonstrations with Rosamond occurs in Chapter 65, from 'It is a terrible moment . . .' to '. . . to say he was her master' (pp. 665–7). Alternatively, you may prefer to develop the analysis of Bulstrode by considering an additional passage from Chapter 70, 'Bulstrode's native imperiousness . . . their common cries for safety' (pp. 704–5).

6

Conclusions

This chapter has two purposes. The first is to consider how Eliot uses the final paragraphs in each novel to resolve the themes she has developed. The second is to formulate some conclusions about the way she works and how she treats the essential themes of her novels; each ending may be expected to reflect the stylistic and technical features as well as the subject matter of the novel it belongs to. In this chapter, it is especially important to consider the immediate context of the passages: each conclusion is a natural outcome of what precedes it; it is part of a larger conclusion.

First, it is worth recalling some of the major features we have noticed thus far:

- Eliot works on a broad canvas, including a general social vision as well as details of natural environment as a setting for her characters. Background is vividly realised and society depicted in detail. In *Middlemarch* especially, there is a strong sense of actuality.
- There a correspondingly broad range of characters: in *Middlemarch* there are many foreground characters. Eliot is capable of empathising equally with men and women, and with characters of different ages. Some characters, like Maggie and Dorothea, are partly autobiographical.
- The society she treats is middle England: a society of working people, but not those of the lowest rank, striving to make their way in the world, and confronting the demands of personal rela-

tionships within and outside marriage. Working life, social class and marriage have great importance in her novels as essential elements in social structure.

- Eliot is a profoundly moral writer, but without a specifically Christian burden. She treats characters in terms of the degree to which they are capable of envisioning themselves and their lives realistically. However, she is conscious of the significance Christianity has in the lives of everybody for historical and social as well as purely ethical reasons.

Part of the task to be done with each ending is to consider how far it matches the individual pattern of the novel it concludes or resolves the questions raised in it.

(i) *The Mill on the Floss*

The final chapter of the novel is brief enough to study in full:

> Nature repairs her ravages – repairs them with her sunshine, and with human labour. The desolation wrought by that flood, had left little visible trace on the face of the earth, five years after. The fifth autumn was rich in golden corn-stacks, rising in thick clusters among the distant hedgerows; the wharves and warehouses on the Floss were busy again, with echoes of eager voices, with hopeful lading and unlading.
>
> And every man and woman mentioned in this history was still living – except those whose end we know.
>
> Nature repairs her ravages – but not all. The uptorn trees are not rooted again – the parted hills are left scarred: if there is a new growth, the trees are not the same as the old, and the hills underneath their green vesture bear the marks of the past rending. To the eyes that have dwelt on the past, there is no thorough repair.
>
> Dorlcote Mill was rebuilt. And Dorlcote churchyard – where the brick grave that held a father whom we know, was found with the stone laid prostrate upon it after the flood – had recovered all its grassy order and decent quiet.
>
> Near that brick grave there was a tomb erected very soon after the flood, for two bodies that were found in close embrace: and it was often visited at different moments by two men who both felt that their

keenest joy and keenest sorrow were for ever buried there.

One of them visited the tomb again with a sweet face beside him – but that was years after.

The other was always solitary. His great companionship was among the trees of the Red Deeps, where the buried joy seemed still to hover – like a revisiting spirit.

The tomb bore the names of Tom and Maggie Tulliver, and below the names it was written –

'In their death they were not divided.'

(pp. 656–7)

The mood and content of this conclusion are complex. Hope mingles with sadness, and these few short paragraphs allude to Tom, Maggie, Mr Tulliver, Stephen, Lucy and Philip as well as the fate of Dorlcote Mill and churchyard. The reminiscent tone of the opening recurs here, five years after the events, with the reference to 'eyes that have dwelt on the past'.

The mood of the conclusion is of sadness controlled and distanced by the pattern of life. The novel ends, as it began, with the natural world. The Floss is mentioned, but now it is nature in general instead of the river that is personified. Nature actively makes good the ravages of the 'face' of the earth with 'her sunshine'. As at the beginning of the novel, nature works together with people. The busy world of the waterside and the ripe corn-stacks show that human life, like the life of nature, has healed the wounds of the flood and is busily constructing the future in a mood of hope. The season is autumn instead of the beginning of spring, but the mood of the first paragraph of the extract emphasises the feeling of ripeness rather than the promise of winter. As in the first chapter of the novel, contrasting seasons and different moods are embraced within a coherent vision. The busyness, the thickness and golden colour of the corn, and the hopeful labour are supported by alliterations in 'rich/rising', 'wharves/warehouses', and 'echoes/eager'. A little later there is reference to the 'grassy order and decent quiet' that have been restored to the churchyard, to the erection of the tomb after the laying 'prostrate' in the flood of Mr Tulliver's stone.

Though Eliot stresses the evidence of restoration and renewal, she cannot forget the sadness of what has passed. The face of the earth smiles, but its heart knows pain. Twice Eliot states that 'Nature repairs her ravages' but only to stress that 'there is no thorough repair' for those closely involved in the Tulliver story. The third paragraph marks the parallel between the human events and the natural environment, refer-ring to 'scarred' hills, new trees to replace those 'uptorn' in the flood, and the general marks of 'past rending' that exist beneath the 'green vesture' of the countryside. The violent language – 'uptorn', 'scarred', 'rending' – matches the violence of the end of Tom and Maggie.

The violence is contained, however. The chapter adopts a general, grave and lofty tone. The individual story finds a place in a greater natural and human evolution. The effect is accentuated by the pre-tence of anonymity that Eliot pursues in a series of coy evasions: she refers to 'those whose end we know', 'two bodies', 'a father whom we know', 'two men', one of whom visited the grave in company with 'a sweet face', while 'The other' came alone; not until the final sentence are the names of Tom and Maggie mentioned. Distance in time contributes, too: although the conclusion begins five years after the flood, it is not until an undefined number of 'years after' that Stephen and Lucy come, while the third paragraph occupies the continuous present of the narrator's imagination. The final sentence mentions the Tulliver children, but counters the specific reference by adopting a biblical style: the redundant 'it' that precedes 'was written' prepares for the concluding quotation from the Book of Samuel, generalising the story of Tom and Maggie as an archetypal pattern.

Within the generalised pattern there is room for particularities. The two men who visit the grave are united in feeling that 'their keenest joy and keenest sorrow were for ever buried there'. In other ways, Stephen and Philip are differentiated. While the relationship between Stephen and Lucy recovers, Philip remains solitary, fre-quenting the Red Deeps that still seem to him inhabited by Maggie's spirit. For both of them, however, the grave contains a buried part of their emotional history. In them, as in nature, the past cannot be erased, and to that extent they exemplify Eliot's deterministic view of the world. The sense of irreversible loss is stressed in the repeated idea that emotion is 'buried' with the bodies in the churchyard.

The conclusion emphasises above all, of course, the fate of Tom and Maggie, the only characters named here. The reference to the discovery of two bodies 'found in close embrace' seems to imply that in death they have at last ironically found reconciliation; perhaps there is a hint, too, of the resolution of the overtones of incest in their relationship. The final sentence, however, expresses the same idea negatively: that they were 'not divided' recalls all the factors – social, psychological, familial, sexual, moral – that presented obstacles to them in their lives; ironically it emphasises the impossibility of their happiness in the real world. The quotation also aggrandises them, coming as it does from the well-known lament of David over the death of Saul and his son Jonathan beginning 'The beauty of Israel is slain upon thy high places: how are the mighty fallen!' (verse 19). Verse 23 runs, 'Saul and Jonathan were lovely and pleasant in their lives, and in their death they were not divided; they were swifter than eagles, they were stronger than lions' (both from Chapter 1 of the Second Book of Samuel). Eliot, it would appear, wishes Maggie and Tom to be seen as victims of a hostile world, as Saul and Jonathan were of the Philistines. To some degree the novel bears this out: Tom's life is changed by the collapse of his father's business; Maggie's relationship with Philip cannot thrive in the resulting familial enmity; otherwise, however, the heroic status of the siblings must depend on symbolic rather than narrative support.

How satisfying, then, is this conclusion? The elegiac mood matches that of the novel as a whole. There is reference to the places that have dominated the novel – the Floss, Dorlcote Mill and the Red Deeps. The final embrace of Maggie and Tom is represented as a resolution of that repeated process of rebellion and retreat that Maggie's history displays. The flood has decisively refuted Tom's dismissal of Maggie, 'You don't belong to me' (p. 612). In other respects, however, the conclusion fails widely to address the concerns of the novel. In the social sphere, Tom's grand ambitions and achievements are narrowed to a single end and set finally at nought. In the moral sphere, the lengthy and minute discussion of duty and passion that dominates the novel after Maggie's return from Mudport is simply ignored. What remains, then, is the dominance of pattern over morality. The novel does not finally involve itself in the specific concerns of its characters: the moralising reminiscences of the narrator ultimately lament and celebrate event; motive and endeavour are set aside. A further dimension of the elevation of pattern here is to set many kinds of human aspiration and endeavour in perspective: among them, Eliot suggests that matters of morality or respectability to which people are exposed may be less important than they are generally considered in a conventional Christian society.

(ii)   *Silas Marner*

The novel ends on a note of optimism with the springtime wedding of Aaron Winthrop and Eppie. This is the 'Conclusion' in full:

> There was one time of the year which was held in Raveloe to be especially suitable for a wedding. It was when the great lilacs and laburnums in the old-fashioned gardens showed their golden and purple wealth above the lichen-tinted walls, and when there were calves still young enough to want bucketfuls of fragrant milk. People were not so busy then as they must become when the full cheese-making and the mowing had set in; and besides, it was a time when a light bridal dress could be worn with comfort and seen to advantage.
>
> Happily the sunshine fell more warmly than usual on the lilac tufts the morning that Eppie was married, for her dress was a very light one. She had often thought, though with a feeling of renunciation, that the perfection of a wedding-dress would be a white cotton, with the tiniest pink sprig at wide intervals; so that when Mrs Godfrey Cass begged to provide one, and asked Eppie to choose what it should be, previous meditation had enabled her to give a decided answer at once.
>
> Seen at a little distance as she walked across the churchyard and down the village, she seemed to be attired in pure white, and her hair looked like the dash of gold on a lily. One hand was on her husband's arm, and with the other she clasped the hand of her father Silas.
>
> 'You won't be giving me away, father,' she had said before they went to church; 'you'll only be taking Aaron to be a son to you.'
>
> Dolly Winthrop walked behind with her husband; and there ended the little bridal procession.
>
> There were many eyes to look at it, and Miss Priscilla Lammeter was glad that she and her father had happened to drive up to the door of the Red House just in time to see this pretty sight. They had come to keep Nancy company to-day, because Mr Cass had had to go away to

Lytherley, for special reasons. That seemed to be a pity, for otherwise he might have gone, as Mr Crackenthorp and Mr Osgood certainly would, to look on at the wedding-feast which he had ordered at the Rainbow, naturally feeling a great interest in the weaver who had been wronged by one of his own family.

'I could ha' wished Nancy had had the luck to find a child like that and bring her up,' said Priscilla to her father, as they sat in the gig; 'I should ha' had something young to think of then, besides the lambs and the calves.'

'Yes, my dear, yes,' said Mr Lammeter; 'one feels that as one gets older. Things look dim to old folks: they'd need have some young eyes about 'em, to let 'em know the world's the same as it used to be.'

Nancy came out now to welcome her father and sister; and the wedding group had passed on beyond the Red House to the humbler part of the village.

Dolly Winthrop was the first to divine that old Mr Macey, who had been set in his arm-chair outside his own door, would expect some special notice as they passed, since he was too old to be at the wedding-feast.

'Mr Macey's looking for a word from us,' said Dolly; 'he'll be hurt if we pass him and say nothing – and him so racked with rheumatiz.'

So they turned aside to shake hands with the old man. He had looked forward to the occasion, and had his premeditated speech.

'Well, Master Marner,' he said, in a voice that quavered a good deal, 'I've lived to see my words come true. I was the first to say there was no harm in you, though your looks might be again' you; and I was the first to say you'd get your money back. And it's nothing but rightful as you should. And I'd ha' said the "Amens", and willing, at the holy matrimony; but Tookey's done it a good while now, and I hope you'll have none the worse luck.'

In the open yard before the Rainbow the party of guests were already assembled, though it was still nearly an hour before the appointed feast-time. But by this means they could not only enjoy the slow advent of their pleasure; they had also ample leisure to talk of Silas Marner's strange history, and arrive by due degrees at the conclusion that he had brought a blessing on himself by acting like a father to a lone mother-less child. Even the farrier did not negative this sentiment: on the contrary, he took it up as peculiarly his own, and invited any hardy person present to contradict him. But he met with no contradiction; and all differences among the company were merged in a general agreement with Mr Snell's sentiment, that when a man had deserved his good luck, it was the part of his neighbours to wish him joy.

As the bridal group approached, a hearty cheer was raised in the Rainbow yard; and Ben Winthrop, whose jokes had retained their acceptable flavour, found it agreeable to turn in there and receive congratulations; not requiring the proposed interval of quiet at the Stone-pits before joining the company.

Eppie had a larger garden than she had ever expected there now; and in other ways there had been alterations at the expense of Mr Cass, the landlord, to suit Silas's larger family. For he and Eppie had declared that they would rather stay at the Stone-pits than go to any new home. The garden was fenced with stones on two sides, but in front there was an open fence, through which the flowers shone with answering gladness, as the four united people came within sight of them.

'O father,' said Eppie, 'what a pretty home ours is! I think nobody could be happier than we are.'

(pp. 181–3)

Many features of this conclusion support the mood of gladness that befits the procession after a homely rural wedding. The setting is spring or early summer with a warm sunshine and the rich colours of laburnum and lilac decorating the walled cottage gardens. The reference to calves drinking bucketfuls of milk suggests fecundity and the prospect of a fruitful marriage, and looks forward to the feasting that is to follow. The fragrance of the milk matches the clemency of the climate. Little is said of Aaron Winthrop – he is referred to only once simply as Eppie's husband, and the open fence of the Stone-pits reveals the flowering of the garden he has built. Eppie herself, however, is described in glowing generality. Dressed in white cotton with pink flowers, she 'seemed to be attired in pure white' in keeping with the virginal innocence of her character, while the reference to her hair as a 'dash of gold on a lily' recalls the traditional biblical vision of the lily as a symbol of natural beauty as well as the well-known (but much misquoted) Shakespearian comment on the wasteful pointlessness of painting the lily (cf. *King John*, IV.ii.11). Silas's neighbours unanimously wish him joy, and the bridal party is greeted with 'a hearty cheer' as it reaches the Rainbow. The language expresses a sense of expansive well-being. The yard is 'open', like one of the fences of the Stone-pits; there is 'ample leisure' to review Silas's story; Ben Winthrop finds it 'agreeable' to stop at the Rainbow to 'receive congratulations'; the flowers at the Stone-pits meet the 'four united people' of the wedding party with 'answering gladness'. All this leads up to the pinnacle of Eppie's concluding exclamation of gratitude for the perfection of her existence.

There is about Eppie's words, of course, a touch of the naivety of Miranda's wide-eyed exclamation on seeing her father's visitors – 'O brave new world, That has such creatures in't' (*The Tempest*, V.i.183–4), and the darker features of Eppie's situation, which she ignores, are apparent to the reader. Mr Macey's back-handed compliment to Silas, 'I was the first to say there was no harm in you, though your looks might be again' you' recalls Silas's 'strange history' and his long insulation from the community of Raveloe. Mr Cass's absence in Lytherley 'for special reasons' shows marked tact to accompany his generosity in paying for the proceedings of the day as well as supporting the Marners generally; it acts also as a reminder of the faults of his past life. The point is underlined by Priscilla's unconscious irony in wishing that her sister 'had had the luck to find a child like [Eppie] and bring her up'. There is, too, the brief reference to the wrong done to Marner by Dunsey Cass. The general sense of well-being is, then, counterpointed by reminders of underlying cruelties past and present.

Thematically the passage relates to some of the central ideas of the novel. The most obvious of these is the theme of marital or sexual fidelity. The wedding of Aaron, the honest working man, and Eppie, dutiful and affectionate daughter, appears destined for success and thus rights the balance upset by Godfrey's treatment of Molly Farren and deception of Nancy Lammeter, and by the sexual rivalry that led to Silas's banishment from Lantern Yard. A more general theme is the opposition of community and ostracism that dominates Silas's history. Here at last Silas, the erstwhile recluse, is fully integrated into the community of Raveloe, is congratulated by all on his adopted daughter's wedding and takes his place in the ceremony and the procession. The wedding is depicted from the outset as a communal and social occasion, not merely a private contract: it takes place at a time 'held in Raveloe to be especially suitable', and the procession and reception at the Rainbow are essential parts of the process. Dolly's sensitivity to the expectations of Mr Macey contributes to the sense of generous community. He voices the changed attitude of the community towards Silas in a 'premeditated' speech like a formal proclamation of approval.

The religious themes of the novel are addressed here, too. The wedding is, of course, a religious ceremony identified as 'holy matrimony' by Mr Macey, but it is not described. There is only Mr Macey's admission that Tookey probably 'said the "Amens"' perfectly adequately. The religious element of the wedding is reduced here to a mere form of words, and not very meaningful at that. There is in the language of the passage a tincture of holiness – Marner has 'brought a blessing on himself' by acting as a father to the motherless child, and Mr Macey considers it 'rightful' that Marner should get his money back – but it is no more significant than the tone of superstitition that colours other phrases; Mr Macey hopes Marner will have 'none the worse luck' for having Tookey say the Amens, Mr Snell comments on Silas's good luck, and Priscilla thinks in terms of luck too when she speaks of her sister's childlessness. The community of Raveloe remains as it was at the beginning of the novel: its religion has more to do with primitive superstitions than with ethical principles; everyone speaks as if religion is a good thing but no one pays much attention to it beyond adopting its forms. Silas's obsession with the standards of Lantern Yard are thus set in a bleak perspective, for he has replaced their unrewarding and hypocritical demands with the simpler requirements of social life in a community dominated by everyday concerns. There is no mention here of the implications of Dolly Winthrop's faith or of the implications of Silas's conviction that he will 'trusten' (p. 180) until his death. Ideas of right and wrong or blessing and cruelty have at this moment a purely practical, secular meaning.

Secular does not mean brutish, however. There is an atmosphere of communal kindness here, expressed in the behaviour of Dolly Winthrop, Mr Macy, Mr Snell who wishes Silas joy, the farrier (Dowlas) who sets aside his scepticism for the day and Ben Winthrop with his 'acceptable' jokes. Godfrey's absence shows not only tact, but an acceptance of the decision made about Eppie's future; his generosity shows his acceptance of his responsibility. Silas's aspirations now exceed his earlier obsession with gold: though Mr Macey speaks of the rightfulness of Silas's recovery of his money, the reference to Eppie's hair as 'like the dash of gold' – the final reference to this thematic symbolism – underlines the moral progress she initiated in his life. It is fitting that the final words of the novel should rest with the virginal Eppie, who has been the occasion of the moral regeneration not only of Silas, but of Godfrey too. Though the novel finishes on a secular note, she in her 'pretty home' is as happy at this point as Eve in Paradise before the Fall.

Though simpler than *Middlemarch*, the novel exemplifies Eliot's characteristic point of view vividly. For her, the principles that guide human existence are a matter of human society rather than revealed truth. Religious life has its place in the community, but is not preeminent. Morality is thus a function of community and not vice versa.

(iii)   *Middlemarch*

The final chapter, rather operatically entitled 'Finale', is too long to deal with fully. It outlines in some detail the fortunes of Fred and Mary, Lydgate and Rosamond, and Dorothea and Ladislaw. This discussion will be restricted largely to the general parts of the conclusion and those that pertain directly to Dorothea.

From a brief summary of its general structure, this conclusion appears to adopt the characteristic device of many Victorian novels: there is the traditional review of the characters. Contrary to the superficial impression of conventionality, however, this ending matches the rigorous intellectuality of the novel as a whole. Eliot pointedly remarks that 'Marriage, which has been the bourne of so many narratives, is still a great beginning') and proceeds far enough beyond that event to envisage Fred with white hair and Lydgate dead at the age of fifty. She argues that her perspective is essential because 'the fragment of a life . . . is not the sample of an even web': a serious attempt to judge behaviour must encompass a lifetime, all the stresses that have affected it and all the responses they have evoked. The

Finale begins, therefore, by reasserting the seriousness of the author's purpose. She speaks of 'promises', 'an ardent outset', 'opportunity', 'past error' and 'grand retrieval' in an effort to reflect the vicissitudes of moral life, and supports her view with a witty reference to Adam and Eve whose experience was passed largely outside Eden, and to the 'Crusaders of old' whose aspirations failed to survive the stresses of their pilgrimage (quotations in this paragraph are all from p. 832).

In addition to her evident moral purpose, Eliot also implies an artistic aim. The statement that opens the Finale, 'Every limit is a beginning as well as an ending', points to the problem that Eliot attempts to meet in *Middlemarch*: seeing the world a web, she tries in this novel to deal not with an individual beginning and ending, but with a part of a continuum. In the choice of the subtitle, 'A Study of Provincial Life', Eliot stresses that the novel is both serious – it is a 'Study . . . of . . . Life' – and partial – it studies a province only and not the whole. At the beginning of the Finale, she stresses also that the novel deals with only a small part of history, beginning and ending at points selected not quite arbitrarily but at least from a number of possibilities. Part of the purpose of this huge novel with its multiple plots, then, is to stress its own littleness. Part of its greatness is that it looks forward to the experimental novels of much later writers more patently concerned with the relationship between life and art.

How, then, does the story of Dorothea fit into this grand pattern? The conclusion recounts the bare bones of her life, including the birth of her child, Ladislaw's successes in public life, the resolution of the conventional matter of the entail on the estate, the visits of Mr and Mrs Ladislaw to the Grange and their playing with their cousins, and the decision of Dorothea's son not to enter political life after he inherits the Brooke estate. Little is said of Dorothea's personal life until these final paragraphs:

> Sir James never ceased to regard Dorothea's second marriage as a mistake; and indeed this remained the tradition concerning it in Middlemarch, where she was spoken of to a younger generation as a fine girl who married a sickly clergyman, old enough to be her father, and in little more than a year after his death gave up her estate to marry

his cousin – young enough to have been his son, with no property, and not well-born. Those who had not seen anything of Dorothea usually observed that she could not have been 'a nice woman,' else she would not have married either the one or the other.

Certainly those determining acts of her life were not ideally beautiful. They were the mixed result of young and noble impulse struggling amidst the conditions of an imperfect social state, in which great feelings will often take the aspect of error, and great faith the aspect of illusion. For there is no creature whose inward being is so strong that it is not greatly determined by what lies outside it. A new Theresa will hardly have the opportunity of reforming a conventual life, any more than a new Antigone will spend her heroic piety in daring all for the sake of a brother's burial: the medium in which their ardent deeds took shape is forever gone. But we insignificant people with our daily words and acts are preparing the lives of many Dorotheas, some of which may present a far sadder sacrifice than that of the Dorothea whose story we know.

Her finely touched spirit had still its fine issues, though they were not widely visible. Her full nature, like that river of which Cyrus broke the strength, spent itself in channels which had no great name on the earth. But the effect of her being on those around her was incalculably diffusive: for the growing good of the world is partly dependent on unhistoric acts; and that things are not so ill with you and me as they might have been, is half owing to the number who lived faithfully a hidden life, and rest in unvisited tombs.

(pp. 837–8)

The use of Sir James to introduce the final portrait of Dorothea stresses the interdependence of the social and personal elements of the fiction that have characterised the whole novel. Her conduct in marrying Ladislaw has already been discussed in Chapter 84. There Sir James expresses his sense of hurt that 'a woman like Dorothea should have done what is wrong' (p. 816), Celia argues that it is 'very dreadful' of her sister to marry Ladislaw when 'She said she *never would* marry again' (p. 817) and Mrs Cadwallader casts aspersions on Ladislaw as born of a stock mingling 'Casaubon cuttle-fish fluid . . . and . . . a rebellious Polish fiddler' (p. 819); Mr Brooke defends not his daughter, but only himself as having pointed out to her the economic and social evils of the marriage; only the Rector expresses the voice of reason, and he is soon compelled to take his wife off with him when she exceeds the bounds of propriety. Dorothea is thus considered broadly from the point of view of her society before Eliot offers a more sympathetic judgement. It is suitably the entirely unremarkable Sir James who is used to express a critical perspective on the thoroughly remarkable character of the protagonist. His simple ideas and stolid character – just a little too limp to be called inflexible – provide a link to the wider view of society that Eliot calls 'the tradition' concerning Dorothea: it is the character of Sir James and of Middlemarch to formulate the unimaginative thumbnail sketch of Dorothea's marital history that appears in the first paragraph quoted. The sketch turns, indeed, into a thumbnail of Middlemarch rather than of Dorothea, revealing a society founded on a witches' brew of prejudice, intolerance and triteness. The phrases 'young enough to have been his son' and 'old enough to be her father' are the common currency of an old-fashioned kind of middle-class comedy. The traditional view mingles romance and error with hard-headed business and common sense in references to Casaubon's sickliness and Ladislaw's lack of gentility and property. This cartoon of the provincial imagination reaches an appropriate climax in cliché when Dorothea is finally categorised as demonstrably not nice.

In contrast, the final two paragraphs of the extract look behind the public perception at a character with which the author clearly feels deep sympathy. Eliot's vision of Dorothea is never in doubt. Prior to her marriage with Ladislaw she is described as a 'queenly young widow' (p. 774) and thus associated with one of the icons of Eliot's time. After the marriage Eliot comments on her being considered 'so substantive and rare a creature' (p. 836) by those who know her. Despite her great gifts Dorothea shows an admirable lack of egoism, having 'no dreams of being praised above other women' (p. 835). Now, in these final paragraphs, Eliot comments directly on the contrast between Dorothea as she is and Dorothea as perceived by society. Dorothea's behaviour, she says, is the effect of 'noble impulse' at war with 'an imperfect social state'; it shows her to be a woman of feeling and faith, and that these qualities are adjudged 'error' and 'illusion' serves merely to reveal the misconceptions of society at large. Eliot sees her as possessed of a 'finely touched spirit' and a 'full nature'.

Furthermore, she sees Dorothea as having a significant social potency. The word 'great' is used twice to describe Dorothea's character, and a third time, negatively, to admit her lack of public stature and her possession of 'no great name on the earth'.

Perversely, it seems, Eliot insists on comparisons between Dorothea and women of historic stature. She refers to Antigone, who dared the wrath of Creon, King of Thebes, by interring the remains of her brother, Polynices, in disobedience of royal decree, and was punished by being buried alive. She alludes, as she did in the Prelude to the novel, to Teresa, who reformed the Carmelite order of nuns. Dorothea's heroism is of a different kind and resides in quietness. She lives in a less heroic world, and less bold 'medium', than Antigone, but her spirit is as 'ardent': the word is a favourite of Eliot's, implying both a fiery spirit and a guiding light for others; though living 'a hidden life' and not 'widely visible', her good influence on her immediate circle is 'incalculably diffusive'. Eliot sees the virtue of such as Dorothea in defining the direction of social evolution. This idea is diffidently suggested, with all the emphasis on negatives – 'partly', 'unhistoric', 'not so ill', 'half owing', 'unvisited' – yet is persuasively adumbrated as 'the growing good of the world'. A third allusion, to Cyrus, deserves comment. The reference is to Cyrus the Great, King of Persia, who conquered the city of Babylon only after drying up the channels of the Euphrates so that his army could cross. By the standards of his time, Cyrus's rule was beneficent, and he brought a semblance of order to his large empire. In suggesting this unlikely parallel between Dorothea and the Euphrates, then, Eliot admits that nobility of nature can withstand political or social power, but implies that it is associated with the force of nature in general: Cyrus is long dead, the Persian Empire no more, while the Euphrates, after all, still flows. And while Will busies himself righting wrongs in the rough-and-tumble of the political arena, his wife remains at home exerting her more subtle but inexorable influence on the future of society.

Here the interdependence of society and individual is deepened. Society misjudges Dorothea, attributing her marriages to foolishness or worse. At the same time, her true nature operates only within the parameters that her society allows: it is the 'medium' in which her actions take shape. Every living thing, Eliot says, is 'greatly determined by what lies outside it'. At the same time, however, 'the growing good of the world' depends on its aggregation of minute goodnesses that Eliot calls 'unhistoric acts': society is formed not by great men, but by the myriad behaviour of unknown individuals. Like her person, and rather like Eliot's, Dorothea's life is not 'ideally beautiful', her deeds not heroic. She, indeed, suffers from a sense of failure, feeling that 'there was always something better which she might have done' (p. 835). To some degree she finds a vicarious fulfilment in supporting her husband in his struggle against wrongs, though those who knew her 'thought it a pity that so substantive and rare a creature should have been absorbed into the life of another, and be only known in a certain circle as a wife and mother' (p. 836). Unattractive though it may appear to those of feminist persuasion, Eliot sees in Dorothea's fate a worthwhile, creative role in the forging of the future of society. Part of the purpose of the conclusion is to consider the meaning of greatness: though she is not great in the public sense, though she is not heroic, performs no historic deeds and will lie in an unvisited tomb, her ardent faith, her beauty of feeling and her fineness of spirit make a deeper contribution to the world.

Although religious and semi-religious language is used freely in the conclusion it is not to any religious end. St Teresa appears not for her beliefs, but for the quality of her life. When Eliot speaks of piety, it is in the pagan context of the 'heroic piety' of Antigone. Thus Dorothea's 'great faith' is not specifically Christian, and the 'number who lived faithfully' does not refer to people adopting an orthodox Christianity. Dorothea lives a secular life far from conventual, yet it constitutes a retreat from the world and her zeal equals that of the saint. Eliot makes no inquiry into the justification for the way of life Dorothea exemplifies: she envisages no glorification in the afterlife and sees no room for miracles in this life; the world is for her a purely material thing with defined limits. Eliot takes a deterministic view of the universe: she speaks of the 'determining acts' of Dorothea's life, of the social medium that limits behaviour; inward life is largely dependent on its environment in the external world. Scope for individual action is therefore limited; individuals can only nudge their world, not revolutionise it. True heroism therefore lies in small matters. At the same time, the effects of action are not foreseeable –

in Eliot's word, they are 'incalculable' – and this imposes a severe responsibility on mankind. If we cannot know the results of our actions, we are constrained to act according to strict principle. True virtue therefore lies in the conscientious exercise of minute rectitude. This is what guides Dorothea's behaviour. No longer dressed as a widow, she nevertheless persists in the kind of self-discipline and steadiness that Victoria's behaviour exemplified. For Dorothea, as for Eliot, serving humanity is a long and incalculable hope: the immediate nobility of life is service to others.

The novel ends on a muted note in keeping with the rest. In particular, it echoes the Prelude which foreshadowed a story of those whose desires for an 'unattained goodness . . . are dispersed among hindrances' (p. 4). Dorothea's story represents the lives of many like her, including those called upon to make 'a far sadder sacrifice'. She is a part of provincial life as provincial life is of regional, national and global life. Despite her exceptional qualities within her sphere, the novel presents the lives of characters all of whom are more or less 'insignificant people': aspiring as Lydgate and Dorothea do to change the world, they actually leave it much as they found it, with the satisfaction only of having done their best towards those close to them. For Lydgate, prone to fits of bitter ill temper to the end, it is not enough; no more is his material success. Dorothea more readily accepts the moderation of the 'lofty conception' (p. 8) of her role with which she began the novel. From a broader ethical perspective, their fate exemplifies different stages of the battle against egoism: only Dorothea achieves the ultimate victory over herself by disappearing into anonymity. No special recognition crowns her achievement. The final words bring the novel to a sombre close, without expectation of redemption or even remembrance.

Conclusions

There are remarkably close links between the ending of *Middlemarch* and that of *The Mill on the Floss*. There is much common ground between the two heroines in personality, and each is dominated by relationships with men. Maggie's life largely hesitates between the claims of Tom, Philip and Stephen; and Eliot speaks of the marriages of Dorothea as the 'determining acts of her life' (p. 838). However, the tendency of their lives shows significant differences, and they die in very different ways: Maggie suddenly in her youth, in a loving embrace with her brother, as an effect of a violent, destructive local catastrophe that seems much in keeping with the wild vicissitudes of her life; and Dorothea quietly after a lifetime of unspectacular service, described pointedly as 'unhistoric acts' (p. 838), devoted to her immediate circle. The detail of the endings underlines the parallel. Both end with water imagery, for example. The flood that destroys the lives of Maggie and Tom is transmuted at the end of *Middlemarch* into the river that reflects the milder but pervasive power of Dorothea's nature. Where the Floss becomes a vengeful force that marks the countryside and the hearts of Stephen and Philip, Dorothea is associated with a gentler but unremitting power as befits her family name. And both endings close with tombs. While we see the tomb of Maggie and Tom visited by those who loved her, Dorothea is destined to lie in an 'unvisited' tomb. These differences point to Eliot's changed outlook. The author who wrote *Middlemarch* was more closely concerned with the faithful representation of everyday experience (see the reference to *Adam Bede* above, p. 113) than was her earlier self. The development goes deeper: the later Eliot is more seriously concerned with the way small acts can contribute to great effects in a realistic social environment in which normality rules. The ending of *The Mill on the Floss* is far more sensational than could be countenanced in *Middlemarch*.

Silas Marner ends differently from the other novels. The marriage, with its associated feasting and bonhomie, brings an optimistic mood to the conclusion. As the analysis indicates, however, Eppie's closing words introduce a false note: her hyperbole suggests delusion, or at least an idealism certain to be severely tested. The mood of the endings of the other novels seems much more in keeping with Eliot's outlook. Both novels end in the grave, and they and *Silas Marner* are much preoccupied with death: not only do they contain deaths – Mr Tulliver's as well as Tom's and Maggie's, Molly's and Dunsey's, Casaubon's, Peter Featherstone's, Raffles's and Lydgate's, to mention only those in the foreground – but the consciousness of death and its certainty form part of their moral world.

Eliot narrates all three novels from a broad social and historical perspective. *The Mill on the Floss* begins and ends in the narrator's recollections; she looks back, at the end, on a time years after the action of the novel has reached its narrative conclusion. *Silas Marner* ends with an long perspective on an unsophisticated rural society with cyclic preoccupations, specifically the time of year most suitable for a wedding, and reliant on traditional ceremonial patterns; this matches the environment of rustic superstition with which the novel began. The final chapter of *Middlemarch*, a novel in which Eliot carefully locates the events in the socio-political reality of her own past, continues to explore the lives of her characters far beyond the pattern the plot demands. Moreover, her imagination expands the meaning of her narrative to embrace a time-scheme extending back to the sixteenth-century Spanish mystic, Teresa of Avila, and even further back to the pagan world of classical Greece, and forward to an incalculable future. The major part of the novel occupies a hiatus in the author's discussion of the place of the Teresa personality in human society.

Though there is much comedy and wit in the novels, the predominant mood of the endings is serious. This is partly because of the content of the endings: Eliot does not blink at failure, loss, ageing or death; even the conventionally happy ending of *Silas Marner* is moderated not only by ironic counterpoint, but by inhabiting a world that remains as grim as at the start of the novel. There is also, however, a nostalgic quality inherent in Eliot's sense of the past. Maggie and Tom and their contemporaries share a romantic intensity in the glow of the author's imagination, and in the epitaph, 'In death they were not divided', there may be a bitter reflection on her own life. There is a comparable expectation of disillusionment in the final words of Eppie, and the idealism of Dorothea seems to belong to a past, comparatively heroic age – not as heroic as the times of Antigone or Cyrus, but more so than the present; not for nothing is she familiarly known to Celia by the nickname of Dodo. These novels, in other words, share a sense of loss – even though, in the case of *Silas Marner*, it is perhaps a loss still to come.

It is hard to divorce this sense of loss from Eliot's renunciation of Christianity. Her novels are far from actively anti-Christian. On the contrary, the values associated with Christianity are strongly upheld, and many of the representatives of Christian belief who appear in the novels are treated sympathetically – Dr Kenn, Mr Farebrother and Mr Cadwallader are obvious examples – and even though Silas Marner and Dolly Winthrop have only a naive understanding of their own beliefs, the essential worth of their values remains unquestioned. Religious language and ideas appear everywhere in Eliot's writing, and not only when she discusses Christian society; they are part of the texture of her mind. There is about her treatment of Christian life and values an element of nostalgia for lost innocence – the kind of innocence Eppie displays at the conclusion of her marriage. Eliot's ideas have evolved beyond orthodox Christianity and beyond Feuerbachian humanism into a more sophisticated and practical moral standpoint, but she retains emotional ties with the religious passion of her early years.

Eliot's humanistic point of view emerges in two ways from the conclusions of the novels. In *The Mill on the Floss* direct fellow-feeling inspires the behaviour of Philip and Stephen in visiting the grave of Tom and Maggie as it moved the conduct of Maggie and Tom in the flood. No attempt is made there, however, to confront the ethical issues raised in the course of the novel. The conclusion of *Middlemarch* goes much further, showing both the beneficent power of personal involvement – in Mary's persistent influence over Fred and in Dorothea's incalculable influence on all those close to her – and the possibility of social evolution that may result. It also admits the difficulty of Lydgate's situation, the hard choices he has to make, the limited success of his efforts and the irredeemable dullness at the heart of Rosamond's superficially bright character. Eschewing Christianity as Eliot did does not mean evading the sense of sin. On the contrary, Eliot's consciousness of personal responsibility is inexorable. Her characters do not escape their past: Lydgate must live with the consequences of his marital choices as Dorothea must with hers.

It is this linkage of cause and effect that constitutes the deterministic nature of the world as perceived by Eliot. The past determines the present, and the only freedom man possesses is to recognise and confront the limits of his freedom. Thus Maggie refuses to go away where she is not known, but must remain in St Ogg's to face equally the scorn, pity or understanding of her community; similarly, her death with Tom recognises the indissoluble relationship between them that he has vainly attempted to disown. In the storm nature itself insists on his acknowledging his sister. Silas Marner spends his life under the yoke of a past that he eventually exorcises when he returns to the scene of Lantern Yard with Eppie to find the scene of his disgrace vanished without trace. Godfrey Cass is bedevilled by dead bodies that give physical form to the evils done by him and his family. In *Middlemarch*, too, the past has a cruel power. Sometimes it is merely the impersonal perversity of fate – 'Destiny stands by sarcastic with our *dramatis personae* folded in her hand' (p. 95) – but more often Eliot suggests the intimate link between fate and character. In wishing the death of Raffles, for example, Bulstrode is wishing to deny the past that in the event betrays him with all the more ferocity for his vain efforts to escape it.

Positive values emerge unemphatically but strongly from these novels. In addition to the importance Eliot attaches to direct fellow-feeling, she upholds the need to perceive things as they are, to grasp the reality both of the world outside and of oneself as the observer. Delusion and disillusionment, or wild expectation and cold fact, are often opposed in the novels. Fred Vincy comes to terms with the realities of his situation under the influence of Mary and Caleb Garth; Dunsey Cass never manages to do so. In personal terms, the greatest vice of Eliot's secular world is egoism. Egoism hinders direct fellow-feeling because it serves only itself. Egoism impedes the perception of reality because it believes itself to be the centre of the universe. Thus egoism becomes more than a personal vice merely because it undervalues the needs of others and so makes any kind of injustice or cruelty possible. The behaviour that seems entirely right and reasonable to characters like Godfrey Cass and Rosamond Vincy has a very destructive impact on the lives of those around them. Conversely, Dorothea's triumph is to see that she can be successful in a modest niche in society without seeking restlessly for social status or economic advantage or even – the most insidious trap – to serve too exalted a cause. If Eliot's secular ideals of service and duty – to community or family – seem simple in the abstract, the detail of her novels reminds us forcibly what rare achievements they are and how difficult to attain. Uncomplicated though her ideas finally appear, it is worth remembering that they were forged by her contact with the finest minds and the strongest characters of her generation.

Methods of Analysis

1. In this chapter the final paragraphs of the novels are used to try to reach some conclusions about the nature of Eliot's work. We have considered them both as endings to the final chapters and as endings to the novels.
2. It is usually useful to look in some detail at the immediate context – that is, the rest of the final chapter in the case of *Middlemarch*, or the previous chapter in the case of the other two novels – to see the effect of the ending more clearly.
3. The endings may be considered from any or all of a range of different points of view:
   - Does our perception of the characters match our earlier ideas about them?
   - How far does the fate of the characters reflect their moral stature?
   - Does the conclusion match the rest of each novel stylistically?
   - How far are the themes of the novel resolved at the end?
   - What is the mood of the conclusion, and how does it affect our interpretation of the whole novel?
4. Finally, what conclusions can we arrive at about the themes, style and mood of each of the novels, and what can we gather about Eliot's moral ideas?

Further Work

The Mill on the Floss

The Conclusion discussed above is in a sense a second ending. An interesting task is to analyse the other ending, the death of Tom and Maggie in the storm. This shows Eliot in a different mood, writing in a different style from the elegiac final chapter. Study the last few paragraphs of the book ironically entitled 'The Final Rescue', beginning with 'It was not till Tom had pushed off . . .' (pp. 654–5). Consider how the style and mood differ from the Conclusion, what the Conclusion adds to the novel, and how it changes the impression the whole novel gives.

Silas Marner

This novel, too, may be said to have another ending. Silas's own story fulfils its pattern with his return to Lantern Yard. Study the passage that concludes Chapter 21, from 'Suddenly he started . . .' to '. . . trusten till I die' (pp. 179–80). It is again an interesting exercise to consider how the final chapter modifies your final impression of the themes and mood of the novel.

Middlemarch

There are several passages worth studying. An obvious option is to take the passage recounting the fate of Fred and Mary from pp. 832–4 of the Finale ('All who have cared for Fred Vincy and Mary Garth . . . Ordered to look out for Mr Lydgate'); the reference to Farebrother is an interesting element in this passage. Another possibility is to follow the history of Lydgate and Rosamond in the single long paragraph on pp. 834–5 ('Lydgate's hair never became white . . . the sharpest crisis of her life'). In either case, consider how the passage helps to resolve the major themes of egoism, service, sacrifice, personal integrity, the conflict between passion and duty, and fatalism. You may prefer to look at an earlier passage, the meeting of Ladislaw and Dorothea in the storm, Chapter 83, pp. 809–10: 'They stood silent . . . loose each other's hands.' Here the dramatic qualities of Eliot's writing are much more in evidence; nevertheless, you will find that the passage has a significant bearing on the themes of the novel.

PART 2

THE CONTEXT
AND THE CRITICS

7

George Eliot's Life and Work

George Eliot's life mirrors the turbulent times she lived in. She led an unconventional life full of vicissitudes, yet there is about her and her work a steady conscientiousness and seriousness that express the highest aspirations of a great period in British history. She thus illuminates the contrary impulses of conservatism and revolution that guided her era. It is perhaps consistent with the depth and complexity of her personality that she should have had difficulty determining her own name. Her choice of a literary pseudonym and her revisions of the spelling of her own name reflect incidentally the issues of gender and faith that troubled her and her contemporaries. Here I shall use her pen name and the 'Mary Anne' spelling of her real name, which she also variously spelled Mary Ann and Marian.

George Eliot was born at South Farm, Arbury, Warwickshire, on 22 November 1819, and christened Mary Anne, as her birth certificate spells her. Her father, Robert Evans, had begun his working life as a builder and carpenter, had bettered himself by reading and study, and had become a forester, and then estate manager to Francis Newdigate, the owner of Arbury Hall. Robert already had two children, Chrissy (or Christiana, born in 1814) and Isaac (born in 1816) by his second wife, Christiana, and in the household also were two children from his first marriage, Robert and Fanny; his first wife had died in 1809. The family shortly moved into Griff House, on the estate of Arbury Hall, and there Mary Anne spent most of the first five years of her life, and much of her time thereafter, when she was not away at school, until she was twenty-one. Her closest playmate was her brother Isaac, with whom she engaged in tomboy activities like fishing; her sister, Christiana, preferred more feminine pursuits. At this stage Mary Anne was a thoroughly contented, outgoing child.

In the next phase of her history, when she no longer had Isaac at her side, Mary Anne became more serious. The happiest times of her childhood came to an end when Mary Anne was parted from Isaac: she was sent to a local boarding school and her brother went away to a school in Coventry. After four unhappy years at Miss Latham's, she went to the Elms School in Nuneaton. In the more congenial environment of Mrs Wallington's school she found a friend in the governess, Maria Lewis, a woman of strong evangelical beliefs, who influenced her deeply. Under Maria's tutelage Mary Anne became rigorously Christian, eschewing personal adornment as vanity; she cut off her curly hair in the pursuit of plainness. Their relationship continued long after Mary Anne's term at the school and even for a time survived Mary Anne's renunciation of Christianity. Mary Anne's third and last school was the Misses Franklin's in Coventry. There she read a great deal, learned to play the piano confidently, wrote stories and poems, and lost her provincial accent. 'Lost' is perhaps inaccurate, since it was here, under the influence of Rebecca Franklin, the younger of the Franklin sisters, that she carefully culti-vated the dignified style of speech, balanced phrasing and musical intonation that struck all those who met her, and indeed frightened some of them. During this period Mary Anne turned into a much more introspective character than she had been in her earlier childhood, became serious, excelling in languages, talented in music and anxious to develop a broad understanding of all the ideas of her time.

Mary Anne's late teens and early twenties introduced a more prac-tical aspect into her life, though her studies continued too. After her mother's death in 1836 and the marriage of Chrissy in 1837, Mary Anne became housekeeper to her father. She took considerable responsibility in the managing of the farm and in the many practical tasks associated with it. In the course of her duties, both indepen-dently and in company with her father, she became acquainted with people of many different ranks, including farm workers, mine workers, shopkeepers, the landowners, and her father's grand employers. She continued to educate herself, however: she read widely and took tuition in German, French, Italian, Greek and Latin, and even taught herself a little Hebrew. Thus she continued until 1841.

These early years had a profound influence on Mary Anne. The woodlands and meadows of the estate, the mining industry that was carried on there, the canal that provided an important means of transport, and the mixture of indigenous and immigrant populations offered a rich experience: these scenes of her youth reappear in her novels. Her early relationships emerge clearly too, especially her relationship with her brother, Isaac. The relationship of Tom and Maggie in *The Mill on the Floss* reflects that of Isaac and Mary Anne, and specific incidents like the cutting of Maggie's hair are taken straight from life; the portraits of Adam Bede and Caleb Garth owe more than a little to the character of her father, as do Mrs Poyser and Mrs Hackitt to her mother; Christiana metamorphoses into Lucy Deane, and her aunt, Elizabeth Evans, into Dinah Morris.

In 1841 time and chance wrought a significant change in Mary Anne's circumstances and activities and in her moral outlook, and coloured the next eight years of her life. Her father retired, leaving Griff House to Isaac, and moved to Bird Grove, Foleshill, in Coventry, taking Mary Anne with him. It happened that their neighbour was the sister of Charles Bray, through whom Mary Anne came into contact with an illustrious group of intellectuals and reformers. Among them were Robert Owen and Ralph Waldo Emerson. Bray himself was a notorious freethinker and helped to develop Mary Anne's independent ideas, which had been undergoing radical change in the previous few months. In less than a year, she moved from passionate orthodox religiosity to a crude state of freethinking. This development reached a crisis with her refusal to accept her father's religious ideas or to attend church with him. The result was a rift of some four months during which she lived with first her sister and then her brother. At length she returned to Coventry on the understanding that she would attend church with her father but retain her right to her own ideas. During this period, too, Mary Anne received her first commission thanks to the good offices of Charles Hennell, Cara Bray's brother; her task was to complete a translation, already begun by Hennell's wife, of *Das Leben Jesu Kritisch Bearbeitet*, an influential work first published in 1838 by the German theologian David Friedrich Strauss. This onerous labour occupied her for two years and was published anonymously in 1846 under the title *The Life of Jesus Critically Examined*. Though the book did not bear Mary Anne's name it nevertheless enhanced her reputation when its authorship became known. She also contributed articles and reviews on theological and philosophical subjects for the *Coventry Herald*, which had been bought by Charles Bray.

Circumstances again changed Mary Anne's life in 1849. After months of nursing by his daughter, Robert Evans died, leaving her an income of £100 a year. She had been devoted to him and was distraught at his passing, but was persuaded shortly after the funeral to embark on a European tour with the Brays, visiting France, Italy and Switzerland. She stayed on in Geneva over the winter after their departure, lodging with M. François Albert Durade, a short, humpbacked painter of attractive and lively personality who may have been the source for the character of Philip Wakem. He was the painter of one of very few portraits of Mary Anne. It hangs in the National Portrait Gallery, and depicts her as fair-complexioned, with light brown hair and grey-blue eyes. It is rather more flattering than most of her portraits, whether graphic or verbal.

Mary Anne returned to England in 1850 and moved to London, which remained the centre of her activities for most of the rest of her life. She stayed first with the Brays, and then with John Chapman at his house, number 142, in the Strand, developing with him a relationship close enough to awaken the jealousy of both his wife and his mistress who also lived there with two children. He invited her to contribute as his unpaid assistant editor to the *Westminster Review*, which he bought in 1851. The arrangement worked reasonably well until Chapman's wife, Susanna, and his mistress, Elisabeth Tilley, determined that the house had become overcrowded. They did not wish their *ménage à cinq* to become six and insisted on Mary Anne's removal. After an intermission of a few months, Chapman became convinced that he could not do without her professional abilities and she returned on a more perceptibly professional footing – not, let it be said, that there is any firm evidence of their relationship having progressed beyond friendship in the first place. In all she spent two years at the house in the Strand, and was instrumental, both as editor and writer (under the name Marian), in restoring to the *Westminster Review* something of the reputation of intellectual importance it had had under the editorship of John Stuart Mill. At Chapman's house she met a dazzling array of influential people including Giuseppe Mazzini, T. H. Huxley, Florence Nightingale, Wilkie Collins, Charles Dickens, Charles Babbage and Herbert Spencer. With Spencer she had something of a brief and unhappy liaison, though its intensity and nature remain in doubt.

There followed, in 1853, the most influential development in Mary Anne's eventful life. She fell in love with George Henry Lewes, a brilliant personality and gifted intellect, an actor, drama critic and novelist who later wrote two books of popular science. He was yet another freethinker among those who helped to mould Mary Anne's experience, was married but living separately from his wife and her lover, Thornton Hunt, and had claimed formal title to fatherhood of both his own and Hunt's children. His relationship with Mary Anne developed quickly and intensely. She met him first at Chapman's house, moved into private lodgings shortly afterwards, and in July 1854 eloped with him to Germany to escape the public scandal their relationship had attracted in London. There she continued to write articles for the *Westminster Review*, and a translation, which remained unpublished, of Spinoza's *Ethica*. In the same month, 'Marian Evans' published the only book that bore her own name, a translation of Ludwig Feuerbach's *Das Wesen des Christentums*, under the title *The Essence of Christianity*; inevitably, this laid her open to the charge of hypocrisy which was indeed freely levelled at her. Mary Anne had foreseen the kinds of difficulties her decision to link her life with Lewes's would attract and remained undeterred. After a period in lodgings in Dover while she awaited confirmation from Lewes's wife, Agnes, that the marriage was effectively and irrevocably ended, she and Lewes took rooms in London as Mr and Mrs Lewes. From then until Lewes's death in 1878 they continued to live together as husband and wife in all but the letter of the law; in effect, Mary Anne

Evans had become Mrs Lewes; she became, in addition, a most devoted mother to the three children Lewes and Hunt had fathered between them.

The repercussions of their unconventional behaviour became speedily apparent after their return to London in 1855. Mary Anne's punctiliousness in seeking the sanction of Agnes before committing herself to Lewes failed to protect her from being labelled a home-breaker. A practical effect of Lewes's many commitments was reduced financial circumstances. Mary Anne's brother, Isaac, was so horrified by her behaviour that he disowned her – as Tom does Maggie in *The Mill on the Floss*. Once her family heard of the nature of her relationship with Lewes, they wrote individually, under Isaac's strenuous incitement, to break off relations with her.

Distressing as this was, of much more importance to Mary Anne was the unfaltering support, encouragement and stimulation that Lewes provided throughout their relationship. Gradually the opprobrium of their behaviour faded. Led by Chapman and Bray, visitors began to visit the their lodgings in Richmond, and Mary Anne began again to contribute to the *Westminster Review*. However, life was quieter than it had been, and it was at this period, with Lewes's encouragement, that she began to write fiction.

About this time Mary Anne invented her alias of George Eliot: George after her quasi-husband, and Eliot because she liked the sound of it; the whole to avoid the disadvantages which her reputation might bring. Her publisher, John Blackwood, who visited Richmond, was persuaded to publish 'The Sad Fortunes of Amos Barton', 'Mr Gilfil's Love Story' and 'Janet's Repentance' in *Blackwood's Magazine* in 1857 in the belief that they were by a male friend of Lewes's who wished to remain anonymous. He did not discover the truth until late in 1858 but agreed to keep the secret of Mary Anne's *nom de plume*. The stories previously printed separately in *Blackwood's Magazine* were published under the collective title *Scenes of Clerical Life* in 1858. The following year was an eventful one in literary and personal terms. Mary Anne began work on *The Mill on the Floss*, but broke off when news came of the death of her sister, Chrissy, whom she loved deeply. She turned her attention for a time to another story, 'The Lifted Veil', published in 1859. In the same year came *Adam*

Bede, her first full-length novel and a great success. George Eliot was born, but the secret of her identity died almost at once. Isaac recognised characters and background details in *Adam Bede*, as did other readers from Arbury. Isaac did not reveal what he knew, but the truth emerged perforce after one Joseph Liggins, a former curate, laid claim to the writings and complained of not having been paid for them. Eliot had no option then but to acknowledge the works as emanating from the pen of the infamous, marriage-breaking lover of George Henry Lewes.

The effects of the success of *Adam Bede* were mixed. With the proceeds from it, the Leweses bought a house in Wandsworth, Holly Lodge at Southfields. However, their social status remained ambiguous. Blackwood was concerned that sales of her second novel, *The Mill on the Floss* (1860), could be harmed by the scandal attaching to the Leweses, but at length was persuaded to publish under the pseudonym. In the event, despite its author's personal reputation, the novel was a popular success.

The identity of George Eliot was now an open secret, but she retained her pseudonym thenceforth. It was as George Eliot that she published all her remaining works, and she even began to use her pseudonym in letters, perhaps in an effort, whether conscious or unconscious, to divorce herself from the recrimination, criticism and acrimony associated with the way of life of 'Mrs Lewes'. Late in the year, finding their new home too removed, the Leweses moved back to London to reside at 16 Blandford Square. There the circle of their acquaintance gradually widened as Eliot's literary reputation grew, but they never achieved full social acceptance. Invitations were often extended to Lewes, but not to Eliot. Visitors indeed there were – and they included Tennyson, Rossetti, Henry James and Edward Burne-Jones among others – but they often left their wives at home. It was Henry James, incidentally, who was responsible for the monstrously double-edged description of Eliot as 'magnificently ugly – deliciously hideous . . . in this vast ugliness resides a most powerful beauty which, in a very few minutes, steals forth and charms the mind, so that you end as I ended, in falling in love with her' (Letter to his father, 1869). The social ostracism of the Leweses weighed heavily on Eliot, who became depressed.

In 1861, after the publication of *Silas Marner*, Eliot went to Italy to begin research for *Romola*, which was to be set in Florence under the governorship of Savonarola in the fifteenth century. The subject had been suggested to her by Lewes during an earlier visit to Italy. Though in conception it was attractive, the demands it made did nothing to relieve her state of mind. The research task she had set herself was enormous, and when early chapters were published serially in the *Cornhill Magazine*, the reviews were not entirely encouraging. When the novel was published in full in 1863, many readers found it unrewarding despite its imaginativeness and insight, its colourful setting and rich characters. Eliot returned to an English setting for *Felix Holt, the Radical* (1866). As with *Romola*, Eliot did thorough research. In *Felix Holt* the public subject that constitutes a major part of the novel was the complex of political issues surrounding the Reform Bill, but she achieved greater success in developing the more personal elements of the narrative.

Eliot's next novel, and by general agreement her greatest, was *Middlemarch*, which she began to work on seriously in 1869. This novel, reverting to a world she knew well, met with rapturous popular approval and brought its author redoubled wealth and fame. In the period following its publication in parts in 1871–2 the Leweses at last began to achieve broad social recognition. Their house, the Priory at 21 Regent's Park, became famous for its fashionable Sunday afternoon gatherings. Among those who visited were artists, actors, philosophers, scientists, writers and political figures such as Herbert Spencer, T. H. Huxley, Barbara Bodichon, Richard Milnes, Ivan Turgenev, Helen Faucit, Edward Burne-Jones, John Everett Millais, Robert Browning and Alfred Tennyson. And, inevitably, having attained the acceptance they desired, the Leweses eventually began to find their popularity oppressive and the Sunday afternoons taxing and to think of escape to some less populous and less central location where they might re-establish a private life.

Instead of taking the step of removal, Eliot began in 1874 to work on another problematical novel, *Daniel Deronda*. Like *Romola* and *Felix Holt*, it mingled political and personal elements without quite integrating them satisfactorily. In the same period, she began to suffer from the kidney ailment that was to remain with her until her death.

After the publication of *Daniel Deronda* in 1876, the Leweses tried to establish a quieter way of life with fewer visitors. One who nevertheless remained always welcome on Sundays was John Cross, who had taken care of Eliot's financial affairs for some years. He found for his hosts a country home at Witley in Surrey that matched their wishes entirely, and there they retired from the punishing glamour of London society. After an idyllic two years, however, Lewes was taken ill with cancer, and died in 1878. Eliot mourned his passing deeply; she was distraught and alone except for Lewes's eldest and last surviving son, Charles. She set up a trust in her husband's name, the George Henry Lewes Studentship in Physiology, and set about completing Lewes's unfinished work, *Problems of Life and Mind*. Her last published work, a collection of essays entitled *Impressions of Theophrastus Such*, appeared in 1879. She continued to see Cross who was of great practical help to her as a financial adviser and an emotional support all the more sympathetic for having lost his mother about the same time as she had lost her husband. In time she began to receive other visitors too.

Eliot's life contained yet another chapter, and a characteristically inconvenient one it was. Her relationship with Cross developed until he proposed marriage. She rejected this and a further proposal from him, but at length, in 1880, accepted a third. Their marriage took place in May, in the august and entirely respectable environment of St George's, Hanover Square. Even after such an unexceptionable ceremony Eliot and her new husband attracted criticism on account of the twenty-year difference in their ages – Cross was only forty while Eliot was in her sixty-first year. On the domestic front, however, all was well: they went off on a honeymoon in Italy, where their newfound respectability was rewarded with the honour of a telegram of congratulation from Eliot's brother, Isaac; this was the first time he had acknowledged her for twenty-three years. On their return to England they moved into a new home at 4 Cheyne Walk in Chelsea and began to enjoy London life. But their happiness did not last long. Soon, a mere seven months after her marriage, Eliot was taken ill and died with unexpected suddenness. She was buried in Highgate Cemetery in London next to her spiritual husband, George Lewes. Isaac attended her funeral, thus publicly signalling familial reconciliation.

A funeral at Westminster Abbey was, of course, incompatible with the social disgrace of her earlier years and she was thus denied the traditional recognition accorded to great writers. There is now, however, a memorial to her in Poets' Corner in the Abbey, placed there a century after her death.

8

The Context of George Eliot's Work

George Eliot is easy to place historically. She was born in the same year as Queen Victoria and lived through the middle sixty years of the nineteenth century. During her lifetime the railway networks were established, the penny post that became uniform in 1840 revolutionised communications, and, in her final years, the first telephone exchange began to operate in London. The Industrial Revolution bore fruit in thriving coal and steel industries and Britain became famous not only as the centre of a great empire but also as the workshop of the world.

Socially the period was equally dynamic. The growth of industry resulted in population movement away from rural areas and occupations into the cities and their factories. The difficult passage of the Reform Bills through Parliament gradually extended voting rights, though women, of course, did not win the right to vote until the twentieth century. The abolition of slavery throughout the British Empire dates from 13 July 1834 (Harriet Beecher Stowe, who published *Uncle Tom's Cabin* in 1852, was roughly contemporary with Eliot).

Eliot's literary environment is a little less easy to sum up. Her contemporaries were Tennyson, Browning and Arnold among the poets, and Thackeray, Dickens, Trollope and Meredith among the novelists. However, the picture is distorted because Eliot turned to fiction rather late in her career. The literary reputations of Dickens and Thackeray were already established before she started writing her novels, and of those mentioned only Trollope's career at all closely matches hers. There is also a generous margin of difference in subject matter between Eliot and her contemporary novelists: none of them attempts the kind of psychological realism that brought Eliot's novels a wide popular readership. Her work has something of the social breadth of Dickens or Thackeray, but psychologically she looks back rather to the world of the Brontës or forwards into the twentieth century, while her descriptive writing, with its powerful sense of place, owes much to her love of the novels of Scott and the poetry of Wordsworth.

Circumstances made Eliot powerfully aware of the large changes that marked the era. Growing up on a great estate where her father was land agent she knew the nature of a feudal society. At the same time, she also came into contact with newcomers attracted to the mines from outlying districts: the clashing of old and new social structures that begins *Silas Marner* was a part of her early experience. Eliot was equally familiar with the day-to-day tasks of farming life, with village shops and inns, the life of the canal that ran through the Arbury estate, and with the routines of the great house her father served. She was fortunate in coming into contact with a broad spectrum of the people and manners of her time; while her own family was comfortable economically, she came into contact on the one hand with the lives of the owners of the Arbury estate, and on the other with the plight of the poor and needy who tried to scratch a living there. The scenes and relationships of Eliot's childhood and adolescence provided a rich source of inspiration for the novels: the brothers and sisters, the uncles and aunts, the clergymen and landowners, her school friends and her reading all resurface in her writing; particularly in *Adam Bede*, characters and locations are closely associated with the people and places she knew. The influence of her strongly religious upbringing and education is apparent in all the novels.

Later in her life, circumstances continued to conspire to make her a touchstone for her era. The removal of her father to Coventry brought her into contact with the Brays, and hence with many of the most influential thinkers of her time: she met T. H. Huxley and Herbert Spencer, for example. Through her contact with the Brays she was commissioned to translate seminal works by Strauss and Feuerbach. She met John Chapman and began to write for the *Westminster Review* which had been recently edited by John Stuart Mill, and included among its contributors George Combe, the phrenologist, and Harriet Martineau, the notorious agnostic, with both of whom Eliot stayed briefly; it gave special prominence to Comtist philosophy, of which Harriet Martineau was an adherent, having translated and abridged his *Cours de philosophie positive.* In her relationship with Spencer, Eliot was exposed to the ideas of another proponent of the thinking of Auguste Comte; and through Huxley she was made strongly aware of the theories of Charles Darwin. The profoundest influence on her life was of course George Henry Lewes, whose thinking took its roots in Spinoza and Comte. In short, George Eliot was a focus for the clash between science and religion that helped to forge her world.

These diverse influences worked on, and changed, a mind formed according to conventional Christian ideas. The most important formative influence on the orthodox Christian outlook Eliot passionately held in her adolescence was her teacher at school in Nuneaton, Maria Lewis, a woman of strong evangelical beliefs, kind nature and severe habits. Though Eliot later parted from Christian practice, she retained the inclination to self-denial, self-abnegation and duty that Maria Lewis inculcated. The echoes of this ethos are easily visible in *The Mill on the Floss* in Maggie's love of Thomas à Kempis and in the tortures she endures later in the novel in finding her way among the conflicting claims of passion and duty. Dorothea, too, illustrates the allure of self-sacrifice when she flings herself blindly into the unyielding embrace of Casaubon's research; and she shows a mature self-command much greater than Maggie's in the precise ethical judgement she exercises in her relationship with Ladislaw later in the novel. The novels are liberally supplied with clergymen of the various shades Eliot had come into contact with, including Unitarians, Methodists and Anabaptists among others.

Eliot's outlook became transformed in a short time when she went to Coventry, though the change was long prepared and longer in formulation. The catalysts were two: the translation work she did, and the people she met. The Brays were instrumental in bringing her into contact with both. They introduced her to the exciting air of a general intellectual climate that was new to her. Eliot absorbed, criticised and adapted the contemporary ideas with which the Brays and their guests were thoroughly conversant. Among the most important of these ideas were those of Comte, whose influence on the Victorian era is hard to overstate. In particular, his thinking inspired Mill and Spencer as well as Lewes. More generally, his rejection of absolutist beliefs helped to open the way to the empiricism underlying new scientific and social theories, and his development of the religion of humanity prepared the way for more general humanist ideas. Positivism of different hues coloured the decades of the middle of the century. Eliot inhaled an intellectual air indelibly tinged with it.

Of Eliot's translations, the earliest and the latest were of works by Benedictus Spinoza, whose ideas were traced forward to Hegel, Strauss and Feuerbach in an article by Lewes. Eliot worked intermittently on translations of his works, including his *Tractatus Theologico-Politicus* of 1670 and his *Ethica* of 1677, for many years, beginning as early as the 1840s, before she began writing novels, and finally (and abortively) preparing *Ethica* for publication in 1878. Spinoza's empiricism, his ideas about religious belief and his sense of the human community link closely with the thinking of Comte. Something that Eliot owes more specifically to him, however, is her deterministic thinking on the relationship between individual freedom and necessity.

David Friedrich Strauss's *Das Leben Jesu Kritisch Bearbeitet*, a two-volume work published in 1835–6, questioned the historical and religious truth of the gospels; it argued that the gospels represented merely the efforts to represent the hopes of early Christians in legendary or mythical forms. Strauss saw Christianity not as revealed truth, but as an expression of man's need to find metaphysical explanations for his own human impulses and conflicts. The publication outraged the German academic world: though Strauss later retracted some of the force of his views by arguing that religion deals with ideas and not facts, he was nevertheless effectively debarred from academic life. By 1842, his ideas were scandalising England, too. Eliot spent nearly two years on the laborious work of translation, publishing in 1846 under the title *The Life of Jesus Critically Examined*. Though she found the task eventually tedious, she was nevertheless drawn to the views Strauss expressed.

Ludwig Feuerbach, who was a significant influence on Strauss, went a step further in *Das Wesen des Christentums*, published in 1841. He took the view that God is not an independent entity, but merely the projection of man's own consciousness, and Christianity no more than a reflection of man's own aspirations. According to Feuerbach's view, God is made in man's image and not vice versa. The attributes of God – such as love, omniscience, or virtue – are simply ways of representing needs inherent in man's nature. Thus the trappings of religious belief, the sacraments, miracles, rituals and so on, are a sham; they serve merely to conceal the anthropological truths from which they spring. Feuerbach influenced Karl Marx as well as Eliot, and it is not hard to see how his ideas became transmuted into the Marxian view of religion as the opium of the people. Denying the atheism of which he was accused, Feuerbach contended that it was merely the Christian encapsulation of God that he wished to reject and not God *per se*. However, there is no necessary place for a God of any denomination in his vision of a materialist world. Human society itself, in his view, contains the seeds of the impulse to good, and human nature has the inherent potential to attain an ideal goodness. Individual morality, then, is a question of properly defining one's place in society, developing a true sense of personal identity as part of a social group and thus making an appropriate contribution to human and social evolution.

Eliot's novels do not echo these ideas naively. She does not use them discursively. Rather, her absorption of the ideas of Spinoza, Strauss and Feuerbach makes itself felt in the moral issues revolved by Maggie and Dorothea, and even by Godfrey Cass. All of them are concerned with right behaviour, with the preservation of good relationships and with the need for a rigorously honest examination of motives. Yet, though principles traditionally associated with Christianity are frequently invoked and the name of God appears not infrequently, we feel little sense, whether in Eliot's characters or in the metalanguage of the novels, of God as a living entity immanent in the world. Clergymen appear, many of them good men, but they are judged from the standpoint of behaviour and not of faith or principle. Eliot also depicts the religious faith of the secular communities with sympathy; but here again she concerns herself with standards of conduct; simple piety holds little interest for her, and indeed, one of the most apparently pious of her characters, Nicholas Bulstrode, is one of her most deeply flawed. One of the more interesting of the minor characters in *Middlemarch* is Mr Farebrother: though he is presented as a man of character and sensitivity these qualities have nothing to do with his calling, and indeed the most powerful expression of his qualities is the quiet, unassuming renunciation of any right in the life of Mary Garth; this act of self-abnegation places him as the male Teresa of the novel, the counterpart of Dorothea – the type of the incalculably diffusive goodness that forges the social future.

The growth of agnosticism encouraged by the works of Feuerbach and Strauss intersected with developments in science. Well before Charles Darwin published *The Origin of Species* (*by Means of Natural Selection*) in 1859, a number of geologists and biologists had already begun to suspect that the biblical seven days might be something of an underestimate of the time required to fashion the earth and the human species that inhabited it together with all its other flora and fauna. Among them were T. H. Huxley and Herbert Spencer. Huxley was a biologist and polymath whose ideas about religion and philosophy had already led him towards agnosticism before he began to promote specifically Darwinist evolutionary theory. Spencer, the philosopher and sociologist, had already developed a theory of evolution that differed radically from Darwin's in assigning evolutionary change to inheritance rather than natural selection. Both men were known to Eliot, and she had a particularly close relationship with Spencer; her interest in science is a feature that distinguishes *Middlemarch* in both content – particularly in the passages concerning Lydgate's research – and style. However, it was with the publication of Darwin's book, in the year before *The Mill on the Floss* came out, that the implications of evolutionary theory burst on the world with such cataclysmic power as to boil into an intense and violent argument that is even now, a century and a half later, still simmering. The problem was essentially simple: Genesis could not be reconciled in any straightforward way with the slow process of development from amoeba to man. Associated as it was with rationalist, scientific and materialist thinking, evolution also meant the abolition of Heaven and it undercut the authority of the Ten Commandments. The intensity of the argument received its most vivid expression in the infamous meeting of the British Association for the Advancement of Science at Oxford University in 1860. There Bishop Samuel Wilberforce thought he saw the opportunity to quash the dangerously anti-religious evolutionary theory by ridicule, and inquired mockingly about the monkeys in Huxley's ancestry; however, he was demolished by a brilliant riposte when Huxley admitted that, faced with a choice between a monkey and a bishop for his ancestors, he would prefer the monkey. As in that instance, though the power of convention was strong, the evolutionists were often a little cleverer than their more staid opponents. Religious opposition notwithstanding, Darwinist theory gained ground.

So, too, did its ramifications. The intense intellectual dialogue of the period nurtured rapid development and cross-fertilisation of ideas. Darwin was influenced by the work of Feuerbach as he influenced others. Among them, relinquishing his own theories, Spencer accepted Darwin's and, indeed, was responsible for coining the phrase 'survival of the fittest' (*The Principles of Biology* (1864), vol. 1, p. 444) which captured the popular imagination more than Darwin's own 'natural selection'. Karl Marx in turn was influenced by Darwin and Spencer. In these exciting times philosophers and scientists of many shades coincided in a creative upsurge released by the promulgation of the evolutionary principle. Spencer's effort to construct a *Synthetic Philosophy* (in *First Principles*, 1862; *The Principles of Biology*, 2 vols, 1864–7; *The Principles of Psychology*, 1855; *The Principles of Sociology*, 3 vols, 1876–96; *The Principles of Ethics*, 2 vols, 1892–3) did not grow out of a tangential pet theory: it was in keeping with the intellectual ambience of the period. The principle of evolution made a direct impact on every area of sociology, biology, psychology and economics as well as on philosophy and religion.

Darwin's influence on social thinking was especially strong: what was valid for the human species should also, it was thought, be true of human society. The term 'sociology' was coined in 1830 by Comte in his *Cours de philosophie positive* (1830–42). He meant by it the scientific and specifically positivistic study of society, but it rapidly came to be used for the systematic study of the development and workings of human social life and social groups. By the 1870s and 1880s, Herbert Spencer was developing sophisticated theories applying evolutionary principles to both general and specific kinds of human organisation, finding direct correspondences between biological organisms and human society. The influence of these ideas on Eliot are most easily seen in *Middlemarch*, which makes clear correspondences between, for example, different systems of communications: the spread of gossip is comparable with the advance of the railways and with the contagion of cholera. Furthermore, the novel as a whole imagines a society evolving under the influence of the Teresa principle: good individuals such as Dorothea, the Garths and Farebrother play a role in steering society as a whole towards a higher, better level of existence. The novel was criticised for being too Darwinist: some of Eliot's reading public would have preferred a happy ending – no matter how unlikely – in which Dorothea and Lydgate would marry. The other novels, too, show the influence of Darwinist theory. A rational view of *The Mill on the Floss* is to see it as tracing the course of Maggie's moral evolution, and she and her brother appear to inhabit a significantly higher moral sphere than their materialistic parents do. *Silas Marner* bears on one questionable extrapolation of Spencer's theory of inheritance as the tool of evolution: the characterisation of the Cass brothers in contrast with Marner, Eppie and Nancy refutes the idea that nobility of birth equated with nobility of character.

Eliot's mind was a fertile medium for all these ideas. Her diverse kinds of work as well as her habits of mind encouraged the cross-fertilisation of different strands of thinking. For example, at about the same time that she was translating Feuerbach, she was also working on her unpublished translation of Spinoza's *Ethica*. These different forms of rationalist thought both worked on a mind well-versed during her childhood in the religious lore of her time. Another strand in her thinking linked the ideas of John Stuart Mill (her work on the *Westminster Review* followed upon his time as editor from 1836 to 1840 in a very practical way) with the democratic realism of Wordsworth and Scott. Her sense of social order grew out of a range of sources including the humanist ideas of Spinoza and Comte and the application of Darwinian principles to human society. Eliot was

immersed in many diverse aspects of the religious, social and political thinking of her time: she knew the thinkers personally and she
understood their ideas; and it is natural that her novels show their
traces.

The ideological background remains background, however. Her
novels contain ideas, but they are experiments in life, not ideological
theses. There is plenty of moralising in her writing, and some would
say too much, but there is no simple regurgitation of received ideas
or transcription of recalled discussions. Eliot's efforts are devoted to
realising a fictional world that will represent as accurately as possible
the real world she knew. Realism is always her aim, and ideas are sub-
servient to it. Her ideological vision emerges naturally from the characters and situations she develops. Thus in *Middlemarch* the use of
scientific imagery and the discussion of science arise from the development of the character of Lydgate; *Silas Marner* takes its impulse
from the dramatisation of a social phenomenon but extends far
beyond it.

Eliot's humanist ideas emerge not in discussion, but in her perception of character and in the balance of her moral outlook. No
simple oppositions of good and evil appear in her work: neither Tom
Tulliver, nor Stephen Guest, nor Nicholas Bulstrode, nor Godfrey
Cass, nor even Dunsey is condemned; each and every character is
treated with understanding and sympathy; in many very imperfect
characters, as well as in the central figures, the possibility of learning
from experience and aspiring to a higher moral condition is present.
Though her characters are often materialistic – the Tulliver aunts,
obsessed with their household goods, and Celia Brooke come to mind
– they are not therefore disparaged; and while religion and its agents
do not dominate the moral landscape, Eliot shows every sign of
valuing the impulse towards good and the power to encourage good
that they represent. The use made of the figure of St Teresa in *Middlemarch* is significant: she is valued not for her Catholicism, but for
exemplifying the ideals of self-sacrifice, duty and service. Eliot's intention is clear from her judgement of the work of Dickens, whom she
valued for his sympathy with the poor and his ability to depict them
vividly, for she thought that if he had been able to 'give us [the] psychological character [of his portraits], their conception of life and

their emotions, with the same truth as, their idiom and manners, his books would be the greatest contribution Art has ever made to the awakening of social sympathies' (quoted in Blind, *George Eliot*, London: W. H. Allen and Co., 1883, p. 107). In Eliot's novels, in contrast, psychological understanding is the first aim: hence the extended treatment of the moral scruples of Maggie and the qualms of Dorothea: even a Nicholas Bulstrode must, above all, be understood. Though the nature of Eliot's ideas developed, she consistently focuses on a single source of unhappiness or misjudgement, which may be generically called egoism. The view of the world that determines Rosamond's ideas is essentially the same as that which, according to Mrs Poyser, defines the mood of Mr Craig who is 'welly like a cock as thinks the sun's rose o' purpose to hear him crow' (*Adam Bede*, Chapter 18, p. 199). Egoism, however, is treated not as an evil, but as a common tendency of character that may often be moderated or conquered, as Fred Vincy exercises discipline over himself, or as Lydgate learns to compensate for Rosamond. In portraying flaws as well as in describing virtues of character or situation, Eliot maintains an emphasis on understanding in her novels.

Though she absorbed the most revolutionary ideas of her era, Eliot remained curiously conservative. She did not fit into the role of agitator. Her novels suggest that personal life is more significant than the public stage: Dorothea and Romola both devote themselves to small causes. For Eliot, the demands of duty take a near, practical and personal form. Lydgate relinquishes his scientific ambitions for the service of one who may, perhaps, be thought ill-deserving of his sacrifice; yet there is no question in Eliot's view that his decision is the right one, no matter what the loss to science, no matter how empty-headed Rosamond may be. In this respect too, then, Eliot avoids great ideas. Her expression of the religion of humanity takes the form of small events in small lives. Eliot's portrait of Maggie Tulliver shows an individual evolving; later, in the portrait of Dorothea, there is a much stronger consciousness of the social effect of action, but the source remains the evolution of Dorothea's personal life. This is not to diminish the importance of small deeds – Mordecai appears to speak for Eliot when he says in *Daniel Deronda*, 'the strongest principle of growth lies in human choice' (Volume 2, Book VI, Chapter

42, p. 404) – but to stress the preeminence for Eliot of the individual mind and character. Eliot remained, like the voice of her novels, complex and contradictory: humanist though she was, she did not accept Comte's theories in anything like totality; she believed in the religion of humanity to the extent of upholding the instinctive power of direct fellow-feeling, but she did not support his more systematic and structural ideas. Democratic though she was by nature, she showed little practical interest in electoral reform. And agnostic though she was, she continued to go to church when she felt inclined.

9

Some Critical Approaches

This chapter presents samples of criticism from a vast field of Eliot scholarship. Rather than attempt to deal with Eliot criticism in general, I have selected pieces that complement Part 1 of this book. The critics represented here deal with Eliot's narrative method, with her sense of history and with the question of gender. The earliest of the pieces is from Barbara Hardy's *Particularities: Readings in George Eliot* (London: Peter Owen, 1982) and deals with the development of Eliot's use of narrators. This topic has been touched on in Chapter 1 in considering the opening paragraphs of the novels; Hardy's essay carries the subject further and deals with additional novels. The second piece is a part of Chapter 4 of Michael Wheeler's *English Fiction of the Victorian Period 1830–1890* (Longman, 1985): this piece, entitled 'Incarnate history and unhistoric acts' refers particularly to *Silas Marner* and *Middlemarch*, and more briefly to *Romola* and *Daniel Deronda*, tracing Eliot's treatment of the impact of fictional history on her characters. Wheeler's analysis extends some of the comments made in Chapters 5 and 6. Finally, we consider an essay by Kate Flint on 'George Eliot and Gender', from *The Cambridge Companion to George Eliot* (ed. George Levine, CUP, 2001): it develops a topic the other critics – indeed, most critics – allude to more briefly.

Barbara Hardy

Barbara Hardy's *Particularities* is a collection of loosely related essays of which 'The Reticent Narrator' is a key example that illustrates the high quality of the work of this most authoritative critic. It covers a crucial issue in Eliot criticism: most readers are uneasily aware of the voice of the narrator in the novels, and unsure of their relationship with it or of its relationship with the author. Hardy's first purpose is to show by chronological analysis of the novels how Eliot's use of narrators developed and matured. Later in the essay, she also shows how the narrators reveal Eliot's changing perception of the nature of the novel as an art form and how they hint at much later developments in narrative technique.

At the outset, Hardy attempts to summarise the nature of the narrative voices in the novels generally. They are not, she says, like characters, for they have no personal involvement in plot: they stand above plot, telling the stories of different characters from an omniscient point of view; the only story they do not tell is their own – hence the 'Reticent' in the title of the essay. When moments of autobiography occur, they are too brief to map out a character. The narrators speak in various moods and voices, yet with a certain consistency across the whole of Eliot's body of fiction. They remain, however, voices rather than persons. This elusive narrative posture is not a function of the adoption of a pseudonym, for it appears in her work before she began to use 'George Eliot' as a pseudonym.

Hardy distinguishes Eliot's omniscient narrator from that of Dickens or Thackeray, and Eliot's narrative method from that of Austen or Charlotte Brontë. She illustrates the complexity of Eliot's attitude to her own names, and suggests that Eliot developed her androgynous persona in her anonymous journalism for a period of ten years before her pseudonym appeared in the two-volume edition of *Scenes of Clerical Life* in 1858. Hardy's contention is twofold: that the autobiographical element in the narrative voice diminishes in the course of Eliot's development as a novelist; and that the narrative voice moves from conscious masculinity to a more abstract mode. This is how Hardy sums up her thesis:

> There is a gradual diminution of autobiographical anecdote; it becomes generalized and eventually vanishes. There is also a gradual disappearance of the masculine allusions which identify the early narrators; they drop from explicit detail into implication, into a form of androgynous

address, with occasional female markings, and finally into an attempt
to speak carefully and comprehensively not for men or for women, but
for human nature.

(p. 128)

After this introductory analysis, Hardy proceeds to investigate individual works. Her approach is simple and persuasive. It consists of
comprehensively selecting and examining instances of narrative intru-
sion in the novels.

First Hardy considers the origins of the masculine narrator in Mary
Anne Evans's earliest work, commenting also on the 'technical self-
consciousness' (p. 129) with which Eliot handles the description and
introduction of characters in her work up to and including *Middlemarch*. Here she considers at some length the masculine identity of
the narrator, the businesslike tone and the comic anecdotal details of
autobiography that appear in *Scenes of Clerical Life*. As in her discussion of other novels, the analysis is pinned to specific evidence.

Turning to *Adam Bede*, Hardy displays a characteristic confidence
and precision in her opening assertion that 'the masculine identification is present in two details' (p. 132). She refers to the conversation
between the narrator and Gedge, a minor character who addresses his
words to 'Sir', and the paean to women in Chapter 33. Elsewhere,
however, Hardy finds that the generalised passages 'tend to be equiv-
ocally phrased, and transcend sexual differentiations' and that they
show 'the thinning down of authorial anecdote' (both p. 132). Here
Hardy introduces the concept of the 'free indirect style [that] merges
authorial narration with the idiolect of characters' (p. 132): this is her
academic description of that flexible movement, initiated in 'Janet's
Repentance', between the voice of the character and the voice of the
narrator that distinguishes Eliot's writing and underlies the complex
impression of sympathy and judgement her writing gives.

In *The Mill on the Floss* the process of development continues. The
masculine details are subdued, anecdote further diminished. Hardy
detects a special kind of emotion, one dissociated from specific personal experience, in the elaborate opening chapter: the address is to
the non-human world of nature, and the experience nothing like the
nostalgic recollection of childhood in *Scenes of Clerical Life*; at the

end of the chapter, dream, reminiscence and fiction merge in a creative whole. There are, however, echoes of Eliot's earlier style. The novel contains one generalised passage of masculine reference (Hardy refers here to Book One, Chapter 7) and one which has the ring of personal female experience (Book Six, Chapter 2).

One of the effects Hardy picks out as characteristic of Eliot's earlier writing is the use of anecdote in reminiscent passages. The last full anecdote, she notes, appears in the first chapter of *Silas Marner*, and has no masculine tones. In the succeeding novels, furthermore, there are no explicit masculine or feminine suggestions in the generalised passages.

In *Romola*, of course, there is no scope for authorial reminiscence for it is set in the fifteenth century. Where first-person narrative is used, it is in the plural. In the Proem Eliot hands the commentary over to a contemporary traveller, the Florentine Spirit, and the generalised passages in the novel as a whole take an impersonal third-person form.

There are, according to Hardy, no masculine references in *Felix Holt*. Two digressions in Chapter 49 show the development of Eliot's rhetoric. One of these, beginning with a portrait of Mrs Transome and moving on to Adam and Eve in Paradise, concludes with a childhood anecdote, nostalgic in mood but generalised and without specific gender characteristics. The other, which begins with Esther's feelings about Transome Court, deals with love in a carefully non-specific manner and considers a universal idea with the urgency of actual but general human experience. It is Hardy's view that these digressions are more subtle and the anecdotal quality less full than in the earlier novels.

Hardy describes *Middlemarch* as Eliot's 'most feminist' novel (p. 138) and finds in it another difference of approach. The discussion of Rosamond's mind in Chapter 43 is not gender-specific but 'emerges from a socially sensitive scrutiny of the conditions which create a woman's imaginative constructions' (p. 138); in other words, it demands both an understanding of how a woman's mind works and a broader understanding of the social world that bears upon it. Hardy refers also to the satirical portrait of Sir James Chettam in Chapter 2. Although she thinks the passage clearly emerges from a woman's mind, she considers it 'in keeping with the double time-sense of the novel' (p. 138) which deals with the late 1820s and early 1830s from the point of view of the late 1860s and early 1870s. The novel contains 'no narrator's anecdote, but . . . continues the subdued narrations . . . used in . . . *Felix Holt*' (p. 139). Both novels, she concludes, use vignette and allegory, achieving 'modes of condensed narration which brim with the pressure of personal experience, but insist on reticence' (p. 139).

In *Daniel Deronda* Hardy finds a similar reticence that invites comparison with that of Tolstoy. There are 'miniature narratives . . . like good metaphors, in which vehicle is not merely subdued to tenor, but asserts a vitality of its own' (p. 140). As usual, Hardy offers specific examples with persuasive focus. Thus her general comments carry conviction when she argues that in the last four novels 'there is an insistence on undifferentiated humanity, on man and woman' (p. 140), but that it is not until *Daniel Deronda* that there appear 'references which carefully disclaim masculinity and femininity, and explicitly link men and women' (pp. 140–1). Daniel, containing within him feminine as well as masculine features, has a stronger discursive voice than has any of Eliot's earlier characters; the role of the omniscient narrator is correspondingly subdued.

Hardy clearly sees in the novels a pattern that works gradually towards a more refined narrative method. She links Eliot and Thomas Hardy as the only great Victorians who never use autobiographical narrative – thus distinguishing themselves from Defoe, Richardson, Charlotte Brontë and Thackeray – yet write one short story as first-person narrative. Having considered this exceptional work, 'The Lifted Veil', Hardy relates it to *Daniel Deronda*, finding in the last novel a deeper, more intense communication between the characters than had appeared in earlier novels. In the light of her analysis of the relationship of Gwendolen and Daniel, she reviews the earlier novels and notes in them what is not told: the reticences in the fictional lives of her protagonists. 'Attention', she says, 'is often drawn to the silences' (p. 144) by contrast with the talkativeness, often comic, of many of the minor characters. She uses as one of several examples of a further dimension of narrative reticence the love of Tom Tulliver for Lucy, which is communicated by hint and suggestion and never explicated. As a final, telling example, Hardy refers to the submerged story of Mr Brooke's love life, hinted at only once in his trivial loquaciousness.

George Eliot has, in Hardy's view, a seminal role in the development of narrative method. She passionately pursues the 'art of reticence' (p. 145) in portraying characters who tell their stories, in adopting narrators who tell everything except their own stories, and in refusing to allow her name to appear on her books. Prior to the appearance of Eliot's novels, Hardy suggests, 'all the stories are told by the end of the story' (p. 146). In choosing a more reticent narrative mode, Eliot uses Victorian conventions, yet nevertheless 'strain[s] towards the conventions and forms of modernism' (p. 146).

Barbara Hardy's is an exemplary piece of critical writing. Though her analysis is light, it is specific and evidently based on thorough knowledge and understanding of the novels; her logic is iron. Her close knowledge of Eliot's work is apparent in the detail and precision of her remarks. She creates links between the content, style and technique of the novels, and their biographical and bibliographical background, to develop a clear argument that moves easily from analysis to evaluation. Though the book from which this discussion comes is quite loosely organised, there are cross-references among its chapters, and the whole is well worth reading both as an example of critical style and for its ideas about Eliot.

Michael Wheeler

Michael Wheeler's essay on 'Incarnate history and unhistoric acts' is one section of Chapter 4 of a general book about *English Fiction of the Victorian Period 1830–1890*. Its function is to place Eliot's work in her literary and historical context. Appropriately, therefore, Wheeler finds it convenient to make comparative reference from time to time to other writers such as Gaskell and Trollope. Wheeler's purpose determines the structure of the essay, which begins by outlining a general pattern of ideas and concludes with analysis of the novels. The title of the section is built on two quotations. 'Incarnate history' is taken from 'The Natural History of German Life', Eliot's

article for the *Westminster Review* on the work of the German sociologist Wilhelm Heinrich von Riehl (quoted on p. 121). 'Unhistoric
acts' comes, of course, from the last sentence of *Middlemarch*.

Wheeler begins with Trollope's assessment of Eliot as a philosopher
rather than a portrait painter; part of his purpose is to contrast the
two novelists. Wheeler explores the idea of Eliot as a 'thinker: medi-
tative, moral, and philosophical' (p. 120) and points out that her
thinking always has a historical dimension. Not a Christian, she was
nevertheless fascinated by the history of religion in the West; her
novels focus on the history of reform in England; *Middlemarch* shows
her knowledge of the history of science; and *Daniel Deronda* explores
racial history.

The meaning of history stands at the heart of Eliot's ideas, according to Wheeler. He notes her habit of calling her stories histories,
implying that she sees her novels as serious works that communicate
philosophical ideas and represent the way people actually behave. The
kernel of Wheeler's argument is that the meaning of history – most
specifically its implications for the principles of determinism and free
will – is the driving force of the novels. Thus history in the form of
the individual's own past determines his future behaviour; but of
course he himself is responsible for his own past, and thus necessity
and freedom may coexist. This paradox is supported by quotations
from several of the novels. So, too, is the emphasis on duty that Eliot
keeps constantly before us; here Eliot's view of history intersects with
her humanist principles. Further extrapolations follow: the perfor-
mance of duty demands a sense of others' needs and hence runs
counter to an egoistic perception of existence; the device of confession is important because it combines admission of personal wrong-
doing with recognition of the rights and powers of another
individual. Confession is a motif sufficiently important to demand
illustration, and there is analysis of the way it is used in *Daniel
Deronda*, 'Janet's Repentance' and *Middlemarch*. In these moments of
confession Wheeler finds Eliot's characters confronting what is essential in their own individual history.

Next Wheeler turns his attention to social history. He focuses on
the influence of the Preface to the 1800 edition of *Lyrical Ballads*, in
which Wordsworth proposes to treat of 'common life' (p. 123), and

he refers to the comparable purposes Mrs Gaskell expressed in the Preface to *Mary Barton*. He notes Eliot's consistent interest in ordinary characters, but stresses too that they harbour aspirations beyond their circumstances. He quotes *The Mill on the Floss* as an example of this abiding interest in the conflict between the ideal and the real that also appears in the later novels.

The concluding section of the general discussion deals with social history. Wheeler sees Eliot as 'fundamentally gradualist rather than catastrophist' (p. 126). This is in keeping with Eliot's sense of the unhistoric acts that add up to a life. Yet, oddly, those unhistoric acts often arise from moments of individual crisis in which reality is perceived sharply and delusion swept away; in which, on the symbolic level, light cuts through darkness.

Up to this point, Wheeler's essay is concise, cohesive and comprehensive. His argument presents Eliot's sense of history as underlying her moral vision and her characteristic methods of presenting characters and their lives. Now he turns to analysis of specific novels, beginning with *Silas Marner*.

What follows is a persuasive analysis of the way history influences the two main narrative threads of the novel. Wheeler considers how Eliot handles the technical difficulties of blending the stories of Silas Marner and Godfrey Cass, and shows how the thematic significance of their individual histories emerges from the narrative method. He draws parallels between Marner's buried history at Lantern Yard, the burial of Dunstan and the gold, and the burial of Godfrey's first marriage. The thematic pattern of the novel is to reconcile the past through confession, and thus achieve regeneration by restoring natural human relationships. The analysis of the novel thus reflects precisely the considerations Wheeler has discussed in the general introductory section of his essay.

Despite the obvious contrasts between *Silas Marner* and *Romola* Wheeler sees a common symbolic pattern in the novels. He shows briefly that both novels are marked by light/dark symbolism, that in both of them history is marked by an extraordinary event, and that Romola is like Silas in her alienation and her need to make a new life. This part of the essay is transitional, and has the quality of a set of extended notes.

Wheeler devotes more space to his next topic, *Middlemarch*. He notices in this novel, too, the importance of a buried past: Edward Casaubon is locked in it; the names of Ladislaw and Naumann, conversely, stress their involvement in the present. As in the earlier novels, light and dark carry symbolic meaning, but more than previously are associated with spiritual hunger. The device of confession is crucial in this novel, too, particularly in the story of Bulstrode. However, Wheeler picks out as distinctive in this novel Eliot's stress on the dominance of the actual world; it is set in a period of great changes that impinge on the lives of the characters; equally, their own circumstances present challenges. In the crises that confront them, both general and personal, Lydgate, Bulstrode and Dorothea illuminate moral dilemmas and the moral qualities required to deal with them. In the discussion of *Middlemarch* Wheeler reverts to the terms of his title: Ladislaw embodies the sense of 'incarnate history' in contrast with Casaubon's absorption in the dead past; and Dorothea expresses in her devotion to 'unhistoric acts' Eliot's faith in the principle of moral duty.

Daniel Deronda receives briefer treatment. Wheeler acknowledges nevertheless that it is 'in several respects George Eliot's *summa* . . . a novel whose massive simplicity contrasts with the complexity of her study of English provincial life, but which distils may of her profoundest themes and ideas' (p. 137). Drawing comparisons with Henry James and Anthony Trollope, and alluding to Carlyle and Ruskin, Wheeler attempts briefly to place Eliot in context as 'the greatest moralist among Victorian novelists' (p. 138).

Wheeler's study ends with the phrases of his title. Thus, though patently part of a larger design, his study of George Eliot has a shape of its own. Though he perhaps need not strive so hard for neatness, he succeeds unquestionably in showing how the awareness of history lies at the heart of Eliot's work.

Kate Flint

Kate Flint's essay in *The Cambridge Companion to George Eliot* employs less perceptible artistry. She takes a direct approach to the question of gender that colours all recent criticism, including the essays considered above. She draws on the sociological ideas of Jane Flax as a measure by which to assess the approach to gender the novels reveal. 'George Eliot and Gender' is a considered discussion of the perceived clash between Eliot's unconventional way of life and her comparatively conservative attitudes. The discussion thus has a biographical as well as a critical aspect. With such intellectual powers herself, why does Eliot not take a bolder stance towards the moral choices faced by her female protagonists?

The introductory section of the essay begins with *Romola*, focusing on the moment when the protagonist turns aside from the glorious promise of intellectual and moral independence to embark instead on a life of self-renunciation. This Flint describes as 'one of the most disheartening moments in all of Eliot's writing' (p. 159). She develops the problem by references to the perceptions of Eliot's biographer, Mathilde Blind, and to Florence Nightingale, both of whom were among those puzzled by and discontented with Eliot's fondness for the principle of resignation and her failure to find more productive roles for her heroines to play in society. This 'reluctance, or inability, to deliver up unequivocally feminist messages' (p. 161) is what the essay seeks then to explain.

The first and perhaps most important of the factors Flint offers is Eliot's desire to avoid publishing work which could be evaluated as specifically a woman's writing. She notes that in the essay on 'Silly Novels by Lady Novelists' of 1856, Eliot's argument appears to prefer universal values as against gendered points of view. Flint does not mention in this connection, nor does she need to, the obvious fact of Eliot's choice of pseudonym; she defers this basic point until the end of the essay.

A second explanation relates to Eliot's realism. Eliot is deeply conscious of social conditions, very aware of social responsibilities, and concerned in her fiction to represent these faithfully. The reference to Dorothea's environment at the end of *Middlemarch* as an 'imperfect social state' is adduced as testimony to Eliot's will to confront the realities of the actual world. Not for Eliot, then, the construction of idealised or utopian fantasies, nor even the representation of exceptional or abnormal circumstances or people: she wished to represent what was typical. The implication is that Eliot avoided presenting in her work the actuality or prospect of a kind of independence that was not a practical possibility for most women. Eliot was evidently painfully conscious of the clash between the injustices of her time and the duties of practical life, and found herself out of sympathy with campaigners with a more simplistic perception of the nature of society. Thus she refused to support John Stuart Mill's petition that women should have the vote on equal footing with men: though she felt that women in general were disadvantaged compared with men, she saw that as an opportunity to practise greater selflessness. Flint finds only one area in which Eliot aligns herself with an identifiably feminist issue, and that is education. *The Mill on the Floss* shows, in its portrayal of the differentiation in education between Tom and Maggie, Eliot's discomfort with a practice that appears in the novel both unfair and inappropriate to the characters: Maggie would revel in the education that she is denied and that Tom has foisted upon him. In *Middlemarch*, Dorothea is drawn to Casaubon by intellectual aspiration. Even on this issue, Eliot's position is complicated. Her correspondence with Emily Davies, who founded Girton College, reveals her suspicion that learning may be unfeminine. However, she shows the consciousness that masculine and feminine traits may be shared by both sexes. The portrayal of Silas Marner's tenderness towards Eppie demonstrates Eliot's understanding that the feelings conventionally associated with women are not restricted exclusively to them.

The introductory section of the essay concludes by suggesting that some of the contradictions that appear in Eliot's position may result from applying to her work the inappropriate standards of twentieth-century feminism. Flint is perhaps in danger of inconsistency here, since her discussion opened with references to the doubts of Eliot's contemporaries. Nevertheless, her caution is one that it seems wise to heed. Furthermore, it leads to the statement of a common factor between Eliot's work and current feminist thinking: Eliot's sensitivity to the interaction between gender, community and ideology; feminist theory, as expressed in the words of Jane Flax, sees gender as a function of changing social processes. In both positions Flint sees comparable 'organicist assumptions' such as Eliot outlines in her essay on 'Notes on Form in Art'.

Middlemarch makes the starting point of the second part of Flint's essay as *Romola* started the first. Flint uses Rosamond Vincy and Dorothea, and Lydgate's view of them, to explore the process of sexual stereotyping. She sees Lydgate's judgements as conditioned by conventional views of feminine roles, quoting his revealing perception that Miss Brooke fails to see things from 'the proper feminine angle' (p. 164). In contrast with Lydgate's relationship with Rosamond, in which there is neither equality nor sharing between the partners, the relationship between Dorothea and Will reveals mutual support. There is some discussion, too, of Dorothea's wider role of exemplifying the potential of women to play an important part in the process of social evolution.

Flint moves on to consider the social function of the key figure of the mother. She sees the role of mother in Eliot's work as representing the principle of duty in its highest form. However, motherhood is only one among many valid social functions, and Eliot rejects differentiation of value between different kinds of contribution: one kind of work is inherently no better than another, and people must find the kind of work appropriate to them. Eliot's attitude to her own work illustrates the idea. Never a biological mother herself, she regarded her fictional characters as spiritual children and spoke of *The Mill on the Floss* as her youngest child. In letters to younger women who followed her ideas, she signed herself 'Mother', and her letters show that she was conscious of thus redirecting her maternal feelings. In Flint's view motherhood is an important concept for Eliot because it expresses, in a particularly strong form, the virtue of sympathy that she often commends. However, Eliot takes a critical view of the conventional popular Victorian perception of motherhood. Many examples in the novels show the failure of motherhood: Molly Farren is more devoted to opium than to her child; Hetty Sorrel abandons her baby. These instances show that Eliot perceives motherhood and the feelings associated with it as fluid and variable, not absolute; nature offers not one, but many solutions. *Daniel Deronda* has an excellent example in the statement by Princess Alchirisi that her feelings as a mother are her own, and not necessarily what other women would feel. This shows both Eliot's awareness of variety of feeling and her sense of the social pressure on women to conform to tradition. Mrs

Transome's feelings towards Harold in *Felix Holt* develop the idea, stressing that women are larger than motherhood, and that restriction to the role of motherhood can be damaging. From this point of view, Flint argues, Eliot presents motherhood as potentially a form of 'emotional bondage' (p. 168) and a source of subjection to men.

The discussion of *Felix Holt* turns to gender differentiation in personal relationships, contrasting the passivity of Esther with the archetypal masculinity that Felix Holt shares with Adam Bede. Flint notes that Felix's radicalism about the social position of women raises a further question implicit in the novel: whether the nature as well as the status of women is determined rather by cultural and social factors than by heredity. She finds in Eliot's much earlier essay on Fuller and Wollstonecraft the basis for the ideas raised in the relationship between Felix and Esther. In this novel, inequality between the sexes is expressed in the idea of love as a form of bondage: in *Daniel Deronda* it is expressed, in the portrait of Grandcourt, in the more violent form of moral and psychological bullying; the crucial requirement in Esther's development is to learn to think for herself and distrust conventional patterns. This love of independence of thought runs throughout Eliot's writing – in her essay on silly novels and in Adam Bede's delusion that Hetty Sorrel's physical beauty must express beauty of character. Flint sees Eliot's dedication to independence of spirit also in her strict adherence to integrity in the style of the writing in the novels. She notes how Eliot generally avoids convention in her plots. Flint finds *Romola* disappointing in this respect as at the beginning of the essay, but praises most of Eliot's endings for their 'defiant [avoidance of] preexistent fictional patterns' (p. 172); she cites in particular the avoidance of orthodox romantic closures in *The Mill on the Floss* and *Middlemarch*. The earlier of these novels she describes as 'a kind of anti-*Bildungsroman*' (p. 173), while the later book refuses to find a suitable husband for Dorothea.

Flint then develops her ideas in relation to *Danield Deronda*, which she considers 'the most eloquent, and radical, of all [Eliot's] treatments of gender' (p. 173). She cites Anna Clay Beecher's sequel, *Gwendolen: or Reclaimed* as evidence that the public wanted a happy ending. In Eliot's novel, however, Flint finds plot used to work out a range of patterns of imaginative potentiality that mingle affective and socioeconomic impulses. Grandcourt views Gwendolen as an economic counter in a world dominated by men interested in power. In his eyes, women and men can never be equal; his sadistic behaviour towards Gwendolen reveals his instrumental view of her as of other women and acts as a condemnation of the unequal balance of power in the gender relations of the Victorian world. The plot underlines the point by relocating the viewpoint of the novel, and by refusing Gwendolen the release of widowhood that Dorothea benefits from. Flint goes on to show that the novel discusses male stereotyping as well as female. Daniel is not the conventional male, but shows marked feminine characteristics; the novel employs him to explore the validity of feminine qualities such as sympathy. His story follows the pattern of a romantic quest, while Gwendolen stands by, feeling insignificant and in need of his guidance. While she finds herself rooted in an uncongenial social system in England, he opts for exclusion from society. The goals of both remain unachieved.

The final section of Flint's essay returns to the writing of Jane Flax, arguing that feminist writing should not simply criticise, but should attempt to compensate for, the consequences of male domination. She sees Eliot's choice of a male pseudonym is significant: Eliot places herself outside female experience, adopts a tone of male authority, and locates her narration in a broader realm of sympathies than is easily available from a gender-specific narrative viewpoint. From this privileged imaginative position, Eliot can pick out, as if objectively, central social injustices and their effects. Her novels offer no simple solutions, for she recognises the interdependence of complex and often contradictory factors in an organic social structure.

Kate Flint's essay adopts an avowedly feminist perspective. It discovers in Eliot, however, no simple feminist message. Rather, it unfolds novels that develop a range of narrative threads including education, personal romantic relationships and motherhood, and it reveals a mature, broad understanding of the social environment within which gender-specific behaviour develops. Rather than a feminist, Eliot emerges as a humanist. This we have probably understood as a general idea already; but our understanding of Eliot's humanism is deepened by the feminist perspective Flint applies to her work.

These three critical essays give a sense of the variety of style as well as of subject that critics apply to Eliot. Her work is rich and responds to very distinct kinds of analysis. Nevertheless, there are common features: all three critics refer to the gender issue, 'the woman question' as it is frequently called; all of them refer to the lacunae, or silences, in the novels; all refer to the device of confession; and all of them perceive a significant relationship between Eliot's fiction and her own actual world. These, then, are central features of Eliot's work. As you extend your study of her novels, you will find it interesting to see how other critics treat these key topics in their own way and form a variety of points of view.

Further Reading

Other than the novels discussed in this book, the most approachable of Eliot's novels is *Adam Bede*. It would be a good idea to read also the early *Scenes of Clerical Life*, and the much-discussed story 'The Lifted Veil'. Of the later novels, *Daniel Deronda* is very highly regarded and there are those who consider it superior to *Middlemarch*. *Felix Holt* is well-known and inhabits much the same general territory as *Middlemarch*, but with a very different theme. *Romola*, though perhaps the least widely read of Eliot's novels, has its devotees who consider it unjustly neglected. However, Eliot was incapable of pointless writing. All of her novels are worth the time and attention careful reading demands.

As I have explained, it is hard to find a precise contemporary for Eliot. Anthony Trollope's Barchester series of novels is closest in time but contrasts sharply with Eliot's writing in almost every respect. Among Victorian writing in general there is a wealth of riches. You should certainly include Dickens in your reading list: perhaps *Oliver Twist* (1837–9) or *David Copperfield* (1849–50) among the earlier novels, and *Hard Times* (1854) or *Our Mutual Friend* (1864–5) among the later. Thackeray is worth reading too, and *Vanity Fair* (1847–8) illustrates a quite different moral world from that of Eliot's novels. The novels of George Meredith offer another contrast: *Beauchamp's Career* (1875) is perhaps his best work, and *The Egoist* (1879) compares interestingly with Eliot's novels because of its theme. A different approach is to try to place Eliot in the tradition of women's writing: this would mean reading the work of Austen, the Brontë sisters, Gaskell and Virginia Woolf.

There are many biographical works available. The earliest is probably Mathilde Blind's interesting and fluent *George Eliot* (1883). Another important source is J. W. Cross, *George Eliot's Life as Related in her Letters and Journals* (1885). An interesting more recent work is Kathryn Hughes, *George Eliot: The Last Victorian* (Fourth Estate, 1998). If you prefer to begin with a more general introduction, try John Purkis, *A Preface to George Eliot* (Harlow: Longman, 1985).

The best place to begin your reading of criticism is with the examples discussed in Chapter 9. 'The Reticent Narrator' is from Barbara Hardy, *Particularities: Readings in George Eliot* (London: Peter Owen, 1982), which discusses several aspects of Eliot's work. Hardy's writing is always lucid and stimulating, and you could go on to explore her other writings on Eliot, especially another complete book, *The Novels of George Eliot: A Study in Form* (London: Athlone Press, 1994). The second essay discussed, 'Incarnate history and unhistoric acts', comes from Michael Wheeler's *English Fiction of the Victorian Period 1830–1890* (Longman, 1985), a useful book for studying the literary context of Eliot's novels. Finally, *The Cambridge Companion to George Eliot* (ed. George Levine, CUP, 2001) deals with several different aspects of Eliot's writing in essays by a number of critics, from which Kate Flint's 'George Eliot and Gender' was selected for discussion.

Beyond this point the field becomes very broad indeed. There is a useful selection of criticism in George C. Creeger, *George Eliot: A Collection of Critical Essays* (Prentice-Hall, 1970). Another useful source is Lucie Armitt's review of criticism in *George Eliot: Adam Bede, The Mill on the Floss, Middlemarch* (Cambridge: Icon Books, 2000). Among recent criticism, the idea of history in the novels is developed in Hao Li, *Memory and History in George Eliot* (Basingstoke: Palgrave Macmillan, 2000). An interesting perspective is Nancy Henry's *George Eliot and the British Empire* (Cambridge, UK/New York: CUP, 2002). This book considers the significance of Eliot's status as a wealthy investor in colonial stocks and a surrogate mother to emigrant sons, and explores the effect of her consciousness of colonialism on the novels. It spends most of its analytical effort on *Daniel*

Deronda, but also has interesting passages on the other novels. The widening range of recent criticism illustrates the richness of Eliot's work. Every generation finds its own new ways of interpreting the novels and subjecting them to the scrutiny of its own perspectives.

You will also find it interesting to consider Eliot's work in relation to Victorian life and literature, and a number of recent books offer ways into this vast subject. Among them you might consider Rick Rylance, *Victorian Psychology and British Culture, 1850–1880* (OUP, 2000), and Harry E. Shaw, *Narrating Reality: Austen, Scott, Eliot* (Ithaca, NY: Cornell University Press, 1999).

Index*

Antigone 159
Armitt, Lucie, *George Eliot: Adam Bede,
      The Mill on the Floss,
      Middlemarch* 208
Arnold, Matthew 181
Austen, Jane 193

Babbage, Charles 175
Beecher, Anna Clay, *Gwendolen: or
      Reclaimed* 204
Bible, the 27, 28, 133, 152, 186
   Adam and Eve 156, 195
   Book of Genesis 186
   Book of Samuel 149
   Book of Tobit 101
   Eve 155
   Revelation of St John 50
Blackwood, John 3, 176, 177
Blackwood's Magazine 176
Blessed Virgin 19, 20, 23, 27
Blind, Mathilde, *George Eliot* 190,
      201, 208
Bodichon, Barbara 178
Bray, Cara 173, 182, 184
Bray, Charles 173, 182, 184
British Association for the
      Advancement of Science
      187
Brontë
   Charlotte 193, 196
   sisters 182, 208
Browning, Robert 178, 181
Bunyan, John 27
   Pilgrim's Progress, The 12
Burne-Jones, Edward 177, 178

Carlyle, Thomas 200
Chapman, John 174, 183

Chapman, Susanna 174–5 *passim*,
      183
Collins, Wilkie 175
Combe, George 183
Communist Manifesto 100
Comte, Auguste 112, 114, 184, 188,
      191
   Cours de philosophie positive 183,
      187
Cornhill Magazine 178
Coventry Herald 173
Creeger, George C., *George Eliot: A
      Collection of Critical Essays* 208
Creon 159
Cross, John 179, 208
   *George Eliot's Life as Related in her
      Letters and Journals* 208
Cyrus 159

Darwin, Charles 114, 183
   The Origin of Species 186, 187
Davies, Emily 202
Defoe, Daniel 196
Dickens, Charles 175, 181, 182, 189,
      193, 208
   David Copperfield 208
   Hard Times 208
   Oliver Twist 208
   Our Mutual Friend 208
Durade, Albert 174

Eliot, George
   Adam Bede x, 113, 173, 176, 177,
      182, 190, 194, 204, 207
   allusion 27
   characters 32–59, 55–7, 83–4, 145
   Christianity 138–9, 163–4
   comedy 25, 112, 163

---

* For ease of reference, page numbers of source material for the passages under discussion
  are given in [square] brackets.

Daniel Deronda   113, 178, 190, 192, 196, 198, 200, 203, 204, 207
determinism   164–5
duty   111, 114, 118, 141, 165, 198
egoism   140, 165, 190, 198
Felix Holt, the Radical   178, 195, 196, 203–4
humanism   164
imagery   66, 98
Impressions of Theophrastus Such   179
irony   29, 55, 56, 114, 123
'Janet's Repentance'   176, 198
marriage   112, 162, 164
morality   27, 110, 117–44, 145
'Mr Gilfil's Love Story'   176
narrative method   27, 55, 56, 114–5
naturalism   54, 55, 56
nature   25–6, 140
'Notes on Form in Art'   202
past, the   26, 139, 141, 163, 165
relationships   60–88, 112, 162
Romola   178, 192, 195, 198, 201, 203, 204, 207
satire   112
Scenes of Clerical Life   176, 193, 194, 207
'Silly Novels by Lady Novelists'   201
society   26, 84, 89–116, 138–9, 145
structure   28
style   27–8
symbolism   55, 58
'The Essence of Christianity'   138, 175
'The Life of Jesus Critically Examined'   174, 184
'The Lifted Veil'   176, 196, 207
'The Sad History of Amos Barton'   176
work   111
Emerson, Ralph Waldo   173
Evans, Christiana   174
Evans, Isaac   174, 179

Evans, Robert   171–4 *passim*, 182

Faucit, Helen   178
Feuerbach, Edward   138, 164, 181–91 *passim*
   Das Wesen des Christentums   175, 185
Fielding, Henry   54, 56, 55
   Tom Jones   56
Flax, Jane, 'George Eliot and Gender'   192, 201–5 *passim*, 208
Flint, Kate, 'George Eliot and Gender',   192, 200–6, 208
Fuller, Margaret   204

Gaskell, Elizabeth   197, 208
   Mary Barton   198
Gender   203

Hardy, Barbara
   Particularities: Readings in George Eliot   208
   The Novels of George Eliot: A Study in Form   208
   'The Reticent Narrator'   192–7
Hardy, Thomas   196
Hennell, Charles   173
Henry, Nancy, *George Eliot and the British Empire*   208
Hughes, Kathryn, *George Eliot: The Last Victorian*   208
Hunt, Thornton   175–6
Huxley, Thomas Henry   175, 178, 182, 186, 187

James, Henry   177, 200

Kempis, Thomas à   124, 183

Levine, George (ed.), *The Cambridge Companion to George Eliot*   192, 200, 208
Lewes, George Henry   9, 175, 183
   Problems of Life and Mind   179
Lewis, Maria   172, 183
Li, Hao, *Memory and History in George Eliot*   208
Liggins, Joseph   177

Maid's Tragedy, The   27
Martineau, Harriet   183
Marx, Karl   185, 187
Mazzini, Giuseppe   175
Meredith, George   181, 208
  Beauchamp's Career   208
  Egoist, The   208
Middlemarch
  [7–8] Dorothea Brooke introduced
    16–25
  [5–6] Saint Theresa   23–5
  [13–14] Dorothea and Celia sort
    their mother's jewels   46–54
  [83–4] Will Ladislaw's prospects
    52–4
  [267–9] Rosamond's perception of
    Lydgate   73–82
  [425] Dorothea links her arm with
    Casaubon's   81–2
  [741–2] social reputation in
    Middlemarch   101–7
  [735–6] Celia's perception of
    Dorothea's widowhood   107–10
  [614–15] Bulstrode's fear   131–5
  [264] the pier-glass   136
  [211] moral stupidity   137–8
  [837–8] the fate of Dorothea
    155–61
  characters   18 *ff*, 46–54
  comedy   77, 103, 106, 108
  duty   109, 134–7
  egoism   80–2, 134–7
  imagery   132
  irony   18, 20–1, 53, 76–7, 101–6
    passim
  marriage   21, 103, 107–9, 155, 157
  morality   131–8
  narrative method   18 *ff*, 50–1,
    53–4, 103–4
  past, the   131
  relationships   73–82
  religion   20–4
  society   18 *ff*, 101–10, 156, 157–61
    passim
  style   22, 77, 103–4
  symbolism   51
Mill, John Stuart   175, 183, 188,
  202

Mill on the Floss, The
  [53–4] the Floss and Dorlcote Mill
    described   4–10
  [119–20] the cutting of Maggie's
    hair   33–40
  [437–8] conversation between
    Maggie and Philip   60–7
  [619–20] Maggie's reputation in St
    Ogg's   90–2
  [611] Tom's face   95–6
  [603–4] Stephen pleas with Maggie
    119–20
  [656–7] nature's ravages repaired
    146–50
  characters   33–40
  Christianity   118, 122, 150
  comedy   7
  duty   123
  egoism   123
  imagery   66
  irony   49–50, 66, 94, 96, 123
  metaphor   65
  morality   118–24, 149
  nature   5–10 *passim*, 147–8
  narrative method   5–10 *passim*,
    93–5
  past, the   5–10 *passim*
  relationships   60–7, 120
  satire   94
  society   90–6, 153
  structure   9–10
  symbolism   37–9, 65
Millais, Sir John Everett   178
Milnes, Richard   178

Nightingale, Florence   175, 201

Pascal, Blaise   18, 22
Positivism   184
  see also Mill, John Stuart
Problems of Life and Mind   179
Purkis, John, *A Preface to George Eliot*
  208

Reform Bill   107, 178, 181
Richardson, Samuel   196
Riehl, Wilhelm Heinrich von   198
  Natural History of German Life, The
    197

Rossetti, Dante Gabriel   177
Ruskin, John   200
Rylance, Rick, *Victorian Psychology and British Culture, 1850–1880*   209

Savonarola, Girolamo   178
Scott, Sir Walter   113, 182, 188
Shakespeare, William
    King John   152
    The Tempest   153
Shaw, Harry E., *Narrating Reality: Austen, Scott, Eliot*   209
Silas Marner
    [5–6] the community of Raveloe   10–16
    [20–1] Silas's solitary life and his pot   40–5
    [114–16] Silas brings the infant to the Red House   67–73
    [23–4] the Cass family of Raveloe   96–101
    [169–70] Godfrey tries to claim Eppie   125–6
    [181–3] Eppie's wedding   150–5
    characters   40–5
    duty   65–6
    egoism   129
    imagery   98
    irony   14, 98, 99, 129
    marriage   153
    morality   124–31, 153
    narrative method   14 *ff*, 45, 99
    nature   129, 152
    past, the   10–15 *passim*, 130–1
    realism   16, 66, 100
    religion   10–15 *passim*, 101
    relationships   67–73
    society   10–15 *passim*, 96–101, 126, 129
    structure   13–14
    style   14–15
    symbolism   44–5

Spencer, Herbert   175, 178, 182, 184, 186, 187, 188
Spinoza, Benedictus   175, 183, 184, 185, 188
    Ethica   175, 184, 188
    Tractatus Theologico-Politicus   184
Stowe, Harriet Beecher, *Uncle Tom's Cabin*   181
Strauss, David Friedrich   173, 181–91 *passim*
    Das Leben Jesu Kritisch Bearbeitet   174, 184

Taylor, Jeremy   18, 22
Tennyson, Alfred Lord   177, 178, 181
Teresa of Avila, Saint   23–4, 25, 117, 137, 163, 186, 188, 189
Thackeray, William Makepeace   181, 182, 193, 196, 208
    Vanity Fair   208
Theresa of Lisieux   15
Tilley, Elizabeth   174
Tolstoy, Leo   196
Trollope, Anthony   181, 182, 197, 198, 200
Turgenev, Ivan   178

Victoria, Queen   161, 181

Westminster Review   174, 175, 176, 183, 188, 198
Wheeler, Michael
    Fiction of the Victorian Period 1830–1890   192, 208
    'Incarnate History and Unhistoric Acts'   192, 197–200
Wilberforce, Bishop Samuel   187
Wollstonecraft, Mary   204
Woolf, Virginia   208
Wordsworth, William   182, 188
    Lyrical Ballads   113, 198
    'Michael'   27
    'Ode to Duty'   113